THE NEW DOMINION

THE NEW DOMINION

The Twentieth-Century Elections That
Shaped Modern Virginia

Edited by John G. Milliken
and Mark J. Rozell

University of Virginia Press • *Charlottesville and London*

University of Virginia Press
© 2023 by the Rector and Visitors of the University of Virginia
All rights reserved
Printed in the United States of America on acid-free paper

First published 2023

9 8 7 6 5 4 3 2 1

Library of Congress Cataloging-in-Publication Data

Names: Milliken, John G., editor. | Rozell, Mark J., editor.
Title: The new dominion : the twentieth-century elections that shaped modern
   Virginia / edited by John G. Milliken and Mark J. Rozell.
Other titles: 20th century elections that shaped modern Virginia
Description: Charlottesville ; London : University of Virginia Press, 2023. |
   Includes bibliographical references and index.
Identifiers: LCCN 2022048809 (print) | LCCN 2022048810 (ebook) | ISBN
   9780813949703 (hardcover : acid-free paper) | ISBN 9780813949710 (paperback :
   acid-free paper) | ISBN 9780813949727 (ebook)
Subjects: LCSH: Elections—Virginia—20th century. | Governors—Election.
   | Democratic Party (Va.)—History—20th century. | Virginia—Politics and
   government—20th century. | Byrd, Harry F., Jr. (Harry Flood), 1914–2013. | Robb,
   Charles S. | Wilder, Lawrence Douglas, 1931– | Allen, George, 1952–
Classification: LCC JK3992 .N4 2023 (print) | LCC JK3992 (ebook) |
   DDC 324.975509/04—dc23/eng/20230302
LC record available at https://lccn.loc.gov/2022048809
LC ebook record available at https://lccn.loc.gov/2022048810

Cover image: pixabay.com/deMysticWay

CONTENTS

THE NEW DOMINION

INTRODUCTION

John G. Milliken and Mark J. Rozell

MANY PEOPLE are familiar with the early history of Virginia, from Jamestown and Williamsburg through the succession of four Virginia-born US presidents, ending in 1828. They are also very familiar with the Virginia of the 1860s, where multiple battles of the American Civil War took place. But for many, history stops there. Twentieth-century Virginia is a blank page. It is as if the commonwealth leaped from the ashes of the Civil War and Reconstruction to become the modern, technology-driven, multicultural, progressive Virginia of today.

How did we get here? What changes took place in the politics of the state in the twentieth century that led to the election outcomes we see today, and what demographic and cultural trends drove those changes? How did we get from Harry Flood Byrd Sr. to Governors Doug Wilder, George Allen, Dr. Ralph Northam, and most recently Glenn Youngkin?

This book looks at the key Virginia elections of the last half of the twentieth century and shows that in each election there was early evidence of the trends that led inexorably to the political Virginia we see today. Whereas many observers tend to see the emergence of a Virginia trending blue to be simply the result of very recent and rapid demographic changes, the process of political transformation of the commonwealth has its roots in the twentieth century and can be seen in the critical elections described and analyzed in this volume. And blue is not its permanent color. The elections of Bob McDonnell in 2009 and Glenn Youngkin in 2021 show clearly that the changes in Virginia are not partisan per se but can be harnessed by either major political party using differing but overlapping geographic and demographic coalitions.

The sport of politics generally has two dominant competing teams, and that certainly has been the case in Virginia for much of its history since the founding of the republic. Whether it was Jefferson and the Democrats versus Marshall and the Federalists in the early 1800s or Billy Mahone and the Readjusters versus Fitzhugh Lee and the Conservatives in 1885, there was a contest, and usually a spirited one.

But for the first sixty-five years of the twentieth century, this was not the case. Virginia was a one-party state dominated by a conservative organization led first by Senator Thomas Martin and later by Governor and then Senator Harry F. Byrd Sr. Frequently, there were multiple candidates for statewide office, but rarely was there a true contest, as the few who were legally able to vote reliably supported the choice of the leadership of what was known as the "organization."

This book establishes the framework for understanding why and how that changed, how Virginia turned into a competitive two-party state, with shifting partisan advantages not unlike what is found in other "purple" states across the country. We have chosen key statewide elections as a means of telling the story in a chronological fashion and have identified common themes throughout the twentieth century and into the twenty-first that explain and point directly to the Virginia politics of today. The contemporary state of Virginia politics and government did not just suddenly emerge out of a shifting landscape but is the product of a historical evolution that has its roots in twentieth-century elections, combined with certain twenty-first-century phenomena.

The volume opens with a detailed overview of the critical Byrd era as a prelude to the key elections that transformed Virginia politics and government. What follows are the chapters on the key elections, and a conclusion that examines the state of twenty-first-century Virginia, showing it to be the natural culmination of its twentieth-century antecedents.

Ronald Heinemann's opening chapter provides the backdrop for understanding the transformation of Old Dominion politics from a closed, single-party structure to an open, competitive, and productive political order with two-party competition. Heinemann investigates the creation and operation of the political machine that dominated Virginia politics for two-thirds of the century, primarily under the leadership of Harry F. Byrd; its structure; its reliance on a controlled turnout based in the rural counties; and the early seeds of its unraveling. The chapter emphasizes the events and elections from the 1930s to the 1950s that weakened the Byrd organization's control and prepared the way for the change that was to come.

Pivotal events, such as President Harry S. Truman handily winning Virginia in the 1948 election over GOP nominee Tom Dewey and Dixiecrat candidate Strom Thurmond, paved the way for later progressive reforms, genuine two-party competition, and eventual empowering of African American voters. Heinemann notes that as early as the beginning of the 1950s, Virginia was beginning to be transformed by urban and suburban growth in the Northern Virginia and Hampton Roads areas, migration into the state, a strengthening of two-party politics, and a rising Black voice. The growing federal presence in Northern Virginia meant more outside money and residents. By the 1950s, for example, there were twice as many federal workers as farmers in the state.

Ultimately, it was Byrd's fervent opposition to the Supreme Court's *Brown v. Board of Education of Topeka* (1954) school desegregation decision and his urging of massive resistance that split the Democratic Party of Virginia, emboldened Republicans, fostered federal intervention, and stimulated Black political participation. Byrd's organization and his legacy faded, "undermined by those economic, demographic, and externally imposed changes that revolutionized Virginia's political culture," Heinemann writes.

The second chapter takes up the underappreciated but profoundly transformative 1966 US Senate election of Bill Spong. In so doing, it describes the various elements of the early anti–Byrd organization group, the entry into politics of the World War II generation, the impact of the politics of massive resistance to court-ordered school desegregation, and the emergence of a significant African American voting population, culminating in the elections of 1965 and 1966, which reshaped the Democratic Party and planted the seeds for a Republican emergence.

The political year was unusual from the outset. The retirement of Senator Harry F. Byrd in late 1965, followed by the appointment of his son and namesake to serve until the next general election, plus the end of the regular term of the state's other US senator meant there would be two US Senate seats on the same ballot in November 1966.

Bill Spong was a member of the state senate and leader of a group of younger, more moderate legislators, mostly from more populated areas. He was part of the World War II generation just achieving political success in Virginia and was born in and represented cities in the growing Tidewater region whose economy was dominated by maritime and defense-related businesses, areas markedly different from the rural, agricultural areas that had produced most of the leaders of the Byrd organization, including its two 1966 US Senate candidates: incumbents Harry Flood Byrd Jr. and A. Willis Robertson. Their opponents, Spong and state senator Armistead Boothe of Alexandria, came from populous and fast-growing parts of the state and spoke to a new generation of Virginians. Spong's victory and Boothe's close race against Senator Byrd provided the first evidence that the locus of political power in Virginia was beginning to shift to the fast-growing urban and suburban areas.

In the third chapter, Frank B. Atkinson takes up the historic 1973 gubernatorial election. Beginning with the gubernatorial election of GOP nominee Linwood Holton in 1969, the back-to-back elections of 1972 and 1973 showed the strength of the new conservative Republican coalition that would dominate state politics for the rest of the decade and beyond. The chapter describes and analyzes the rapid changes that took place in both Virginia political parties in the 1970s as the inverted but fraying Byrd-era alignment (Democrats as conservative "Southern Democrats," Republicans as the more progressive alternative in state elections) finally collapsed and was replaced by a more standard setting in which the two state parties' issue positions came to closely resemble those of their national counterparts. The transition, though a product of forces at work for some time, could more aptly be described as a convulsion, with former Democrats running successfully as independents and winning highly contested statewide elections from the right (Senator Harry F. Byrd Jr.) and left (Lieutenant Governor Henry E. Howell Jr.) in 1970 and 1971, respectively, and with a former Democratic governor, Mills Godwin, switching to the GOP to win an unprecedented second term in 1973.

The 1972–74 period was most consequential in this realignment: The Senator George McGovern–led liberal/antiwar takeover of the national Democratic Party in 1972 and like shifts in the Virginia Democratic Party hastened the exodus of conservatives from that party, and the ascension of a conservative GOP state chairman (Richard Obenshain), who defeated the more moderate incumbent party chief favored by progressive Republican governor Linwood Holton in 1972, made the GOP more welcoming for conservative former Democrats like Godwin. It appeared that a wholesale shift was about to occur, but the dramatic realignment was never consummated. Watergate and the resulting unpopularity of the Republican label in 1974 abruptly halted the Democratic crossover.

The result was that many conservative former Democrats chose to remain independents, following the Byrd rather than the Godwin example. These conservatives generally supported Republicans for the remainder of the decade. They forged a coalition that dominated state elections and made the Virginia Republican Party the winningest state party, Republican or Democrat, in the country by 1980, barely a decade after its first statewide win since Reconstruction. But the coalition proved fleeting, and even as Ronald Reagan was forging a similar coalition to win nationally in 1980, the stage was set for the resurgence of moderate Democrats in the 1980s. The decade was remarkable not only for what happened but for what might have been. The sudden death of young Lieutenant Governor

J. Sargeant Reynolds in 1971 deprived Virginia Democrats of a Kennedy-esque moderate leader who almost certainly would have won the governorship in 1973 and changed party fortunes in Virginia.

Then, in 1978, Republicans likewise lost their dynamic leader, Dick Obenshain, denying them the Reaganesque champion who might well have aligned Virginia with the dominant national GOP and reversed Virginia party fortunes in the 1980s. Thus did broad trends conspire with dramatic and unexpected events to produce a decade of consequential change in Virginia, the main effect of which was to usher in a sustained period of intense two-party competition and closely contested state elections.

In chapter 4, authors Stephen J. Farnsworth, Stephen P. Hanna, and Sally Burkley present an analysis of Charles S. "Chuck" Robb's 1981 gubernatorial campaign and the Democratic realignment that followed his victory. Democrats held the governor's office throughout the decade of the 1980s, relying on a coalition first assembled by Robb that combined strong support in the African American community with acceptability in many parts of the conservative business and professional community.

As Virginia had emerged from the one-party-dominated Byrd era to be two-party competitive at the state level, Robb configured an electoral and governing coalition that effectively captured both the progressive wing of his party while attracting proponents of fiscal conservatism. This coalition positioned the Democratic Party to be dominant in state politics in Virginia during the Reagan-Bush era of national Republican dominance. This was no small feat, as much of the Deep South and the Rim South states such as Virginia were moving increasingly Republican as the national Democratic Party shifted more to the left and was centered in the northeastern and midwestern industrial states and on the West Coast.

The Robb-built coalition made possible the continued success of the Democratic Party in Virginia statewide elections, as Gerald Baliles succeeded to the governorship in 1985 and L. Douglas Wilder in 1989. Although Robb himself governed as a fiscal conservative, his progressive views on social issues and race helped pave the way for an inclusive Democratic Party that represented an emerging evolution in social and cultural values in the state. Governor Baliles continued to help solidify the progressive-to-moderate and moderately conservative Robb coalition in Virginia and effectively helped protect Doug Wilder's gubernatorial quest from charges of Wilder being an ultraliberal, out of touch with mainstream Virginia.

In chapter 5, Julian Hayter takes up the political rise and 1989 gubernatorial election of L. Douglas Wilder, the nation's first elected Black governor. The continued growth in size and importance of the African

American voting population culminated in the election of Doug Wilder first as lieutenant governor in 1985 and then as governor in 1989.

Many leading observers had dismissed Wilder's chances of winning statewide office in 1985 because of his race. That assessment reflected a common belief at the time that Virginia, the capital of the former Confederacy, simply was not yet ready to elect a Black man statewide. Wilder's victory positioned him to be the leading candidate for governor four years later, with questions still remaining whether his race would undercut his electoral chances for the governorship. Wilder won a historically close gubernatorial election that was widely touted as a major breakthrough in racial politics, both in Virginia and nationally. This chapter traces the path of African American voting participation from the early 1950s through 1989, using the rise of Doug Wilder as a means of telling the story of how his elections reflected evolving political trends over a period of time.

Doug Wilder is one of the most important African American political figures of the twentieth century, not merely for his individual political achievements but also for what his achievements symbolized as the first African American governor to be elected in the Commonwealth of Virginia and the first elected Black governor in US history. On the one hand, Wilder's election in 1989—he served from 1990 to 1994—confirmed the clout of Black voters in Virginia. In fact, Wilder did not emerge out of thin air. Even prior to the American civil rights movement, Virginia's and Richmond's African Americans had long since organized one of the most effective voting blocs below the Mason-Dixon line. By the late 1980s, Black voters were poised to transform state politics.

On the other hand, Wilder's election revealed the limitations of electoral victories, epitomized the crisis of rising Black expectations, and affirmed the challenges that Black candidates faced in winning White voters. His election also helped reinitiate a tidal wave of White resistance to African American ballots that had been building in the commonwealth since the 1960s. Moments of political permissiveness and symbolic electoral victories are often followed by eras of restriction. No American politician encapsulates this dilemma quite like Wilder. His story is as much a cautionary tale about the nature of race and American political development as it is the story of a historic political victory.

The 1980s era thus saw the Democratic Party sweep all three statewide offices—governor, lieutenant governor, and attorney general—in all three election cycles (1981, 1985, 1989). In positioning the party in the political center as the Virginia GOP moved far to the right, Governors Robb,

Baliles, and Wilder created what many considered an unbeatable coalition in state politics. Thus, in 1993, Virginia appeared ready for another historic breakthrough with the Democrats nominating two-term attorney general Mary Sue Terry for governor, who ran to become the commonwealth's first woman chief executive.

It was not to be, as told by Warren Fiske and Robert Holsworth in chapter 6 on the 1993 landslide gubernatorial election of Republican George Allen. In the 1990s, Republicans elected back-to-back governors, including one sweep of all three statewide offices, took control of both houses of the legislature for the first time in more than a century (commencing, remarkably, a two-decade-long House of Delegates majority), won a second US Senate seat, and possessed a substantial GOP majority in the congressional House delegation. The Virginia Republican Party's ascendancy even exceeded what the party had achieved by the end of the 1970s and what the Democrats had achieved in the 1980s. This period was a time of significant policy innovation at the state level, led by Republicans but accomplished with bipartisan support, and much of it survived later changes in partisan control. And it was a time when individual Virginia Republicans gained a degree of prominence in Congress not matched since the Byrd era, including, among others, a Senate Armed Services Committee chair and a House of Representatives majority leadership.

The key catalyst for all this change was the 1993 election of George Allen as governor. Allen gained office, after three successive Democratic governors, by the largest landslide in modern competitive Virginia politics after reversing a thirty-point polling deficit. Also elected that year was James Gilmore as attorney general. Gilmore went on to win the governorship in 1997, extending the GOP's fortunes. The GOP dominance of the 1990s, though, did not sustain beyond that decade as the party became identified with extreme conservative positions on social issues such as abortion and on criminal justice issues, leading to a political backlash beginning in the 2000s that commenced the now long period of Democratic dominance of the state.

With Mark Warner's gubernatorial win in 2001, the Democrats began a period of dominance, winning the governorship again in 2005, and then in 2013 and 2017, and winning US Senate races in 2006, 2008, 2012, 2014, 2018, and 2020. The GOP captured the governorship in 2009 but did not win any election statewide again until 2021. Prior to 2021, this GOP statewide electoral drought had led many to wrongly conclude that the transformation of Virginia into a progressive-leaning Democratic state was complete. As the election case studies in this volume make clear, what appears to be a straight-line political transformation at one period in time can be interrupted or derailed altogether.

The concluding chapter discusses the practical impact in Virginia of an axiom of politics: *let me decide who can vote and I will decide who will win.* It sounds obvious, and it is. And it was the cardinal principle that underlay the success of the Martin and Byrd organizations that dominated Virginia politics for more than forty years beginning in the 1920s. Constitutional provisions, laws, and practices in place in Virginia sharply limited the electorate, allowing a Byrd organization–supported candidate to win the Democratic nomination (and hence, for all practical purposes, the election) with the support of between 6 and 9 percent of the adult population.

All of that began to change in the late 1950s, driven by explosive population growth in the urban areas and significant increases in the number of African American voters. In short, the Byrd organization lost control of the size and demographic shape of the electorate. These demographic trends persisted year after year, election after election, though their impact on elections was sometimes obscured by the more immediate ups and downs of national politics and local personalities.

The closing chapter explores these two trends in more detail, taking up common themes from the earlier chapters. Its thesis is that changing demographics and the emergence of the African American vote drove the politics of the commonwealth in an inevitable direction, but not a permanently Democratic-controlled one. It pulls together the strands of political history and shows how they combined with rapid growth in the urban corridor—an area reaching south from Washington, DC, to Arlington—to produce in the twenty-first century six governors (four Democrats and two Republicans) and successive US senators (John Warner, Jim Webb, Mark Warner, Tim Kaine) from the corridor.

As the center of politics shifted over time to the urban corridor, the Democrats benefited simply because they appealed more successfully to the needs and desires of those living in the corridor, many of whom were new to Virginia. The Democratic Party in Virginia had a remarkable run of victories—so much so that many observers counted the Old Dominion a solid blue (Democratic) state. Just as no Republican candidate running statewide won an election in Virginia between 2009 and 2020, Democratic presidential nominees carried Virginia in four consecutive elections (2008, 2012, 2016, 2020), with Joe Biden winning the state by double digits in 2020. Prior to 2008, Virginia had not voted for a Democrat for president since 1964 and was the only state of the South not to vote for native son southerner Jimmy Carter in 1976.

Yet, as the chapters in this volume caution, whether Virginia is now, and for the long term, a truly "blue," Democratic state, is unanswerable, as it really does not ask the right question. The twentieth-century elections covered in this volume show that the trend toward Democratic dominance was not a continual straight line but one with shifts in partisan fortunes over time as the two parties competed to find the best way to appeal to the growing and changing electorate. The common denominator of all the elections, however, has been the twin impacts of population growth almost exclusively in the urban corridor and the growing participation of African American and other racial and ethnic groups.

The analyses that suggest that Virginia is now a blue state assume a kind of permanency to voting patterns in particular geographic regions and among certain demographic groups, and also assume that the parties' appeal to the electorate will remain static. As Governor Glenn Youngkin's election confirmed, Republican statewide candidates can win in Virginia, just as George Allen, James Gilmore, and Bob McDonnell did in 1993, 1997, and 2009, respectively, by basing their appeals on those issues that matter in the large population centers. The axiom of "you go where the votes are" will remain true. Is it inevitable that, for example, migrants and younger voters will remain loyal in the long term to the Democratic Party? More than likely, the party that can best appeal to voters in the newest growth areas—such as Loudoun, Prince William, Stafford, and Spotsylvania in Northern Virginia and James City County, Chesapeake, and Virginia Beach in Hampton Roads—will become the next dominant party in Virginia.

Youngkin's win makes the point. He appealed with enough success to voters in the counties and cities of the urban corridor that, in combination with his unprecedented numbers in the rural areas, he was able to eke out the small but comfortable 51–49 win. Digging a little deeper reveals some fascinating aspects of the 2021 election year.

First, and most important, the percentage of registered voters casting ballots reached an all-time high, at least in the modern era.

Just as remarkably, in all but two jurisdictions, Charlottesville and Portsmouth, voters turned out in higher percentages than they had in the previous gubernatorial election in 2017. And herein lies one of the keys to Youngkin's election. Of the thirty-nine jurisdictions whose turnout exceeded 60 percent, Youngkin won thirty-six (thirty-five counties and one small city, Poquoson). Of the jurisdictions Democratic nominee Terry

TABLE 1. Percentage of registered voters casting ballots in gubernatorial elections, 2001–21

Election year	Percentage (%) of registered voters voting
2001	46.4
2005	44.9
2009	40.4
2013	43.0
2017	47.6
2021	54.9

Source: Data from Virginia State Board of Elections.

McAuliffe carried, only Charles City County, Albemarle County, and the City of Falls Church exceeded 60 percent in turnout.

From McAuliffe's perspective, he carried the jurisdictions he needed to carry, many (e.g., Arlington, Fairfax, Alexandria) by margins close to or greater than those realized by Governor Ralph Northam, the winning Democratic candidate in 2017. But in others (Loudoun, Prince William) the 2017 margins that had propelled a statewide Democratic win were reduced, and critically, in still others (Virginia Beach, Chesterfield), 2017 wins became 2021 losses.

For Youngkin, enormous wins in the many rural counties were not enough. He needed to (and did) win, or reduce Republican loss margins, in many of the suburban counties in the urban corridor. And he did so by addressing directly the issues that mattered on the sidelines of the soccer fields and in the homeroom settings of PTA meetings. The content of the political message may have been different from election to election, but Youngkin's formula was the same as it had been for McDonnell and Allen, and as it had been for Northam, Kaine, Warner, and for McAuliffe in his successful run for governor in 2013. If you are a Republican, run up your margins in the rural communities, to offset declining total populations in those areas, and hold your own in the urban corridor. If you are a Democrat, fatten your wins in the big urban corridor jurisdictions, building on their growing populations, and squeeze whatever you can get out of the rural areas. The same formula had been working for more than fifty years, with population growth driving it toward the Democrats.

What follows in this book is the history of that Virginia geographic and demographic evolution, told through the stories of the transformative elections from 1949 through the first part of the twenty-first century.

1

Prelude to Revolution

THE RISE AND FALL OF THE BYRD ORGANIZATION, 1925-49

RONALD HEINEMANN

THE POLITICAL machine that dominated Old Dominion politics for two-thirds of the twentieth century had its birth in the post-Reconstruction era as Conservatives, the heirs of antebellum planters, battled Readjusters and Republicans over issues of funding the state debt and Black political participation. In 1883, Conservatives, now assuming the label of Democrats, overwhelmed Republicans by playing the race card to win control of the legislature. They proceeded to use patronage, gerrymandering, and new election laws to solidify their power and end Virginia's brief fling with two-party competition. Republicans would not win the governorship for another eighty-six years.

During the next century, Democrats would create and perfect a political organization to perpetuate their authority. Preferring the more refined term "organization" to the more negative label "machine," Virginia's Democratic leaders over time came to think of themselves as a group of like-minded men who agreed on conservative economic policies and paternalistic politics. A part of this imagery of personal virtue was their association with the myth of the "Lost Cause."

As devastating as the Civil War had been to Virginia, it had not eroded the antebellum social and political order that inhibited steps necessary for a real emancipation. Indeed, the Confederate cult or Lost Cause myth strengthened Virginians' veneration of a past history in which, in James Branch Cabell's words, "there had been no imperfection, but only beauty and chivalry and contentment."[1] And for their efforts to preserve this paradise, Confederate soldiers were romanticized as honorable if doomed fighters for a way of life. Richmond, as the capital of the Confederacy, became the shrine of this cult with its Confederate White House and Monument Avenue, soon to be lined with the statues of the great Confederate leaders. By denying that slavery was the cause of the war and blaming the defeat solely on overwhelming Union Army numbers, the Lost Cause myth allowed Southerners to escape responsibility for the war and defeat while basking in the glow of heroic behavior and smug superiority. More practically, the nostalgic cult was also used by Democratic politicians to recapture power by vilifying Republicans and African Americans for their disloyalty to the Cause and their efforts to overturn the old order. The message was sounded at the dedication of every Confederate monument across the Old Dominion, and for the last quarter of the century, Virginians elected Confederate veterans to be their governor. The Lost Cause myth was another weighty anchor that prevented the state from realizing its potential for nearly a century.[2]

The man most responsible for consolidating the Democrats' new authority was Thomas Staples Martin, a modest, dignified lawyer from Scottsville who had an amazing facility for organization. After building a successful legal practice in Central Virginia, he became counsel for the Chesapeake and Ohio Railroad, whose money he dispensed to candidates who promised to support legislation beneficial to his client. Martin's railroad interests propelled him into state politics. Working closely with US senator John S. Barbour, who had revitalized the Democratic Party, he was elected to the executive committee in 1885. When Barbour died in 1892, the relatively unknown Martin pursued his Senate seat. He called on his considerable resources—including railroad money—to curry favor with the state legislators, who at that time selected US senators. He defeated former governor Fitzhugh Lee, nephew of Robert E. Lee, for the position, thus establishing himself as the leader of the Democratic Party in the Old Dominion. Although charges of bribery were made at the time, it was only years later that correspondence was published that established the money trail and Martin's complicity.

Martin's power was never total, confronting as he did the challenges of populists and progressives and the volatile issues of free silver and Prohibition, but he shrewdly chose his battles, his pragmatism frequently overriding his personal sentiments. In the controversial election of 1896, he made a last-minute conversion to support the free silver candidacy of William Jennings Bryan in order to preserve Democratic unity. And in the early years of the century, he entered into an alliance with Methodist minister James Cannon, leader of the Anti-Saloon League, to defuse the Prohibition issue and protect the Martin organization. Favorable to his control was the absence of a strong Republican Party in the state, which, except in the Shenandoah Valley and the Southwest, could not overcome the legacy of Reconstruction.[3]

Aided by the growing reform impulse, and especially incensed by the charges of vote buying levied against Martin, progressives elected independent Andrew Jackson Montague to the governorship in 1901 and won popular support for a constitutional convention to revamp state government and eliminate the Black vote, which, they believed, was corrupting politics. The convention, attended by twelve Republicans and eighty-eight Democrats, met in Richmond from June 1901 to June 1902. The major achievement was the disfranchisement of most Black Virginians and about half of the White electorate through the imposition of a poll tax and other constitutional restrictions, including literacy tests and understanding clauses that would be interpreted by White voting officials. The poll tax was $1.50 per year for up to three years and had to be paid six months before the general election. The convention also restructured state and local government and created a State Corporation Commission to regulate railroads and other corporations. At the end of the session, delegates arrogantly proclaimed their handiwork to be in effect rather than submit it to the electorate as had been promised. Ostensibly designed to liberalize politics and overthrow the machine, the new constitution, ironically, strengthened the Martin organization, producing a very undemocratic political order in Virginia. It eliminated voters who were more likely to vote against the machine; it undermined weaker parties and independent candidates by creating a smaller electorate that was more easily controlled by the group with the best organization and most money; and it placed a premium on control of patronage and election machinery. The percentage of Virginians voting in presidential elections would not get back to 1904 levels until 1952.[4]

Organization authority was further enhanced through the creation of a circuit court system. Appointed by the General Assembly, the new judges had the power to select county electoral boards and other local officials. They complemented the preexisting "ring" of local county or "courthouse" officials—the commonwealth's attorney, treasurer, commissioner of revenue, clerk of the circuit court, and sheriff—who, along with their prescribed duties, were responsible for getting out the vote and dispensing patronage. An infamous fee system rewarded many of these local officials by allowing them to keep a portion of the fees they charged for their services. The interlocking network of General Assembly members, circuit judges, "courthouse ring," and machine leaders, dependent on one another for job security, salaries, and election support—and now under-girded by a constitution that kept the electorate small—became the key to the Martin organization's power for the next sixty years.[5]

The progressive movement that swept the country in the first two de-cades of the twentieth century under the leadership of Presidents Theo-dore Roosevelt and native Virginian Woodrow Wilson did achieve some modest results in the Old Dominion. Demonstrating some independence from Senator Martin's control, Governor Claude Swanson, himself a member of the organization, pushed through increased funding for new schools, teacher salaries, and longer school terms. But Virginia was still spending only half the national average, and much of the increase was not trickling down to Black schools. To address a road system labeled "the worst known to civilization," Swanson pressed for the creation of a state highway commission and monies to deal with an exploding automo-bile population. Gains were also made in public health, agriculture, and regulation of big business, but these achievements were compromised by racism, localism, and paternalism, while one-party politics prevented the competition that might have produced better services. In historian Ray-mond Pulley's view, progressivism in Virginia did more "to conserve and strengthen the Old Virginia order than to rid the state of political bosses and broaden the base of popular government." Virginia would change, but slowly, and certainly not at the expense of the ruling class.[6]

Another group that suffered from paternalism and prejudice was women. Opposition to women's suffrage in the Old Dominion rested on tradition and politics. Earlier votes against equal education for women and equal access to the professions clearly indicated a male bias in the legislature against upsetting time-honored gender distinctions that risked control of the political order. Conservatives also believed that women were more likely to support costly social welfare programs such as child labor laws. In the 1919 special session, the House of Delegates condemned the proposed Nineteenth Amendment to the US Constitution as an "un-warranted, unnecessary, undemocratic, and dangerous interference with the rights reserved to the states." As if these hurdles were not substantial enough, opponents of women's suffrage, including many female antisuf-fragists, played on racist fears by claiming that the amendment would open the doors to voting by Black women. Despite ratification at the national level, which allowed women to vote for the first time in 1920, Virginia's legislators did not approve the amendment until 1952. Although women gained access to political and professional domains long off limits to them, they did not assume important public roles in the life of the common-wealth for another three decades.[7]

When Martin unexpectedly died in November, 1919, a struggle en-sued for control of the Democratic Party between Martin's allies and renegade governor Westmoreland Davis. Debates over Prohibition en-forcement, women's suffrage, and better roads had splintered organiza-tion unity, allowing the independent Davis to win a close three-man race for the governorship in 1917.

After two contentious legislative sessions, the Davis and Martin organi-zation forces began jockeying for position in the governor's race in 1921 and the contest for Swanson's US Senate seat in 1922. Westmoreland Davis initially appeared to hold a commanding lead. Defiantly, he had maneu-vered much of his legislative program through an obstinate assembly, win-ning public praise for his executive budget process, which had worked so effectively for the first time in the 1920 session. And he had filled Senator Martin's vacated seat with Carter Glass, a longtime opponent of the ma-chine, who Davis believed would now become his ally in the battle with the organization.

Martin's death left the already disarrayed organization leaderless. Preoccupation with the Prohibition issue had caused the organization to ignore demands for improved state services, while wartime exigencies had forced Martin to attend to congressional responsibilities and neglect important fence-mending tasks. Yet the machine still commanded the loyalties of the courthouse people and the state Democratic Commit-tee, and it had a talented group of battle-tested leaders who would not concede easily. The triumvirate of Congressman Hal Flood, now Senator Claude Swanson, and party chairman Rorer James moved to restore au-thority. They wooed Carter Glass to a position of neutrality by allowing him to fill out the remainder of Martin's term, a position he held until his death in 1946. They enthusiastically supported the successful candidacy of E. Lee Trinkle for governor in 1921 against another independent, Henry St. George Tucker, whom Governor Davis had backed. Unfortunately, these taxing efforts contributed to the deaths of James and Flood and led to the selection in 1922 of Flood's nephew, Harry Flood Byrd, to be the next party chairman. Few could have guessed how portentous that choice would be.[8]

Harry Byrd Takes Over

Elected to the state senate in 1915 from Winchester, young Byrd was an un-
tested commodity in state races. The loss of tested leadership was just one
of the problems confronting the organization. The machine had no money.
Many bills were in arrears, and the committee was saddled with a $5,500
deficit from the 1921 gubernatorial campaign at a time when funds were
needed for the elections of 1922, which included Davis's effort to unseat an
ailing Senator Swanson. Whoever could provide the organizational skills
and savvy decision-making in a victorious election effort would be in a
position to replace Martin as the acknowledged leader of the organization.

It was an opportunity that Harry Byrd did not let pass. At once he dis-
played the political pragmatism for which Martin and Flood had been
so well known. Laying aside his personal preference for Senate colleague
Willis Robertson, Byrd conceded Flood's congressional seat to Henry
Tucker, thus appeasing and silencing another old independent. Relying
on the courthouse crowd and the friendships he had made as state fuel
administrator during World War I, Byrd applied the organizational techniques he had developed for his own elections to the state senate: precinct
organization, poll tax paying, voter registration, voter lists, and letter writ-
ing. Overcoming his opposition to women's suffrage, he now made a special effort to qualify women voters. To raise money, he recommended that
party leaders contribute $250 each; his was the first donation. Instead of
using the money to pay the old bills, he channeled it to the local chairmen
to pay the poll taxes of "reliable Democrats."[9]

The fight to redeem the "Fighting Ninth" may have been the most crucial for Byrd's subsequent rise to power. Republicans Campbell Slemp and
his son, C. Bascom Slemp, had controlled the Ninth District for twenty
years, perfecting an organization that was the equal of the Democrats'
organization in qualifying voters and distributing patronage. However,
the untiring efforts of new district chairman George Peery had enabled
Trinkle to carry the Ninth in 1921, and Democrats looked forward to defeating Bascom Slemp the following year. As a reward for his efforts, Peery
was nominated to run against the Republican. Everett Randolph "Ebbie"
Combs, clerk of Russell County, replaced Peery and assumed control of
his campaign. Byrd's relationship with Combs, begun on the hilly, wind-
ing roads of Southwest Virginia, deepened into a friendship and political
association that lasted thirty-five years.

Because of the bitter competition between the parties in the Ninth District, its politics were the dirtiest in the Old Dominion. Voting irregularities

were common, particularly abuses of absentee voting and the requirement for block payment of poll taxes, which voters had come to expect despite its illegality. "Qualifying" voters meant ensuring that their poll taxes were paid six months before the general election in the fall, and then registering them. Money was essential for this practice. Soliciting contributions from state employees, Byrd directed state committee secretary James Hayes "to write each of the more important employees a circular letter requesting a contribution to the Ninth District campaign." But, he cautioned, "Use the utmost care not to send letters to any Republican as a copy of the letter might be published." Estimating that the Democrats had spent $20,000 to $25,000 in their poll tax campaign, a disconsolate Slemp withdrew from the race in favor of John Hassinger, state senator from Abingdon.

Byrd made a personal appearance in the district in June—when he met Combs for the first time—and returned in August and October, making new friends and impressing all with his energy and advice. He lined up speakers for the Ninth, distributed ten thousand cards presenting information on the candidate and the issues, welcomed the support of organized labor, and sent personal letters to local officials urging them to get out the vote. Assisted by the nationwide "Republican recession," Peery won a decisive victory over Hassinger, ending Republican hegemony in the Ninth, and a solid Democratic congressional delegation was sent to Washington in 1923 for the first time in memory, along with the reelected Senator Swanson, who had easily turned aside Westmoreland Davis. Acclaimed for his work in restoring organization authority, Harry Byrd now turned to the road question to consolidate his emerging status as the heir to Tom Martin.[10]

In actuality, the issue of bonds to finance new roads had never been far from his mind during the summer and fall campaigns. He had acceded, if somewhat unenthusiastically, to building roads with borrowed money before 1920, but at this point several factors, all undergirded by his visceral objection to debt and the waste of interest payments, combined to turn him into a vigorous foe of state borrowing. Harry Byrd believed in economy in government. Public indebtedness, he feared, would cultivate a spendthrift mentality, affecting not only road building but all other state services. Higher taxes and wasteful spending would result. He particularly disliked the long-term nature of bonds, which, like Virginia's nineteenth-century debt, could remain a burden for generations to come and hinder the state's development. Byrd's deliberations on road building revealed the competing forces that were a part of his early career: a conservative preference for traditional practices, especially when it came to spending money, versus a zest for progress, for growth, for the utilization of resources in the most efficient and productive manner possible. Roads were necessary for development, but one had to be careful not to overextend in financing them.[11]

To counter new bond proposals, Byrd and his rural friends offered a three cents per gallon alternative that would build the highways in almost the same time but without bonded indebtedness. As soon as Governor Trinkle summoned the legislature to convene on February 28, 1923, Byrd began arranging for antibond men to be placed on the Roads and Finance Committees. Not surprisingly, Byrd was appointed chairman of the Roads Committee, from where he orchestrated a reorganization of the highway department. The debate between the competing plans—the three-cent gas tax versus a $50 million bond issue—raged on for the duration of the monthlong session, each side challenging the figures of the other, each side looking for the votes to sustain its position. After a very bitter contest, the three-cent gas tax bill won, but in a spirit of compromise, the General Assembly passed a referendum bill that allowed a statewide vote on a $50 million bond issue in November. It was a risk that Byrd and the pay-as-you-go advocates were now willing to take.

Although wet weather on Election Day eve turned roads into quagmires, dampening the spirits of the antibond people, they need not have worried. Their victory was substantial: 127,187 to 81,220. As predicted, only in the cities and in some mountain counties did the bond issue do well. The rural sections of the Valley and Southside, where taxes and debt were anathema, overwhelmingly rejected the proposal. The only consolation for the bond people was the fulfillment of their prediction that the roads would not be built on time. However, the 1923 bond referendum had a significance far beyond that of the speed with which roads would be built in Virginia. Everyone recognized Harry Byrd as the driving force behind the victory, as a man of rare organizational ability and indefatigable energy. This effort confirmed his leadership of the organization and launched his campaign for the governorship in 1925. Years later Byrd said his political career would have died had he lost that election. The vote also solidified a pay-as-you-go mentality in the Old Dominion that would be the ideological basis for the state's fiscal policy for the next several decades.[12]

In the two years since he had taken the helm of the state committee, Harry Byrd had assumed total command of the organization. This had been no fluke; he had worked diligently to restore life to the machine and impose his leadership on it. He continued to rely on the "lists"—the rolls

of loyal Democratic workers and voters in every county down to the precinct level that revealed the full extent of the machine's authority. Byrd
often sent each of these people three separate letters over the course of
a campaign, requesting their assistance, emphasizing the need to get out
the vote, and thanking them for their efforts. In matters of finance Byrd
proved adept at raising funds from businessmen and party leaders. There
were few political activities in the state that he did not direct or influence.

His apprenticeship with the Martin machine made Byrd remarkably
well prepared to assume its command. Tutored by his father and uncle,
he had mastered the arts of politics: tenacity, compromise, loyalty, and
teamwork. Having watched Flood subordinate his personal ambitions for
the good of the organization, curry favor with people in high places, and
deftly carve up his opponents, Harry Byrd became just as adept at playing
the game. He too would be a tough, ruthless machine politician. But Byrd
also shared some of the softer qualities of his predecessor, Senator Martin,
whom he greatly admired. Both projected the image of a selfless public
servant who did not run for office but was sought by the office, who did
not dictate policies but consulted experts and suggested solutions. Theirs
was a quiet, noncharismatic leadership, devoid of public demagoguery
and display, reflecting personal integrity both in private and in public life.
Distrustful of the masses, neither was committed to a freewheeling democratic political order but preferred the comfort of a controlled electorate
whose will they could read with uncanny skill.

The most significant difference between the Martin machine and the
new Byrd machine was the close personal supervision that Byrd exercised
over his forces. Control of the courthouse, the assembly, and the network
of patronage and fees that sustained the loyalty between commanders and
lieutenants remained the key to power, while constitutional limitations
restricted the electorate, keeping it small and controllable. What Byrd
brought to a revived organization was an intimate approach. Whereas
Martin had left much of the routine operation to Hal Flood and Claude
Swanson, preferring to hobnob with railroad executives rather than clerks
of the court, Byrd comfortably mingled with local officeholders, relishing
their Brunswick stews and talk of weather and farm prices. In addition
to the officeholders and farmers, Byrd cultivated friends in the business
and banking communities and among journalists, to whom he catered with
his news releases. His way of leading was not to coerce but to reward
with praise, jobs, roads, and legislation. When he moved to the US Senate
in 1933, he had to reduce his participation in local affairs, but he never lost

the personal touch. What he created was a political organization that ran smoothly, efficiently, and powerfully, and was beholden to one man for its direction for forty years, an oligarchy far more dominant than the one Thomas Martin had ruled over.[13]

Byrd used these organizational skills and his success with the roads issue to easily win a term as governor of Virginia from 1925 to 1929. His governorship reflected what historian George Tindall has called the "business progressivism" of the 1920s in the South—no fundamental changes in the role of government but a tinkering in the realm of economy and efficiency. This reflected Byrd's view of the role of politics. The responsibility of government, he believed, was to provide an environment in which individual opportunity might flourish and to facilitate the creation of wealth with minimal taxation and regulation, a view not unlike that of Virginia's leaders.[14]

Consistent with this philosophy, his "Program of Progress" led to a reorganization of state government, advanced road building, and industrial development and tourism, but little was done for education, agriculture, or the structure of county government, which was wallowing in the abusive fee system by which local officials were paid. Though he moved Virginia forward, he did not move it very far. For all the bright lights—and unquestionably the excitement of the twenties contributed to a sense of forward motion—Virginia changed very little. Its industrial growth was impressive, but the commonwealth continued to languish at the bottom of the states in school and public welfare appropriations, state hospital care, and correctional facilities. While the improvements in fiscal accountability produced real savings through centralized accounting procedures, the attention to patronage did not shrink the bureaucracy.

That attitude endured, and its legacy was even more negative than its immediate results. Byrd left Virginia's finances in good order for the Great Depression—low tax rates and low indebtedness were desirable attributes for bad economic times—but the absence of a broader social conscience and an unwillingness to spend restricted the commonwealth's ability to assist its citizens in that time of need. The state constitutional amendments, especially the restrictions on borrowing and tax segregation, straitjacketed the state, costing it flexibility as economic conditions changed. These factors kept Virginia locked into a 1920s mode for another generation, a backward state with untapped potential.[15]

The "Antis"

When Byrd left the governorship in 1930, he retired to his apple orchards, but he did not relinquish his influence with his successors or his leadership of the organization. And his direct involvement in political life was restored with his appointment to the US Senate in 1933, a position he would hold through six successive elections until his retirement in 1965. His new office would bring him into direct conflict with the progressive, activist new president, Franklin Roosevelt and his New Deal, which was directed at ameliorating the problems of the Great Depression that had hit the country in 1930. By the end of Roosevelt's first term, Byrd had become one of his harshest critics.

The Great Depression did not strike Virginia as hard as it did the industrial states of the Northeast and the one-crop farm states of the South and Midwest, but by 1932 it clearly was affecting the state's economy. Unemployment was rising, soup kitchens were appearing, and farm prices were declining. Governor John Garland Pollard's response, with Byrd's approval, was to impose budget reductions and rely on private charities. They feared that public efforts to deal with the crisis would undermine individual character and the "Virginia way." One of Byrd's closest advisers, Billy Reed, said, "We must keep Virginia like she is without any changes." And the senator agreed.

Byrd's animosity toward the New Deal programs, especially the farm and relief programs, support for labor, and eventually Social Security, reflected his concerns over their intrusion into state affairs, their costs, and their popularity, all of which threatened his political power in the Old Dominion and challenged his views on the proper role of government. But his fears were not shared by all Virginians, and an opposition to his authority in the state emerged.[16]

This opposition seemed insignificant in 1934, but three years later it was a menace to the organization. There had always been a difference of opinion between moderate reformers and conservatives within the machine dating back to the Martin years, but Byrd's rise to power and the progressive nature of his governorship had unified the two wings of the party, leaving only a few renegades and discontented office seekers such as Westmoreland Davis and Walter Mapp on the outside. However, the scarcity of top political jobs at the state level, the lengthening lines of candidates for those positions, and a difference of opinion over ways to combat the Great Depression produced a growing number of dissatisfied followers, who would soon come to be called anti-organization men or "antis"—enemies of the machine.

The "antis" eventually included former governors Davis and Trinkle, Lieutenant Governor James Price, Congressman John Flannagan, party secretary Martin Hutchinson, and editors Norman Hamilton and Charles Harkrader. Although they remained loyal Democrats, their political ambitions and personal philosophies were incompatible with Byrd organization objectives. While a few of them had liberal backgrounds, most were fiscal conservatives who simply believed that more money should be made available for services other than highways. The allegiance Byrd demanded precluded their kind of independence, and while many of them remained on the fringes of the organization because there was no alternative, they chafed at their forced subservience. Worth Smith characterized their frustration: "Personally, I tried to be loyal to Senator Byrd, but after a few years I found out that in order to be loyal to him I'd have to become a bullfrog and jump every time he said jump, regardless of my personal views on any subject." For the antis, the New Deal offered hope of political emancipation.

The major challenge was Jim Price's decision to run for governor without Byrd's blessing. Handsome, gregarious, and active in several fraternal organizations, Price had represented Richmond in the House of Delegates for seven terms before the machine selected him to be Pollard's running mate in the crucial 1929 race. While his popularity had made him acceptable to the leadership, he did not move into the inner circle primarily because he had taken positions at variance with those of the Byrd organization. The silence with which the organization received his candidacy revealed Byrd's surprise and dismay. Cognizant of Price's ambition, the senator floated a few trial balloons of his own, none of which found a favorable wind. After further attempts to find a competitor proved futile, Byrd conceded Price's election. For the only time in his forty-year reign as head of the organization, Byrd would not personally influence the selection of the governor, adhering to the principle that entering a race and losing was worse than not entering at all.

Price's first session with the General Assembly in 1938 proved to be the pinnacle of his success against the machine. Much of his legislative program passed in the face of minimal opposition: social security (Virginia became the last state to join the federal system), a forty-eight-hour workweek for women, and increased aid to schools. The major controversy came when he fired Ebbie Combs from his two positions as comptroller and chairman of the new Compensation Board that had been created to fix the salaries and expenses of local officials, replacing the discredited fee system. Coming as it did just a day before a private meeting between Price and Roosevelt, the firing reignited the struggle for supremacy between the organization and the antis. Although the governor also replaced the heads of several other departments, his action against Combs, Harry Byrd's longtime friend, was deemed most offensive and threatening, especially because of the crucial patronage power held by the Compensation Board.

Organization leaders had their guard up, concerned about renewed reports out of Washington that the administration was out to challenge Byrd's rule in Virginia and replace him in the Senate. The major blow to Price's challenge came in the 1940 legislative session. Price planned a thorough reorganization of the executive branch: a consolidation of departments, notably in conservation and welfare, with the duties of the Division of Motor Vehicles to be taken over by the Department of Taxation; he estimated savings of $350,000. It was a masterful proposal, but the threat to patronage in the lucrative conservation agencies and the Division of Motor Vehicles was obvious. Led by Byrd's allies, the House of Delegates killed the governor's plan. A bitter Price blamed his loss on "thinly disguised political activity." The organization once again reigned supreme in Virginia, and Price was so discredited that Harry Byrd was reelected to the Senate in 1940 without any opposition.[17]

A New Day Dawning

As in the world and nation, World War II produced significant economic and social changes in Virginia. Federal income payments in the Old Dominion rose from $122 million in 1939 to $902 million in 1945, a sum that constituted 30 percent of all the money Virginians were earning; as a result, per capita income rose almost 150 percent. The war proved to be a particular boon to shipbuilding and the production of chemicals, clothing, furniture, and tobacco in the state. Farm prices were up markedly, tobacco rising from fifteen to forty-three cents per pound. Farmers prospered, but the number of farms declined, indicative of new migratory patterns and growing mechanization. By the end of the decade, the commonwealth's urban population exceeded its rural population for the first time. While organized labor and Blacks improved their situations, their gains produced increased tensions that would play out in the postwar years. Now less rural, more crowded, and wealthier, the Old Dominion would have to adjust to these changes, but the conservatism of the state's political and social systems ensured a delayed response.

During the war, Senator Byrd paid less attention to what was happening in Richmond than at any time since his election to the state senate in 1915. Wartime issues, lengthier congressional sessions, and national politics had absorbed his interest. Fortunately, he could afford to be preoccupied elsewhere. Political opposition in the state had been effectively quieted by the defeat of Governor Price's legislative program in the 1940 General Assembly and the loss of New Deal patronage. With attention focused on events abroad, political debate, at least at the state level, was set aside for the sake of national unity.

The organization had secured ascendancy once again, but the selection of a new governor in 1941 was important in maintaining that control and minimizing factional squabbles. The process by which Harry Byrd selected governors—"giving the nod," as it was called—was complex but orderly. The names of prospects were floated before the courthouse crowd, whose sentiments carried great weight because their enthusiasm for the nominee would be crucial in the primary. Demanding integrity, loyalty, and electability in his candidates, Byrd gave consideration to longevity of service and place of residence. Within the bounds of fiscal conservatism, he accepted persons who had demonstrated streaks of independence but were the men most likely to unite the party and win elections. "Success in politics," he reportedly said, "is the candidate—don't ever try to carry a dead horse." Though the final decision was likely made by consensus, Benjamin Muse was close to the truth when he declared, with only slight exaggeration, that "governors of Virginia are appointed by Harry Byrd, subject to confirmation by the electorate. . . . He ruled not with a command but with a nod." It was not without justification that the organization was frequently labeled the Byrd machine.[18]

In 1940 the two leading contenders for Byrd's nod were Bill Tuck and Colgate Darden. Tuck had the stronger organization credentials, but his partisanship in the struggles against Price had alienated moderates and antis whom Byrd was trying to win back to the organization. Pragmatically, Byrd settled on Darden, who had recaptured the Second District congressional seat from Norman Hamilton in 1938 and had been uninvolved in assembly politics. His heroic World War I record and his current service on a naval affairs subcommittee were attractive attributes for the times. He won easy victories in the primary and general elections. Aided by the war and the weakness of the antis, who lacked money, candidates, and issues, Byrd's control of Virginia politics would never be more secure than it was during Darden's governorship.

Not so close to the day-to-day operations as he once was, Byrd ruled from afar, relying on the telephone and advisers Combs and "Peachy" Menefee for passing on advice and information. E. Blackburn "Blackie" Moore, his neighbor and fellow apple grower, was his contact in the House of Delegates. Moore had been in the House since 1933 and would become its Speaker in 1950. Darden summed up the keys to Byrd's success as the leader of the organization: "Nobody in the world ever loved politics like Harry loved politics. He just lived on it. He loved the organizing, loved working on it. . . . He'd work at it morning, noon, and night. Harry would talk to you about doing something in the middle of the day and he'd call you by supper and want to know if you'd gotten it done. . . . But he was one who took into account what the Organization as a whole wanted." It did not hurt that there was near unanimity among organization leaders concerning what policies would be good for Virginia: low taxes, frugal and honest government, and local autonomy. Unlike other political machines, there were few scandals in the commonwealth during the organization's life, but that was easy enough to achieve without an opposition. With good reason the organization was once labeled "the Great Virginia Officeholders Mutual Protection Agency."[19]

Even as it reached the pinnacle of its success, however, the organization was growing complacent in its authority. The apathy of the electorate had carried over to the politicians, who were paying little attention to local issues. This complacency was occurring at a time when Virginia was undergoing significant economic and demographic changes. The war had had an incredible migratory effect on the population as Virginians left for military training and factory jobs elsewhere before returning. Making contact with the outside world was a transforming experience—uplifting, challenging, and threatening—causing many to reevaluate perpetuation of the status quo. Furthermore, thousands of "Yankees" had come south for soldiering and jobs, and many of them stayed after the war, marrying and settling down—modern carpetbaggers not used to unresponsive government. The new electorate meant that older methods of campaigning would no longer be effective. Issues were emerging, such as schools and poll taxes, that could no longer be ignored. There was growing criticism of the failure of state government to deliver. Although they offered little more than the organization, the antis caught the scent of dissatisfaction and resurrected their challenge to the Byrd machine.[20]

For the first time in his Senate career, Harry Byrd faced opposition in the primary in 1946. He won a relatively easy victory, but Martin Hutchinson made a respectable showing, especially in the cities, where he took almost 45 percent of the vote. Consoling themselves with the thought that thousands of Republicans had voted for Byrd, the antis looked forward to the next contest, but they were never able to obtain more than 37 percent of the vote in any election against the machine. The senator's victory over the Republicans in the fall was effortless.

A more significant issue consumed Byrd's attention in 1946: renewed interest in changing the election laws, specifically repealing the poll tax. Virginia was one of only eight states still using the poll tax as a weapon to restrict Black voting and keep the electorate small. Despite a concerted effort by the antis and leading editorial opinion in the state, the organization had been powerful enough to spurn these overtures on several occasions. Byrd insisted that the tax was a necessary source of income for schools that could not easily be replaced, but he could not adequately explain why it had to be tied to voting. His intention was clear. The poll tax was an electoral mechanism that obstructed the mobilization of poor voters who would likely oppose organization economic and social policies. Byrd cited the repeal movement as an effort to "New-Dealize our State Government." Only a "motley group of Republicans, Negroes, CIOs, Communists, ardent New Dealers, and 'antis' were for it," he noted in correspondence.[21]

But the desires of Byrd and the organization to preserve a restricted electorate were running counter to the democratic spirit ignited by the war. Such pressure increased with the revelations of voting fraud in Wise County and the publicity given the extremely low voter participation in Virginia. North Carolinian Jonathan Daniels ridiculed the Old Dominion as "the birthplace and grave of democracy." In an article titled "Carry Me Back to Dear Ole Bulgaria," he scathingly indicted political bossism and the block payment of poll taxes. Virginia might be getting efficient government, he said, "but trains have run on time where democracy has died." Indeed, Virginia ranked forty-third in the nation in the percentage of its adult population voting in the 1940 election: 22 percent. From 1920 to 1946 an average of 12 percent of eligible voters participated in Democratic gubernatorial primaries, the lowest percentage in the nation.[22]

Such criticism struck a raw nerve in the organization, which was searching for some replacement for the poll tax without giving up a limited suffrage. Having been appointed to a new commission to study the question, Byrd adviser Frank Wysor warned of the consequences: "To liberalize further will . . . be about equal to 'Unconditional Surrender' to the forces which have opposed the democratic party and the democratic organization for forty years."[23] Byrd worried about the effect that repeal would have on the Black vote. Nevertheless, the commission recommended abolition of the tax as a requirement for voting, replacing it with an annual registration procedure and a literacy test. The changes passed the General Assembly with strong backing from organization leaders, but the "Campbell Amendments" were so complicated and so patently undemocratic that voters overwhelmingly rejected them in a 1949 referendum. The poll tax survived.[24]

The obsession of Harry Byrd and the organization with balanced budgets, treasury surpluses, and low taxes created another crisis in the Old Dominion that was worsening with postwar population growth: deteriorating schools. In spite of modest advances made during the Darden administration, Virginia still languished near the bottom of the states in its commitment to education. As documented by the 1944 Denny Commission on education, Virginia ranked forty-fourth in percentage of income spent on education, forty-fourth in percentage of persons receiving welfare assistance, and last in old age assistance. School building needs were estimated at $396 million over the next ten years; more than one thousand schools were deemed fire or health hazards and were labeled "unsuitable" for students. The problem was compounded by Virginia's maintenance of separate public schools for Black and White children. Conditions were so unequal that even friendly judges were now ruling that the state would have to improve the Black schools at considerable cost or risk integration. The modest expenditure increases of the Darden and Tuck administrations for education only enabled the commonwealth to hold its ground at the bottom of the rankings.[25]

"Golden Silences"

Byrd's problems with a changing Virginia were compounded by political chaos at the national level. President Harry Truman from the Jim Crow border state of Missouri was an unlikely candidate to become a civil rights advocate, but his basic decency toward people, an understanding of the international implications of America's discrimination against Blacks, and a pinch of politics converted him. A spate of racial violence in the South caused Truman to create the President's Committee on Civil Rights in December 1946 to investigate ways of protecting the civil rights of American citizens. A year later, in a stunning recommendation, the committee urged an immediate end to segregation in American life. Truman also initiated the desegregation of the armed forces, and his Commission on Higher Education proposed an end to segregated schools. Most southerners were shocked by such developments, including Harry Byrd.[26]

The senator came out swinging at the Jefferson-Jackson Day dinner on February 19, 1948, with a tirade against a "mass invasion of states' rights never before even suggested . . . by any previous President of any party affiliation in the nation's history." Itemizing Truman's proposals, he condemned the coercive nature of the Federal Employment Practices Commission (FEPC), defended Virginia's antilynching record, and compared federal interference with election laws to the dictatorships of Hitler and Stalin. He forecast an invasion of the South by a host of federal officials who would strike down all segregation laws. Faced with possible loss of federal funds if the states did not remove such laws, Virginia, he said, should "lead the Southern States in renouncing for all time every dollar of Federal aid. We must not sell our right of self-government for a mess of Federal pottage." Having aroused his audience to resistance, Byrd then closed with a call for calm deliberation and a defense of his own record of racial tolerance.[27]

Byrd and Governor Bill Tuck, who had succeeded Darden, then set out to obstruct President Truman's reelection. They devised a scheme called the "anti-Truman" bill to keep the president's name off the November ballot and allow the state party to instruct electors on whom to vote for. Although most of the organization leaders in the General Assembly dutifully endorsed the proposal, opposition was immediate and vociferous, even among other party notables. Newspapers across the Old Dominion likewise excoriated the idea; Douglas Southall Freeman in the *Richmond News Leader* concluded, "No more undemocratic proposal ever was advanced responsibly in the General Assembly of Virginia." Clearly, Senator Byrd was attempting to blackmail the national party into rejecting President Truman's renomination or at least watering down the civil rights platform by threatening to withhold Virginia's support from the party. It constituted nothing less than a brazen attempt to deny Virginians an opportunity to cast their ballots for whomever they pleased.

Surprised by the vehemence of the opposition, the leadership offered modifications to the bill and pressured the assembly to approve it. In its final form the law tolerated a wide array of candidates, but it left open the possibility that Virginia voters might be denied a full expression of their choice by party leaders. As criticism of the bill continued, Byrd and Tuck conducted a "campaign of enlightenment" to combat the "deliberate misrepresentations" of the press. As part of this effort, the House of Delegates passed a resolution that called for an SCC investigation of the Richmond newspapers for their "iniquitous editorials." Nothing came of this, but such a blatant assault on a free press revealed a bumbling, antiquated machine relying on old-time political head-bashing to preserve its authority. The anti-Truman bill was the first of several missteps that the organization made in the next decade that would lead to its eventual demise.[28]

From the beginning, Byrd believed that such activity against Truman would force him out of the 1948 presidential election, but the feisty president would not be denied. No other Democrat emerged to challenge him within the party, and he had begun traveling around the country preparing the ground for his eventual "give 'em hell" attack on the GOP. Aware that the "stop Truman" effort had faltered, Byrd moved to consolidate organization forces preparatory to the governor's race in 1949. Since a tough contest with the anti-organization forces appeared likely, the risk of further splitting state Democrats by bolting the national party was inadvisable. On June 4 at the governor's mansion, Tuck, Byrd, and Combs decided not to desert the party at the national convention or in the November election. They agreed that the state convention would instruct against Truman and empower the state committee to call it back into session if necessary, but these were essentially face-saving measures. Coming on the heels of the anti-Truman bill, the high-handed tactics of the convention reinforced the public perception of a machine running roughshod over its members and invigorated the efforts of the anti-organization forces to challenge the organization.

After the 1948 Democratic National Convention in Philadelphia endorsed the president and his civil rights program, southern dissidents met in Birmingham, Alabama, amid a bevy of Confederate flags to create the National States' Rights Party and nominate Governor Strom Thurmond of South Carolina for president. Angered at the loss of southern influence in the Democratic Party and upset with federal intrusion into state affairs, the "Dixiecrats" hoped to unite the South behind Thurmond and throw the election into the House of Representatives, where they might bargain with both parties over the choice of the next president and the elimination of civil rights legislation.[29]

The emergence of a southern party threw organization leaders, who had chosen not to attend the Birmingham gathering, into a quandary. They desperately wanted to defeat Truman, but a public defection from the Democratic Party posed substantial risks. It would threaten the fall campaigns of Senator Willis Robertson, who had replaced Senator Glass, and seven Old Dominion congressmen who had Republican opposition, but more important, it risked the race for governor the following year. The anti-organization forces traditionally began each contest with a solid third of the electorate in their column, and increasing political participation by Blacks and labor would add to their numbers. Moreover, loyal Democrats, already angered by the anti-Truman bill and the "cooked" resolutions at the state convention, might choose to join them if the national party was so cavalierly rejected for a third-party fling. On the other hand, support for Truman, no matter how grudging, would alienate states' rights advocates, possibly causing them to refrain from voting for organization candidates.

While Governor Tuck was inclined to join the Dixiecrats, Senator Byrd opted for a middle course that he hoped would defeat Truman and still leave the organization forces intact: a "golden silence." By not committing to a candidate, he would allow his followers to support either Truman or Thurmond, but his silence would imply a rejection of the president and encourage those so inclined to vote for the Dixiecrats. With an inactive state committee, Democrats' chances of carrying the state would be greatly diminished, and either Republican Tom Dewey or Thurmond could win Virginia, thus delivering a devastating blow to Truman.[30]

But Byrd had not counted on the antis. Martin Hutchinson had predicted this "sit-down strike" by the organization and urged his colleagues to organize for Truman if the regulars did not. Angered by the capricious and dictatorial methods of party leaders throughout the year and not unmindful that their loyalty might be rewarded with national support in the future, they organized a Straight Democratic Ticket Committee to back the president. Their leaders included Hutchinson, Francis Pickens Miller, and state senators Robert Whitehead and Lloyd Robinette. They were aided by a small group of organization Democrats in Richmond whose speakers included Attorney General Lindsay Almond and Third District representative J. Vaughan Gary.

Throughout the campaign, Byrd maintained his silence, but most of the Democrats running for office generally aligned themselves with Truman. Attorney General Almond offered a colorful defense for loyalty when he hyperbolized: "The only sane and constructive course to follow is to remain in the house of our fathers—even though the roof leaks and there may be bats in the belfry, rats in the pantry, a cockroach waltz in the kitchen, and skunks in the parlor. . . . We cannot take our inheritance and depart into a far country." Despite all the polls predicting a GOP triumph—even in Virginia—Truman won a smashing upset. Peace, prosperity, and interest group politics won the day. Thurmond and Henry Wallace ran far behind, although the Dixiecrat did win four Deep South states with thirty-nine electoral votes, a result far short of his goal of a united South. Surprisingly, Truman's margin of victory in Virginia was substantial: 48 percent to 41 percent for Dewey and 10 percent for Thurmond. Senator Robertson and the other Democratic congressmen also won handily. Traditional party loyalty and the hard work of the Straight Ticket people were largely responsible for these results, but the antis exaggerated the extent of their victory over the organization. Forecasting a new day in Virginia politics, Francis Pickens Miller predicted that leadership of the Democratic Party in Virginia was within their grasp, but his hope that this would translate into patronage and financial support from the national party was never fulfilled.

The election of 1948 was highly significant. It further liberalized the Democratic Party, opening doors long closed to Black Americans; it began the realignment of politics in the South that would end the long run of one-party rule and restore the region's importance in presidential elections; and it initiated the era of "massive resistance" in which race came to dominate southern elections. In Virginia, Truman's success in the face of machine opposition was a major blow to Byrd's prestige and an encouragement to his opponents, but it did not mortally wound the organization. It did, however, accelerate Byrd's shift away from the national party; more golden silences were in the offing. Lulled into complacency by the easy gubernatorial victories of the early forties and the absence of any political competition, organization leaders had arrogantly tried to impose their wishes on a changing electorate. Shocked into reality by the consequences of their own blunders, they prepared for upcoming contests with renewed vigor. It had been a bad year, but the organization had recovered from such reverses before.[31]

The Politics of Self-Preservation

The postwar changes in Virginia, combined with the schism within the national Democratic Party, caused Byrd to be unduly concerned about the election of the next governor. Organization authority depended on a victory. To avoid repeating the last contentious selection process when

Tuck had preempted the nod, Byrd and his advisers determined to select a successor well before the election to unify organization forces and forestall any opposition. Nevertheless, despite their well-laid plans, political conditions in Virginia and events elsewhere produced a multicandidate race that threatened to defeat the machine.

The man chosen to lead the organization into the fray was John S. Battle, state senator from Charlottesville. A quintessential-looking governor, the tall, handsome, dignified, and mild-mannered fifty-nine-year-old Battle had impeccable credentials as a longtime supporter of the machine, but he also had a moderate legislative record that would attract independents. With the full support of Byrd and the organization, Battle formally announced his candidacy in June 1948, over a year before the primary.

Within weeks it was a crowded field. Horace Edwards, the forty-six-year-old state party chairman, former state legislator, and mayor of Richmond, entered the race as a representative of younger organization members who had grown impatient with a selection process that seemed to reward only seniority. Fearing the damage such a split would cause, both Byrd and Combs attempted to persuade him to wait his turn, but without success.[32]

Buoyed by the Truman victory and the prospect of an organization split, the anti-organization forces confidently backed the candidacy of Francis Pickens Miller, a longtime opponent of the machine, who entered the contest in late July. Miller had a distinguished Virginia background, had served in both world wars, and, as a devout Christian, had been involved with the ecumenical movement. He had served two terms in the General Assembly but had been defeated for reelection in 1941 by a smear campaign that misidentified his wife with a woman of the same name who was a Communist. The only incumbent Democrat to lose that year, Miller vowed "to destroy a system which could destroy men." His campaign slogan was "To set Virginia Free."

A fourth candidate joined the field in November: Remmie Arnold, a wealthy businessman from Petersburg who promised to bring business practices to the governor's mansion. He was a relative unknown, but his conservative rhetoric threatened to attract votes away from Battle. Very much aware of this, both Byrd and Combs told Arnold, who had asked for their support, that it would be a mistake for him to run, but as with Edwards, their pleas were ignored. Thus, despite all his efforts, Byrd confronted a difficult four-man contest for the governorship in 1949 that raised the possibility of defeat for the organization since there was no runoff provision.[33]

Byrd threw himself and the full weight of the organization into the campaign with an intensity not witnessed since John Garland Pollard's election in 1929. The election, he warned, "was one of the most momentous we have ever had in Virginia." His major problem was Battle's easygoing nature and lack of competitive campaign experience. Byrd and Combs began advising the candidate about his correspondence, campaign management, issues, and publicity. They instructed him to secure a manager in every county and city, announce his platform, appoint a treasurer, answer his mail promptly, and place his picture and biography in the local newspapers. Worried by the possible consequences of an imperfect campaign organization, the master campaigner was teaching the novice the catechism of organization politics.[34]

To undermine Edwards's campaign, Combs suggested that Battle put forward a $74 million bill for public school construction that combined a treasury surplus with low-interest loans; this proposal competed favorably with Edwards's similar plan to aid education but which would be financed with a 2 percent sales tax. They also let it be known that a vote for Edwards was a vote for Miller, a move that Edwards called an act of desperation designed to derail his candidacy. It not only did that, it effectively ended his political career.

To blunt Miller's attacks on the machine, the organization defended its honest and solvent record and portrayed Miller as a radical bent on upsetting this secure environment. In its defense, Battle offered what came to be the standard description of the organization: "It is nothing more nor less than a loosely knit group of Virginians . . . who usually think alike, who are interested in the welfare of the Commonwealth, who are supremely interested in giving Virginia good government and good public servants, and they usually act together." Byrd frequently referred to this statement in future years when asked to explain his political machine.[35]

Although Miller campaigned aggressively on the machine issue, it paled in significance to the charge that he was the pawn of organized labor. Correctly gauging the anti-union sentiment in the state after years of strikes and aggressive CIO PAC lobbying, Byrd chose to inject life into the Battle campaign by utilizing the issue that had propelled him to victory over Hutchinson three years earlier. Breaking his pledge not to interfere in Democratic primaries, Byrd addressed a Harrisonburg rally in July and warned against giving the election to "a CIO-supported candidate." He ranted about "outside labor leaders" gaining control of Virginia and repealing the recently passed state right-to-work law.

The coup de grâce was the publication late in the race of a letter reputedly sent by James C. Petrillo, president of the American Federation of Musicians, to his several hundred union members in the state asking them to vote for Miller. Used by Battle, the letter reinforced the image of a "labor thug" attempting to dictate Virginia's politics. Although Miller labeled this the "worn-out trick of conjuring up ghosts" and vowed to enforce Virginia's labor laws, he could not recover from the impression that he was in labor's pocket.

The final organization ploy to win the election for Battle involved the encouragement of Republican voters to participate in the Democratic primary. Years before, Combs had shrewdly advised against separate party registration because Republicans had always been friendly to the organization in Democratic primaries. The Republicans were having their own primary on the same day, but their races had elicited no enthusiasm. On July 13 Henry Wise, a prominent Republican from the Eastern Shore who had once run against Byrd, urged his fellow Republicans to enter the Democratic primary and vote for Battle in order to turn away this "invasion by aliens." The Miller forces charged that Byrd had made a deal with Wise, but there is no evidence to substantiate the claim. Republicans agreed with organization policies, and knowing that the Democratic nominee would be victorious in the fall election, they preferred Battle to Miller.

The events of the final month of the campaign—Harry Byrd's public endorsement, the Petrillo letter, and the entry of the Republicans—turned the election in Battle's favor. In the largest primary turnout in Virginia history to that time, he won a sizable plurality, gaining 43 percent of the vote to Miller's 35 percent, Edward's 15 percent, and Arnold's 7 percent. Most commentators, including Miller and his supporters, believed the Republican vote turned the tide that had been running in favor of the anti-organization forces, an assessment confirmed by the large turnouts for Battle in heavily Republican areas. But even more important was the work of Harry Byrd, who quite correctly referred to "my election success in Virginia" when he described the victory to his brother. Had he chosen to remain uninvolved, Miller likely would have won. His advice, his active participation in the campaign, his selection of the labor issue, and his possible influence with Republicans added up to another triumph for the organization. The leader and his machine were not yet dead.[36]

In the early 1950s, Byrd confronted new challenges to the organization from the antis, national Democrats, and Republicans who threatened his domination of commonwealth politics. Each time he overcame his opponents, but those victories may have insulated him from the growing dissatisfaction in Virginia with the pace of progress and the wielding of authoritarian control. He allowed himself the satisfaction of believing that all was well. He particularly liked the tax reduction plan authored by young Harry Jr., recently elected to the state senate, that would reduce taxes if state surpluses exceeded revenues. During that 1950 General Assembly session the legislators also approved a $45 million appropriation for school construction that attempted to deal with inadequate and crowded facilities, but the gains barely kept pace with population growth. Although state expenditures for education doubled during Battle's administration, teacher salaries and per pupil expenditures remained below national averages. The state was last in the percentage of its students attending high school and next to last in the percentage of its college-age children going to college. Faced with rising inflation and growing populations, localities were strapped for funds with which to provide basic services in education, health, and safety. While the state debt remained low, cities and counties had debts of over $200 million by 1952.[37]

However, a movement was afoot to address these problems. Behind this reform effort was a group of young organization members, many of them veterans of World War II representing urban areas, who realized the need to change Virginia's tax and spending policies. Not content with the stand-pattism of the machine or the long apprenticeship of being seen and not heard, several of these "Young Turks" opposed the tax reduction plan authored by Harry Byrd. Jr. but favored repeal of the poll tax, more equitable redistricting, and a more enlightened policy in dealing with racial segregation. But they faced an obstinate leadership, and the General Assembly acceded to none of their requests in the 1950 and 1952 sessions.

The legislature was still controlled by Byrd loyalists, traditionalists from the rural areas who were committed to maintaining fiscal solvency and who were insensitive to the changes that had been taking place in the Old Dominion since the end of the war: urban and suburban growth in the Northern Virginia and Hampton Roads areas (up 40 percent in the 1950s), migration into the state, the strengthening of the Republican Party, and a rising Black voice. The growing federal presence also meant more outside money and residents. There were now twice as many federal workers as farmers in the state. Organization leaders believed that the poll tax was still necessary to safeguard a restricted electorate. On redistricting, rural elements presumed that the balance of power in the Old Dominion should remain, in Charles Moses's words, "with the men who feed the hogs and milk the cows." Pressure from Francis Miller in the 1952 primary forced Byrd to agree to a special legislative session to deal with redistricting in December 1952, but the result was far short of a fair apportionment for urban areas. As for race relations, the leadership judged them to be good and so rejected legislation introduced by Delegate Armistead Boothe of Alexandria to end segregation on all forms of transportation and to create a state civil rights commission. "Non-segregation," Byrd wrote N. C. McGinnis of Kenbridge, "would be most unwise and I will certainly oppose it in every way I can." Faced with the prospect of federal action, the reactionaries within the organization talked of closing parks and schools or turning them over to private firms in the event of desegregation.[38]

Byrd's problem was typical of political machines that hold power over a long period of time with limited competition; growing old and complacent, they atrophy. In light of the mini-revolt in the assembly, he was getting more suggestions now about bringing young men and women into the organization, giving them opportunities for service, and sharing patronage with them, but whether it was his distrust of youth, his own torpor, or preoccupation with Washington activities, Byrd continued to rely on traditional practices for rewarding supporters. According to William Spong, "New leadership was not nurtured or encouraged." There was no consideration of modifying the time-honored organization policies of pay-as-you-go, low taxes, limited spending, and the poll tax. Colgate Darden put it best: "Organizations don't reform from within. An organization reflects the power of an individual and his friends. They are grouped together. They stay their day and go their way." The old men of the organization were running against history, and they proved remarkably inept at dealing with change.[39]

Francis Pickens Miller, preparing for a US Senate race in 1952 against Byrd, emphasized this complacency when he referred to the "dry rot" in the Virginia democracy: the "anti-Truman" bill, the invitation to Republicans to vote in Democratic primaries, and the rejection of poll tax repeal. Faced with such charges, Byrd saw no machine candidate, with the possible exception of Bill Tuck, who could fend off Miller. Putting aside his preference for retirement, he announced his intention to run for a fourth term "to preserve the fundamental principles of government."

Miller declared his candidacy, vowing a "hot fight" against a record of "isolationism and indifference." Citing Byrd's votes against the Marshall Plan and the Truman Doctrine, he accused Byrd of joining the Taft wing of the Republican Party. The other issue of his campaign would be the organization's control of Virginia politics. Although there had been some reservations in the anti-organization camp about making a fruitless race against the popular incumbent, Miller could rely on the avid support of that intrepid band led by Robert Whitehead, who was considering a run of his own for the governorship the following year. They had little money and had to rely on their enthusiasm and an implacable hatred of the machine.[40]

Byrd organized his campaign as diligently as any he had ever run. To his campaign managers, Byrd wrote: "Take nothing for granted. . . . Effect a thorough organization to get our vote to the polls on election day. . . . Leave no stone unturned." The old network of local officeholders was revived, the poll taxes of dependable voters were paid, and the channels of correspondence to precinct workers were reopened. Byrd's commitment to his reelection campaign was so intense that his Senate chores suffered; he was on hand for only 60 percent of the roll calls, one of the lowest attendance figures in the Senate.

Byrd's strategy in the campaign was to tie Miller to the Truman administration and run against that record. Although Miller was aware of the liability of his association with Truman, he opened himself to attack when he offhandedly said, "On every one of the great issues which have confronted him, the President has made the right decision." After that comment, he never succeeded in shaking the label of "Trumanite." Moreover, his statement about "dry rot" in Virginia politics was turned against him as a disparaging remark about Virginia itself, something a true native son would never say about the Old Dominion. Harry Byrd was "not ashamed of Virginia"; as he told his campaign managers, "Mr. Miller has never had a kind word to say about Virginia, but apparently approves of practically everything being done at Washington." Finally, Byrd used Miller's prolabor record to good advantage, reminding his listeners of the efforts of organized labor to take over the state.[41]

Motivated by Miller's aggressive campaign and his own personal tragedy, the death of his daughter, Byrd turned the Old Dominion into a "burned-over" district, delivering over three hundred speeches—sometimes as many as eight a day—in all corners of the state. Dressed in his double-breasted white suit, he spoke rapidly, occasionally gesturing or pounding the podium, his face reddening as he moved to the attack. Time after time he threw the "dry rot" statement in Miller's face, along with an impressive set of statistics showing the progress in the state and its secure financial position, asserting that Virginia was "like an oasis in a desert of corruption." "Dry rot" was "tommy-rot." To lay to rest the implication that he too might be over the hill, Byrd challenged Miller to a climb up Old Rag Mountain. Columnists began rating the candidates' mountain climbing abilities and predicting the finish, but the hike was never held.

As the campaign progressed, it degenerated into a name-calling contest that endured to the end. Claiming that he had never had so many charges and misrepresentations thrown at him, Byrd lamented that he was being blamed for everything that had happened in Virginia since 1775. Old Dominion voters felt otherwise. In a record vote for a Virginia primary, Byrd won 63 percent of the total, taking every district but the Ninth. The antis blamed "Trumanism" and the Republicans for their defeat, but in reality it was Harry Byrd who had defeated Miller. His record of economy and efficiency and his independence and incorruptibility still proved congenial to a majority of the voters.[42]

Perhaps the most significant result of the 1952 primary was the death of the anti-organization movement in Virginia. Having emerged in the 1930s to challenge Harry Byrd's control of Virginia politics, the antis had occasionally created consternation among organization leaders, but they had achieved little, with the possible exception of Jim Price's victory in 1937, which was more a personal triumph than a group success. Relatively liberal in a very conservative state, without adequate funds, and confronting a powerful machine that denied them access to all levers of power, they won no major election after 1937 and did not push the organization to a more liberal position. Only the missteps of the organization in the 1948 effort to defeat President Truman and the multicandidate gubernatorial election in 1949 offered them any real opportunity to succeed. But the passage of a runoff primary law in 1952 that prevented victory by plurality, the moderate record of Governor Battle, Harry Truman's unpopularity, and Harry Byrd's prestige rendered them impotent. The subsequent struggle over school desegregation in the Old Dominion overwhelmed further liberal efforts to move Virginia forward. The only consolation for the antis was that in time, the goals that they had been fighting for—abolition of the poll tax, more funding for education, an end to machine rule—came to pass in the 1960s.[43]

Byrd had little time to savor his victory over Miller, for within the week he had to attend the state and national party conventions that would determine his and Virginia's course in the upcoming presidential election. Over his objections, Governor Adlai Stevenson of Illinois won the Democratic

PRELUDE TO REVOLUTION   39

nomination and faced General Dwight Eisenhower in the November election. Byrd's Senate voting record clearly demonstrated a greater affinity for the Republican position than for Stevenson's position. He had voted with the Democrats on only 22 percent of the major Senate roll calls, the lowest figure for party unity in the body, which well explains why Virginia Republicans chose not to challenge his reelection to the Senate. As Lester Stovall succinctly put it, "He's the best Republican we've got."

Toward the end of August, the presidential battle lines in Virginia were drawn more firmly. Governor Battle endorsed Stevenson, and the state committee indicated its intention to work for all Democratic candidates. However, state chairman Bill Tuck resigned, claiming that he could not commit to the party's nominee until his positions were more clearly delineated. At the same time a Virginia Democrats for Eisenhower group was formed. At this point, Byrd and Tuck seemed to have decided on another golden silence, similar to that of 1948.

Byrd made known his choice in an October radio address to a Virginia audience. "Trumanism," he said, was the dominant issue in "the most momentous political campaign in the history of our nation"; the FEPC, the Taft-Hartley veto, and high taxes were all leading to socialism; and Stevenson had not moved to an independent position or repudiated the president. Unable to violate his primary pledges against these policies, Byrd concluded, "I will not, and cannot, in good conscience, endorse the Democratic platform or the Stevenson-Sparkman ticket. Endorsement means to recommend, and this I cannot do." While he did not recommend a vote for either candidate or indicate how he would vote, Byrd's intention was clear. Ending his golden silence, he worked to defeat the nominees of his own party. As he told his brother, "A change in Washington is the most essential thing." But more essential was perpetuation of the Byrd organization's power. A more forthright man would have switched parties, knowing that he and his party were no longer compatible. But Harry wanted it both ways. Attempting to blend principles and personal interest, he preferred Republican national victories that helped him preserve the status quo in the commonwealth.

On Election Day Eisenhower won an overwhelming national victory and took Virginia handily in a record turnout. Byrd thought the result was "magnificent," even though Democrats suffered defeat in three congressional races, the Sixth, Ninth, and newly created Tenth—the first losses to Republicans since 1930. The Republicans also narrowly seized control of Congress, costing the Democrats chairmanships and committee control. In his own reelection bid, Byrd won easily, but one-fourth of the vote went to two unknowns, indicative of the anti-Byrd sentiment in the state. Although it is likely Eisenhower would have carried the Old Dominion without Byrd's assistance because of his personal popularity and the dissatisfaction with Harry Truman, the senator's indirect support contributed to the size of his victory. Richmond attorney Lewis F. Powell Jr., a Democrat who had defected to Eisenhower, wrote Byrd, "I believe your speech was a turning point in the campaign, as it influenced a number of other leaders as well as countless thousands of voters."[44]

But it was also a turning point in Virginia politics by contributing to the development of a competitive two-party system. After years of being little more than a protest vote in general elections, the Republican Party began to challenge the Democrats in the Eisenhower years. Traditional Republican strength in Southwest Virginia and the Valley was augmented by newcomers in the suburbs who preferred the fiscal conservatism of the national Republicans. Their emergence was fostered by the liberalization of the national Democratic Party, which had alienated many southern Democrats, including Harry Byrd. Given Byrd's blessing through his golden silences, they began voting Republican in national elections.[45]

Fresh from his triumph, Byrd now contemplated the upcoming governor's race, which, in light of the party defections in the assembly and the recent campaign, took on new significance. In the selection of a new governor, Byrd gave the nod to another faithful retainer, although it may have been that a previous obligation tied his hands. For over a decade Byrd had turned Tom Stanley aside in favor of Darden, then Tuck, then Battle. An affable, wealthy businessman, Stanley had served nine terms in the House of Delegates—three as Speaker of the House—and three terms as a congressman from the Fifth District, but he was a bland politician, inarticulate and awkward in formal press conferences and not very imaginative. Stanley had graciously stepped aside at Byrd's request in 1949, and there was little doubt that he would run in 1953 with organization support. Byrd might have preferred a more dynamic figure, but none was acceptable to him. Lulled into a false sense of security by Battle's success in dealing with the assembly, Byrd hoped that the maintenance of such calm would enable Virginia to survive a Stanley governorship, and so he gave his blessing to the Henry County native shortly after the presidential election.

Coming on the heels of Republican successes in state and nation the preceding year, the gubernatorial election of 1953 was reminiscent of that in 1929. Although Hoover's coattails had proved weak in the twenties,

Virginia Republicans were hopeful that Eisenhower's popularity would translate into victory. Their hopes were further buoyed by the selection of Ted Dalton of Radford as their nominee. A former Montgomery County commonwealth's attorney, state senator for ten years, and Republican National Committeeman, Dalton was a popular and vigorous campaigner known for his candor on the issues. He immediately put Stanley on the defensive by calling for repeal of the poll tax, a voting age of eighteen, a review of absentee voter laws, and revisions to the state tax system. He appeared to be more flexible on public financing than Stanley and prudently suggested that Virginia be prepared to act when desegregation cases now before the Supreme Court were decided. Stung by such hard-hitting tactics, Stanley became evasive and often responded to reporters' questions with a simple "no comment." He and his handlers accused the Republicans of "pulling figures out of the air" and "using cry-baby tactics"; they even waved the flag of Black Reconstruction to frighten Old Dominion voters with memories of "carpetbaggers and Republicans."

As the campaign moved into its final stage, Dalton raised one issue too many. Seeking an alternative to raising gasoline taxes to pay for highways, Dalton offered a "pay-as-you-use" program for road building to be financed with special construction revenue bonds totaling $100 million over a five-year period. Senator Byrd, who had played an insignificant role in the campaign to that point, immediately branded the plan unconstitutional and said he would "oppose with all the vigor I possess this plan of Senator Dalton to junk our sound fiscal system based upon freedom from debt." Given the sorry state of the Stanley campaign, Byrd was itching to get into the fight, and Dalton's support for bonds gave him the perfect rationale to break his silence. Said one Seventh District Democrat, "Dalton couldn't have hurt himself more if he'd come out for licensed prostitution." With Byrd leading the way, Stanley swept to a 43,000-vote victory in the largest turnout in a gubernatorial election since 1889, but his 10 percent margin of success was the smallest ever for an organization candidate seeking statewide office.

Dalton attributed his defeat to an error of conviction, but it is questionable whether his blunder changed the outcome. Byrd's entry certainly stimulated vigorous debate and attracted many of his supporters to the polls, but it was organization muscle and money, not issues, that decided the result. Bonds were no longer so critical an issue to Virginia voters as they had been in the 1920s. The diminished margin was mainly attributable to Stanley's "colorless and disappointing campaign" and to

Ted Dalton's vigor. Bolstered by a temporarily reinvigorated Republican Party, Dalton benefited from dissatisfaction that reflected the changing nature of Virginia society. Perhaps the real loser was Tom Stanley, who emerged a discredited politician, the figurehead of a political machine whose power seemed to be ebbing.[46]

The major issue of the 1954 assembly session was a renewed effort by the Young Turks to abolish the Byrd Automatic Tax Reduction Act—to get a start, said Senator Edward Breeden, on the things Virginia needed. Demanding larger appropriations for schools and hospitals, they introduced legislation to divert to these areas the estimated $7 million that would be returned to taxpayers. A bitter struggle ensued between these moderate organization men, who had near control of the House, and their more conservative elders, who were dominant in the Senate. In an arduous final session that lasted thirty-seven hours, involved five conference committees, and required stopping the clocks in the legislative chambers, a compromise was finally arranged that permitted a diversion of $2.2 million of the $7 million for teachers' salaries and other educational expenditures. The assembly then adjourned, leaving the leadership to ponder its future.[47]

A major split over a cornerstone of orthodoxy associated with the Byrd name, a governor who would not or could not lead, and the narrow victory in the recent election all portended ill for the organization. E. Ray Richardson warned the senator: "I am concerned with the present state of affairs here in our Virginia. This last session of our legislature confirms . . . impotent leadership. I heard it all through the session that things were badly confused at the top with no force and leadership. . . . The rank and file are not pleased and we are losing too many votes." Byrd acknowledged that the session had hurt the organization, but he seemed powerless to respond except to retaliate against the Young Turks. Rather than acknowledge the legitimacy of their demands, organization leaders chose to discipline them for their independence by denying them key committee assignments and support for statewide office, creating even more animosity. Moreover, losses to the Republicans, more frequent changes in the congressional delegation, and the emergence of a more independent electorate suggested that the Byrd organization was losing its control over Virginia politics. Only the emergence of the volatile desegregation issue would grant it an extended life.[48]

Massive Resistance

The decision of the US Supreme Court in May 1954 to end segregation in the public schools of America was greeted with hostility in the Old Dominion. Senator Byrd publicly responded to the court's decision in a restrained if somewhat critical way, warning that it was "the most serious blow that has yet been struck against the rights of the states in a matter vitally affecting their authority and welfare." Within days the governor's office was deluged with hundreds of letters protesting the decision, expressing fears of race mixing, and charging communist plots. Said one, "The Parent Teachers Association of Crewe prefers, as the lesser of two evils, the end of public education, rather than unsegregated schools." Garland Gray, who was to figure prominently in the massive resistance movement, urged Stanley to make a fight against the decision or face the "destruction of our culture" and "intermarriage between the races."[49]

Over the next five years, Byrd and most organization leaders were consumed by an effort to obstruct the court's decision. Influenced by the editorials of James J. Kilpatrick, editor of the *Richmond News Leader*, Byrd moved to a more defiant position. In a February 1956 speech, he coined the phrase that would represent the "final solution": "If we can organize the Southern States for massive resistance to this order, I think that in time the rest of the country will realize that racial integration is not going to be accepted in the South. . . . In interposition the South has a perfectly legal means of appeal from the Supreme Court's order." Instead of channeling the South's frustration in a positive direction, he pushed it toward defiance. And he set the tone for Virginia's response as well.[50]

Traditional racial attitudes were certainly a factor in the creation of Virginia's response. Age-old customs and attitudes that had been legalized for half a century were being challenged by the *Brown* decision. The loudest voices defending the overturned separate-but-equal policy came from the Southside, the heartland of the Byrd machine, where the Black percentage of the population was highest and where fears of racial mixing were strongest. The key representatives of this region—Congressmen Watkins Abbitt and Bill Tuck and state senators Garland Gray and Mills Godwin—were highly placed organization leaders whose views would become even more influential in the next few years. The economic and political changes taking place in Virginia forced Byrd to be attentive to Southside interests. He could not afford to antagonize his rural power base, and this gave the region and its racism an influence on policymaking out of proportion to its population in the state. As Lindsay Almond said years later, "There would have been no hard, unyielding core of massive resistance in Virginia if there were no Southside. Virginia as a whole was opposed to racial mixing in the public schools, but outside of the Southside the state evinced more of a willingness to face reality."[51]

But more than racism was involved in the shift to radical obstructionism. For years, Virginia's leaders had disdained the racial demagoguery so common in the rest of the South. The Ku Klux Klan had little clout, and racial violence was minimal thanks in large measure to the effective antilynching bill passed during Byrd's governorship. Paternalistic editorial voices praised the good relations between Whites and Blacks and supported improvements in the Black community, albeit of the separate kind. Although poll tax requirements and a White electoral structure proved intimidating and kept participation low, Blacks were allowed to vote in Democratic primaries. Byrd himself had only rarely resorted to the race issue for political purposes, such as in the bitter 1928 presidential campaign, and he did not use disparaging or rabble-rousing racial language in his speeches or private correspondence. Invariably, his opposition to integration was couched in the rhetoric of states' rights.[52]

Why did the Old Dominion suddenly forgo its tradition of racial moderation? It appears that Byrd and other organization leaders perceived race as an issue with which to maintain their political hegemony that had so recently been threatened by Miller, Dalton, and the Young Turks. Fears were expressed that if the organization did not take a forceful stand on the issue, it would lose the initiative to moderates like Ted Dalton or Robert Whitehead. Massive resistance was designed, in effect, to revitalize a dying political machine. The gradual policy shifts and planning over a two-year period confirm the ulterior purpose. Had race prejudice alone been the primary motive, Virginia's resort to massive resistance would have been much more immediate and emotional, as it was elsewhere in the South. Throughout their time in power, Byrd and the organization used race only when they were in political trouble. Now they would turn to it again in the fight over school desegregation.

Race and politics, therefore, were reinforcing elements in organization thinking because Black emancipation, particularly through increased political participation, threatened machine hegemony. Black Virginians had been contesting discrimination for much of the century. In 1929 they won a district court ruling that allowed them to vote in the Democratic primary and a decade later gained equal pay for Black teachers. In the post–World War II years, they overcame segregated interstate bus transportation (*Morgan v. Virginia,* 1946), elected Oliver Hill to the Richmond City Council in 1948, and protested inferior schools in Prince Edward County, an action that led to the celebrated *Brown* decision. Such protesters would undoubtedly vote for Byrd's opponents. Opposing an amendment that would terminate the poll tax, Willis Robertson had commented to Byrd, "Every man who knows anything about Virginia politics is bound to realize that if you suddenly give the vote to several hundred thousand who have not had it before, they are going to use it as directed by their group leader—labor or racial." Predictably, then, organization leaders fought changes in the poll tax or any civil rights legislation that promised to improve Black voting opportunities.

Finally, Byrd also believed the court's ruling was another dangerous example of federal interference in state affairs that would undermine the political and social status quo in Virginia, an act reminiscent of the Civil War and Reconstruction. For Byrd, who had spent all of his Senate years fighting this federal octopus, the decision overturned legal precedent and time-honored custom and was another blow to states' rights. It was the final humiliation, and he reacted angrily and bitterly, his frustration producing an unreasonable and overwrought defiance. The 1954 *Brown* decision, Louis Rubin said, "not only symbolized all the changes that were being forced upon Virginia . . . but it struck at the heart of the social and economic institutions that had seemed to make possible the old order and which reflected the values and attitudes embodied in the old order." A resolve to preserve this traditional way of life, along with political profit and racial conviction, dictated Byrd's response to desegregation.[53]

Byrd's rhetoric over the next five years and his unwarranted confidence that the *Brown* decision could be rolled back indicate the degree to which emotion had replaced reason in his thinking. His hyperbolic statements about villainous federal judges, a ruthless president, and an apocalyptic vision of the end of segregation were the delusions of an embittered, frustrated man whose world was collapsing around him. He encouraged the General Assembly in the summer of 1956 to pass legislation to close schools in the event of court-ordered integration, which occurred in the fall of 1958. Years later Almond explained the senator's motives: "I think he was determined to preserve his power and his hold on the people of Virginia. He saw the seeds of the destruction of his organization." While massive resistance led to short-term school closings (they were reopened by court order in January 1959) and may have produced a few more election victories, it did not prolong the life of the organization but contributed to its demise by further dividing the Democratic Party, stimulating Black political participation, and encouraging more federal interference. It also tarnished the image of the Old Dominion and complicated what was truly inevitable: the end of state-imposed racial discrimination. Virginia did not need time; it needed leaders with vision and a sense of justice.[54]

Despite his forty years in power, Byrd's legacy did not endure. He was not yet in his grave and the structure was coming down, undermined by those economic, demographic, and externally imposed changes that revolutionized Virginia's political culture. African Americans, Republicans, and Yankees, invisible since Reconstruction, were emerging from the shadows to create an opposition to the machine. The foundations of the organization—a small, controllable electorate, the courthouse crowd, a one-party General Assembly—had eroded. Soon to go were the poll tax and one-sided reapportionment that favored rural areas, always the strength of the organization. Harry Byrd's world was disappearing.

Notes

1. James Branch Cabell, "New Rumblings in the Old Dominion," *New York Times,* June 19, 1949, Sunday Magazine.
2. Ronald L. Heinemann, John G. Kolp, Anthony S. Parent, and William Shade, *Old Dominion, New Commonwealth: A History of Virginia, 1607-2007* (Charlottesville: University of Virginia Press, 2008), 259, 261.
3. Wythe W. Holt Jr., "The Senator from Virginia and the Democratic Floor Leadership: Thomas S. Martin and Conservatism in the Progressive Era," *Virginia Magazine of History and Biography* 83 (January 1975): 3–21; Paschal Reeves, "Thomas S. Martin: Committee Statesman," *Virginia Magazine of History and Biography* 68 (July 1960): 344–64; Burton Kaufman, "Henry De La Warr Flood" (Ph.D. diss., Rice University, 1966), 2–24.
4. Heinemann et al., *Old Dominion, New Commonwealth,* 276–78; Brent Tarter, *The Grandees of Government: The Origins and Persistence of Undemocratic Politics in Virginia* (Charlottesville: University of Virginia Press, 2013), 262–72.
5. Heinemann et al., *Old Dominion, New Commonwealth,* 278.
6. Ibid., 278–82; Raymond Pulley, *Old Dominion Restored: An Interpretation of the Progressive Impulse, 1870–1930* (Charlottesville: University Press of Virginia, 1968), 83–89, 114.
7. Heinemann et al., *Old Dominion, New Commonwealth,* 295–97.
8. Ronald L. Heinemann, *Harry Byrd of Virginia* (Charlottesville: University Press of Virginia, 1996), 28–31.

9. Ibid., 37.

10. Joseph A. Fry and Brent Tarter, "The Redemption of the Fighting Ninth," *South Atlantic Quarterly* 76 (Summer 1978): 352–70; Harry F. Byrd to A. K. Morison, May 11, 1922, Harry F. Byrd to Hayes, August 22, October 9, 1922, Box 76, Papers of Harry Flood Byrd, Sr. (Charlottesville: University of Virginia Library, Special Collections) (hereafter Byrd Papers).

11. Heinemann, *Harry Byrd of Virginia*, 32–33.

12. Stanley L. Willis, "To Lead Virginia Out of the Mud," *Virginia Magazine of History and Biography* 94 (October 1986): 425–52; Robert T. Hawkes Jr., "The Career of Harry Flood Byrd, Sr., to 1933" (Ph.D. diss., University of Virginia, 1975), 60–62.

13. Heinemann, *Harry Byrd of Virginia*, 44–46; Allen W. Moger, *Virginia: Bourbonism to Byrd, 1870–1925* (Charlottesville: University Press of Virginia, 1968), 334–61.

14. Heinemann, *Harry Byrd of Virginia*, 10, 102.

15. Heinemann, *Harry Byrd of Virginia*, 103–5; Robert Hawkes, "Harry F. Byrd: Leadership and Reform," in *The Governors of Virginia, 1860–1978*, ed. James Tice Moore and Edward Younger (Charlottesville: University Press of Virginia, 1982), 233–46; Leslie Lipson, *The American Governor: From Figurehead to Leader* (Whitefish, MT: Literary Licensing LLC, 2012), 101, 113–14.

16. Heinemann, *Harry Byrd of Virginia*, 120; see Ronald L. Heinemann, *Depression and New Deal in Virginia: The Enduring Dominion* (Charlottesville: University Press of Virginia, 1983).

17. Heinemann, *Harry Byrd of Virginia*, 185–98; Alvin Hall, "James Hubert Price: New Dealer in the Old Dominion," in *The Governors of Virginia*, 277–90; John Syrett, "The Politics of Preservation," *Virginia Magazine of History and Biography* 97 (October 1989): 437–62.

18. Heinemann, *Harry Byrd of Virginia*, 265–66; Benjamin Muse, "The Durability of Harry Flood Byrd," *Reporter* 17 (October 8, 1957): 26–30; Muse, *Washington Post,* July 28, 1966.

19. Heinemann, *Harry Byrd of Virginia*, 266–70; James Latimer, interviews with Colgate Darden, *Richmond Times-Dispatch,* May 5, 1964.

20. Heinemann et al., *Old Dominion, New Commonwealth,* 331.

21. Ibid., 272–77; Byrd to Wysor, September 13, 1944, Box 183, Byrd Papers.

22. Jonathan Daniels, "Virginia Democracy," *Nation* 153 (July 26, 1941): 74.

23. Wysor to Byrd, September 13, 1945, Box 185, Byrd Papers.

24. Heinemann, *Harry Byrd of Virginia*, 272–73.

25. Ibid., 278–80.

26. Ibid., 255–56.

27. Byrd, speech, February 19, 1948, Box 368, Byrd Papers.

28. Heinemann, *Harry Byrd of Virginia*, 257–59.

29. Ibid., 259–63; William Crawley Jr., "William Munford Tuck: The Organization's Rustic Rara Avis," in *Governors of Virginia*, 308–19.

30. Ben Beagle and Ozzie Osborne, *J. Lindsay Almond: Virginia's Reluctant Rebel* (Roanoke, VA: Full Court Press, 1984), 50.

31. James R. Sweeney, "The Golden Silence: The Virginia Democratic Party and the Presidential Election of 1948," *Virginia Magazine of History and Biography* 82 (July 1974): 351–71; Heinemann, *Harry Byrd of Virginia*, 262–64.

32. Peter Henriques, "The Organization Challenged," *Virginia Magazine of History and Biography* 82 (July 1974): 372–406.

33. Ibid., 373–77; Francis Pickens Miller, *Man from the Valley* (Chapel Hill: University of North Carolina Press, 1971), 173–74.

34. Heinemann, *Harry Byrd of Virginia*, 281.

35. Henriques, "The Organization Challenged," 390–96; Heinemann, interview with Harry Byrd Jr.

36. Heinemann, *Harry Byrd of Virginia*, 280–85; Henriques, "The Organization Challenged," 398–406; James R. Sweeney, "Byrd and Anti-Byrd: The Struggle for Political Supremacy in Virginia, 1945–1954" (Ph.D. diss., University of Notre Dame, 1973).

37. Heinemann, *Harry Byrd of Virginia*, 317–18.

38. Ibid., 318; Byrd to McGinnis, May 24, 1951, Box 196, Byrd Papers; Douglas Smith, "When Reason Collides with Prejudice: Armistead Lloyd Boothe and the Politics of Desegregation in Virginia, 1948–1963," *Virginia Magazine of History and Biography* 102 (January 1994): 9–15.

39. Heinemann, *Harry Byrd of Virginia*, 318–19; Sweeney, "Byrd and Anti-Byrd," 197–203.

40. Heinemann, *Harry Byrd of Virginia*, 306.

41. Peter Henriques, "The Byrd Organization Crushes a Liberal Challenge, 1950–1953," *Virginia Magazine of History and Biography* 87 (January 1979): 3–29.

42. Ibid., 20–25.

43. Ibid., 25–29; Heinemann, *Harry Byrd of Virginia*, 309.

44. Heinemann, *Harry Byrd of Virginia*, 310–16; James R. Sweeney, "Revolt in Virginia: Harry Byrd and the 1952 Presidential Election," *Virginia Magazine of History and Biography* 86 (April 1978): 180–95.

45. See Frank Atkinson, *The Dynamic Dominion: Realignment and the Rise of Virginia's Republican Party since 1945* (Fairfax, VA: George Mason University Press, 1992).

46. Heinemann, "Thomas B. Stanley: Reluctant Resister," in *Governors of Virginia*, 333–47; J. Harvie Wilkinson III, *Harry Byrd and the Changing Face of Virginia Politics, 1945–1966* (Charlottesville: University Press of Virginia, 1984), 98–105.

47. Heinemann, *Harry Byrd of Virginia*, 323–24. The tax reduction law was repealed in 1956.

48. Ibid., 324. Richardson to Byrd, March 19, 1954, Box 231, Byrd Papers.

49. Heinemann, *Harry Byrd of Virginia,* 325–26.
50. *Richmond Times-Dispatch,* February 15, 1956.
51. Heinemann, *Harry Byrd of Virginia,* 328.
52. See J. Douglas Smith, *Managing White Supremacy: Race, Politics, and Citizenship in Jim Crow Virginia.* (Chapel Hill: University of North Carolina Press, 2003).
53. Heinemann, *Harry Byrd of Virginia,* 329–30; Wilkinson, *Byrd,* 150–54; Robertson to Byrd, June 28, 1957, Box 249, Byrd Papers; Lewis Rubin, *Virginia: A Bicentennial History* (New York: Norton, 1977), 196–97. See also Andrew Buni, *The Negro in Virginia Politics, 1902–1965* (Charlottesville: University Press of Virginia, 1967).
54. Heinemann, *Harry Byrd of Virginia,* 330–54. For a thorough discussion of Virginia's massive resistance, see James Ely, *The Crisis of Conservative Virginia: The Byrd Organization and the Politics of Massive Resistance* (Knoxville: University of Tennessee Press, 1976); Robbins Gates, *The Making of Massive Resistance: Virginia's Politics of Public School Desegregation, 1954–1956* (Chapel Hill: University of North Carolina Press, 1965); Matthew Lassiter and Andrew Lewis, eds., *The Moderates' Dilemma: Massive Resistance to School Desegregation in Virginia* (Charlottesville: University Press of Virginia, 1998); Benjamin Muse, *Virginia's Massive Resistance.* (Bloomington: Indiana University Press, 1961); and Bob Smith, *They Closed Their Schools: Prince Edward County, Virginia, 1951–1964* (M. E. Forrester Council of Women, 1996).

2

The Emergence of the Modern Democratic Party

BILL SPONG AND THE ELECTION OF 1966

John G. Milliken

VIRGINIA MADE the political transition to the World War II generation later than much of the rest of the nation. While the New Frontier was in full swing across the nation in 1961, the "museum piece"[1]—in V. O. Key's memorable description—that was Virginia was still in the grip of the generation that came of age in the years immediately following World War I, and its politics were dominated by a rural conservative coalition led by US senator Harry Flood Byrd Sr., first elected to the state senate in Virginia in 1916.

The Byrd organization (as it was known) was based in the rural counties where a majority of Virginians lived in the 1920s and 1930s when Byrd was governor and first inherited the leadership of the coalition from Thomas Staples Martin, US senator from Virginia from 1895 to 1919. The organization held a firm grip on state politics for more than half a century, finally succumbing to changing demographics and the rise of the role played by African Americans in the politics of the commonwealth.

The 1966 Democratic Primary for the US Senate

The retirement of Senator Harry Byrd in the fall of 1965 and the appointment of his son to his Senate seat led to a special election being called for November 1966 to fill his unexpired term. Since the term of Virginia's other senator, A. Willis Robertson, ended in 1966, voters were faced with the unusual circumstance of having two US Senate seats appear on the same ballot. There was immediate scrambling among Democrats opposed to the organization to contest one or both seats in the Democratic primary.

The results of that primary provided the first indication of the impacts that changing demographics would have on the state's politics over the next fifty years. These changes were most obvious in the fast-growing areas of Northern Virginia and Hampton Roads, where job opportunities in and around the nation's capital and around the Navy base and maritime facilities in Hampton Roads brought new people to the commonwealth and attracted many rural Virginians to relocate. New people meant new perspectives. Many of these newcomers were younger and just starting families, and their concerns centered on issues of education and quality of life in their new suburban homes. They became active, and their activity forced even incumbent officeholders to take notice. The primary candidates divided sharply between organization and antiorganization. But they also divided between urban and rural, between fast-growing and shrinking. The antiorganization candidates came from Northern Virginia and Hampton Roads, and the incumbents came from the organization's base in the rural areas.

The results reflected that split. The two counties and three cities constituting what was then defined as Northern Virginia provided the opponents of the organization margins of more than 20,000 votes. The margins were only slightly lower in the six cities of Hampton Roads. In those cities, as well as in Richmond, the antiorganization margins were increased significantly by the votes of a growing number of African Americans, whose numbers had increased with the ending of the poll tax in national elections and with increased voter registration spurred by the civil rights movement. The candidates of the organization relied as always on their rural base, and though they carried those seventy-plus counties by large percentages, the numerical margins were small.

These demographic trends of uneven population growth and increasing African American participation were first evident in the outcomes in 1966 but would have an increasing impact in succeeding elections, as shown in more detail in this book's concluding chapter.

The Young Turks and the Beginnings of Virginia's Transformation

As early as the mid-1950s, rumblings among some younger, more urban members of the Byrd organization led to what became known as the "Young Turk" revolt in the state House of Delegates. Led by Delegate Armistead Boothe of Alexandria, these men, many of whom were World

War II veterans in their thirties, considered themselves members of the Byrd organization. That was certainly true of Boothe, who had first been elected to the House of Delegates in 1948. His father, Gardner Boothe, was a prominent Alexandria lawyer and close personal and political friend of Harry Byrd Sr. Rather than overthrowing the organization, Boothe and the Young Turks sought to modernize its policies. Their ranks included then newly elected delegate William B. Spong Jr. of Portsmouth, one of the port cities of Hampton Roads.

The Young Turks focused their attention on the issues of state spending and debt, especially spending for schools. Over several sessions of the General Assembly they tried without success to increase state support for education, the issue they heard about most often in their increasingly urban constituencies. But in 1954 the education funding question was pushed aside by the issue that would dominate Virginia politics for the remainder of the 1950s and postpone the impact of the demographic shifts that would change the state's politics. That issue was the US Supreme Court's decision in *Brown v. Board of Education of Topeka*[2] and Virginia's adoption of a policy of massive resistance to its implementation. The term "massive resistance" was first used by Senator Harry F. Byrd Sr. in a statement issued in February 1956. It referred to what Byrd hoped would be a collective action by the southern states to convince the rest of the country that the South would never accept racial integration. Organization leaders in the Southside, where the African American population was greatest, had already voiced their clear opposition to compliance with the court's decision. Following Byrd's statement, the rest of the organization fell in line, interpreting his statement as meaning that every possible means should be used to frustrate the desegregation of the public schools in the state.[3] The issue became a rallying cry, and its use papered over many of the divisions that had begun to show in the organization.

In June 1954, within a month of the court's decision, Governor Thomas B. Stanley appointed a commission chaired by state senator Garland Gray (the Gray Commission) to recommend proposals to respond to *Brown*. The proposal offered by the commission suggested a measured approach to opposition but included a call for a statewide referendum to revise section 141 of the Virginia Constitution, which prohibited the spending of public money on private schools, potentially paving the way for tuition grants to families who did not want their children to attend an integrated public school. A special session of the legislature was set for late November 1955 to act on the commission's recommendations. The Young

Turks and other moderates were in a bind. They did not like aspects of the Gray Commission recommendations but feared that the more strident opponents of the court's decision would push the state into even more militant opposition. As a result, many of the Young Turks supported the Gray Commission recommendations, including the referendum to repeal section 141.

The opposition to the Gray Plan was led by Delegate Armistead Boothe. But he could muster only five votes in the House of Delegates and only one, Republican Ted Dalton's, in the state senate in opposition to the plan.[4] He then did what no loyal member of the organization could ever do. He took his opposition directly to the voters. He became chairman of the Virginia Society for the Preservation of Public Schools and traveled the state in opposition to the referendum. But his was a lonely voice, and the referendum passed 304,154 to 146,164. Some even applied the dreaded word "liberal" to him and his policies. And the issue was moving headlong in the opposite direction. Byrd's call for "massive resistance" was followed by the legislature's adoption of a series of measures much more restrictive and strident than those proposed by the Gray Commission, including the elimination of state funding for any school district in which even one school was integrated. Moderate voices were either silenced or ignored, and the issue dominated elections and political debate through the remainder of the decade.

Ending Massive Resistance and the Byrd Organization's Dominance

In September 1958, schools in three Virginia jurisdictions—Charlottesville, Norfolk, and Warren County—were closed. They remained closed for five months, and the issue was resolved only when both the Virginia Supreme Court and a three-judge federal district court in Norfolk declared the massive resistance laws unconstitutional.[5] At that point, prodded by leaders of the business community, Governor J. Lindsay Almond called a special session of the General Assembly and secured the repeal of the principal massive resistance laws.[6] Leaders of the Byrd organization, including the senator himself, his son, and many of the leaders of the General Assembly, remained bitter about what they considered to be Almond's abandonment. Where you stood and whose side you chose in the era of massive resistance defined the politics of the decade of the 1950s and much of the 1960s in the commonwealth. As an issue it would return in the election of 1966.

But slowly, with the end of massive resistance, more normal political discourse resumed. And increasingly that discourse was about issues that mattered most to the fast-growing parts of the commonwealth, particularly the Northern Virginia suburbs and Hampton Roads, where large numbers of young families were finding jobs and buying and renting homes near the governmental and military installations that were growing in both areas. More and more, the discussion was about government services, and particularly about education. Newcomers to the state with experience in other places complained that Virginia lagged far behind many of its sister states in the quality of its services and the level of state financial support for education.[7]

Those same young families were forcing a broadening of the focus of Virginia elections. Traditionally, Virginia politics was all about the government of the commonwealth. And, while Virginia sent "ambassadors" to Washington in the form of senators and representatives, their principal task was to limit what negative impact the federal government with its laws and regulations might have on state affairs. But beginning in the 1950s, for an increasing number of residents of Hampton Roads and Northern Virginia who worked for or around government and the military, national politics mattered. That shift in the focus of politics was obscured during the years of struggle over the *Brown* decision and massive resistance but became apparent with the new decade and the new president with his "New Frontier." These new Northern Virginia and Hampton Roads residents paid attention in even-numbered federal election years, not as much in state election, odd-numbered years.[8] The issues that interested them were not the traditional Byrd organization issues of fiscal austerity, opposition to social change, and support for a rural life and economy. And the new residents were moving into areas where their neighbors were already less likely to be a part of the organization.[9] The influence of this growing demographic adding its voice and vote to the traditional antiorganization forces and the still resentful remnants of the Young Turks began to chip away at the organization.

Some leaders of the organization saw the need to bring in these younger people and to moderate the organization's image. In the 1964 presidential race, Sidney Kellam of Virginia Beach, a key leader of the organization, wove together a remarkable (for Virginia) and successful coalition involving many of those younger Democrats that carried the state for the Johnson-Humphrey ticket. The outcome of the 1964 election and the disparate distribution of its vote across the state resulted from the impact of three trends that had been building and would have a decisive impact on the elections to follow in 1965 and 1966 and beyond:

- The growth in the size of the electorate, particularly in the urban corridor stretching from Northern Virginia to Hampton Roads;
- Defections from the Democrats in Southside and other traditional areas of conservative Democratic strength; and
- Dramatic growth in the size and one-sided nature of the African American vote.

Virginia's voting-age population had grown 9.4 percent from 1960 to 1964, and the percentage of that population that participated in elections had shot up from 33.35 percent in 1960 to 41.2 percent in 1964, driven largely by significant increases in fast-growing Northern Virginia and larger turnouts in the predominantly African American precincts in the cities and in rural Southside. The Johnson-Humphrey ticket carried the city of Richmond by 35,662 to 27,196. In 1960 the Kennedy-Johnson ticket had lost the city, 17,642 to 27,307. The Republican vote in the city was virtually unchanged from 1960 to 1964, while the Democratic vote doubled. A substantial part of that vote came from the fifteen precincts having the largest numbers of African American voters. That total was 18,807 votes for President Johnson and only 424 votes for Barry Goldwater, his Republican opponent.[10]

The Twenty-Fourth Amendment to the Constitution, ratified in January 1964, had banned the poll tax as a prerequisite to vote in federal elections, and its absence, both practical and symbolic, combined with aggressive voter registration drives, contributed greatly to the increased turnout. Of the more than 224,000 new voters registered between April and October 1964, more than 150,000 registered for federal elections only (a poll tax was still required to register for state elections).[11] These were the presidential year voters that added to the Johnson margin, and they came mostly from the two fast-growing areas of Northern Virginia and Hampton Roads.

In contrast, the Democratic presidential candidate had carried the Fourth Congressional District in Southside Virginia in every modern election, even in 1952, 1956, and 1960, when the Republican nominee won the state handily. But Lyndon Johnson, the 1964 Civil Rights Act, and the increasing assertiveness of the local Black political leadership were too much for the traditional conservative Byrd organization voter in

Southside, and he broke ranks, resulting in Goldwater carrying the Fourth District, while at the same time Fourth District voters reelected both Senator Harry Byrd and the local congressman and organization leader Watkins Abbitt. Senator Byrd, running for his sixth term, had remained silent on the presidential race, though both sides trumpeted their support for him and signs for "Barry and Harry" vied with "Vote for Johnson-Byrd November Third" at Byrd rallies.[12]

No Virginia politician was more attentive to the changing Virginia political landscape than Mills E. Godwin, then lieutenant governor and anxious aspirant to the governorship in the election of 1965. Godwin, raised in Chuckatuck, in rural Nansemond County (now the City of Suffolk) in the same Fourth Congressional District, had been the organization's spokesman in the state senate, supporting massive resistance. In his race for lieutenant governor in 1961, Godwin attacked his opponent, state senator Armistead Boothe, the AFL-CIO, the NAACP, and Bobby Kennedy interchangeably. But that same Godwin as lieutenant governor climbed aboard the *Lady Bird Special,* the train carrying President Johnson's wife through Virginia and much of the South. For the ardent conservatives of the organization, that was the ultimate apostasy.

But Godwin was making a careful and gradual shift from Southside segregationist and organization spokesman to straight-ticket Democrat, open to discussing heretofore forbidden topics such as a statewide retail sales tax and bonded indebtedness. And the political coalition assembled for his 1965 election reflected that shift, though in his case it was more of a straddle. Many organization leaders, among them Sidney Kellam, quickly supported his early efforts, frustrating what might otherwise have been a candidacy by Harry Byrd Jr. To that organization base was added many of the 1950s-era Young Turks and the national straight-ticket Democrats, who then dominated the party in vote-rich Northern Virginia. They gravitated to Godwin because he had shown clear signs of moderation in his views and because they feared a Byrd Jr. candidacy.

All that togetherness was too much for some in the Southside, and in the summer of 1965 the Virginia Conservative Party was founded by those who thought the Democratic Party, including the Byrd organization, had lost its way. The new party fielded a full slate of candidates for statewide office, determined to save the Old Dominion from Godwin, that man who had ridden the *Lady Bird Special.*[13] Their emergence shut the door on the traditional dominance of the Democratic Party and the state by rural Southside interests. And their emergence hastened the move of both organized labor (in the form of COPE, the political affiliate of the

AFL-CIO) and the Richmond Crusade for Voters and the Independent Voters League, the state's two largest African American political groups, into the Godwin camp. The irony of African American political support for the former chief spokesman for massive resistance was lost on no one.[14]

Godwin's coalition won convincingly, but with only a plurality of the vote (269,526 votes representing 47.9 percent). The newly formed Conservative Party polled more than 13 percent (75,307 votes), and Linwood Holton, the Republican nominee, received more votes than any statewide Republican in history (212,207, or 37.7 percent). Holton's votes came from traditional Republican areas west of the mountains but also from the suburban counties of Arlington, Fairfax, and Henrico.[15] Holton ran as a "liberal" alternative on race and spending to the Godwin of the 1950s. But this was not the Godwin of massive resistance, and with Holton on his left and the Conservative Party on his right, Godwin's straddle succeeded. Sidney Kellam had masterminded back-to-back victories for President Johnson and Godwin by recognizing that the organization had to change and that an organization-based coalition could be built somewhere in the middle with the "liberal" Republicans on one side and the unreconstructed Conservatives on the other.

While most of the focus in political 1965 was on the governor's race, a Virginia Supreme Court of Appeals decision in January required General Assembly action to redraw congressional district lines to recognize the disproportionate growth that had occurred in the urban and suburban areas, particularly in the Eighth Congressional District, a largely rural area that was then represented by Howard W. Smith, a nineteen-term veteran who was chairman of the Rules Committee in the US House of Representatives.[16] Responding to the state Supreme Court decision in September 1965, the General Assembly removed several western, rural counties of his constituency and placed them in the Seventh District. In their place, Smith was given approximately 36,000 new voters in suburban, fast-growing Fairfax County plus several counties on the Middle Peninsula with large African American populations.[17] Those changes, coinciding with newly invigorated voter registration of African Americans in the eastern rural counties in the Eighth District, led to a clash in the 1966 Democratic primary that was to have a significant impact on the statewide election that year and on the Virginia political landscape for the next decade.

The opening step on the path to the 1966 election actually occurred the prior year and entirely changed the dynamic of the political year to come. On November 11, 1965, after Godwin's election but prior to his taking office, Harry Flood Byrd Sr. announced his retirement from the US Senate.

Governor Albertis Harrison, long an organization stalwart, promptly appointed state senator Harry Flood Byrd Jr. to fill his father's seat until the next general election, set for a year hence. This resulted in both US Senate seats being on the same ballot since the term of the seat held by Senator A. Willis Robertson was ending that same year.[18]

With Harry Byrd Jr. a certain candidate to fill the reminder of the term for the seat to which he had just been appointed, the organization's attention focused on incumbent senator Robertson, then aged seventy-nine. Robertson had never been part of the organization's inner circle, but he shared the organization's basic values, and his voting record closely followed that of his senior colleague, Senator Harry Byrd Sr. Despite that, some of the organization's leaders yearned for a younger candidate, sensing that a bridge to that generation was needed. Sidney Kellam, hoping to repeat his successful strategy of 1964 and 1965, urged a local Hampton Roads congressman, Thomas N. Downing of the First District, to run.[19] He understood better than most that the Virginia electorate had changed and that a ticket of two unbending conservatives would not appeal to a broad enough segment of the expanded voting population to win a Democratic primary.

Robertson, who had not faced real opposition since his arrival in the Senate in 1946, busied himself lining up support among local organization leaders and, importantly in his calculations, leaders in the banking and business community. As chairman of the Senate Banking Committee, Robertson was a reliable supporter of banking interests. J. Harvie Wilkinson Jr., a prominent Richmond banker, assumed the task of Finance Committee member and organizer of the business community for Robertson. On June 20, 1965, the Virginia Bankers Association adopted a resolution urging him to run for reelection.[20] In Robertson's view, this early effort to line up support in the business community would discourage efforts within the organization to replace him with a younger candidate.

Potential opposition to Byrd and to Robertson was slower to emerge because of the number of possible candidates, the fact that there was no single acknowledged leader to follow, and because the "tradition" was that such candidacies were not announced until after the annual General Assembly session. While the leaders of the old Byrd organization quietly discussed possibly replacing Robertson with a younger candidate,[21] the more diverse, less cohesive nonorganization elements of the Democratic Party broke roughly into two groups: the liberals who had long fought the organization and the self-described moderates, whose rhetoric was softer, whose policies were less ideological, and whose ranks included some who thought of themselves as supporters of the organization, or at least of Harry Byrd senior and junior.

The Henry Howell Liberal Challenge

The more liberal group included state senator Henry E. Howell of Norfolk, Congressman W. Pat Jennings from the far Southwest, Delegate George C. Rawlings of Fredericksburg, and state senator Armistead L. Boothe of Alexandria. Howell, only recently elected to the state senate, was the most voluble of the group and a gifted speaker. Addressing a young and largely African American audience at Virginia State University on December 2, 1965, Howell laid down a challenge:

> Yes, Virginia is faced with a political problem . . . how to find, encourage and elect a U.S. Senator that will lead Virginia forward into the mainstream of national life. There are many timid political leaders. There are those who aspire to the office but who are afraid to run up the flag of progressive government. . . . There are too many political leaders in Virginia looking for the middle road. . . .[22]
>
> Many persons have urged me to offer for the high office of U.S. Senator so I might make a contribution on a statewide basis to remold a new Virginia during this transitional period when political influence in Virginia can be caused to pass from the conservative regime of the Organization to a new vital Democratic force.[23]

Howell's continuing very public efforts put pressure on the moderates. That faction included state senator Bill Spong of Portsmouth, attorney Bill Battle of Charlottesville, state senator Bill Hopkins of Roanoke, and a number of younger elected officials, professionals, and businessmen around the state who, twenty years earlier, would have naturally gravitated to the organization. But the organization no longer spoke to their needs or interests. They did not share the organization's stridency on race or its aversion to spending on critical state domestic programs, principally education. And they viewed the organization as out of touch with the Virginia they saw every day in their professional and personal lives. Many still rankled from the treatment they and their friends had received in the wake of the Young Turk rebellion a decade before.

Henry Howell ramped up the pressure at an event in Fredericksburg on February 15 and said he would run if Jennings and Spong did not, and set a two-week deadline for making a decision.[24] Behind the scenes,

Howell and his allies had plotted out a full scale campaign and lined up support among labor and other liberal groups for a Howell candidacy. His threats to run forced Bill Spong and the moderates to move up their decision timetable.[25]

On February 25, Bill Spong, responding to the pressure from Howell and others to declare his intentions, issued a two-sentence statement saying he would run against Senator Robertson and would make a formal announcement following adjournment of the General Assembly in mid-March. Henry Howell endorsed him two hours later, saying he would not run himself and endorsing Congressman Jennings for the race against Senator Byrd.[26] There was every expectation that Jennings would soon announce against Byrd, and he announced his intention to make a statement on March 2.[27]

Spong, Boothe, and Jennings met in Fredericksburg the evening of March 1 and agreed on what had apparently been decided between Boothe and Jennings in the hourlong drive that afternoon from Alexandria: Boothe would run for the US Senate against Byrd, and Jennings would seek reelection to Congress from the Ninth District.[28]

Boothe, a silver-haired, smiling, courtly gentleman, appeared a traditional Virginia politician, often in seersucker suit and bow tie. But to most of the state he was remembered only as a leader of the Young Turks and as having led the opposition to massive resistance. He made his formal announcement the following day, surprising most political activists outside Richmond. Staff for Congressman Jennings cited four reasons for his decision to defer to Boothe: Boothe would be better financed, was from a more populous area, was better known statewide, and had a more moderate image. Critical to his thinking, according to those same sources, was Sidney Kellam's decision to support Byrd. Jennings and many others saw Kellam as symbolic of the broad coalition that had elected Godwin, and his supporting Byrd, while at the same time seeking a younger alternative to Robertson, sent the message to Jennings that he could not win.[29] In Jennings's view, Kellam would have been the key to raising money as Jennings did not have the financial base in his home area of the Southwest that Boothe had in Northern Virginia.

With the focus on the unusual circumstance of a simultaneous election of two US senators, little attention was being paid statewide to the line-ups for the congressional seats. In the newly reconfigured Eighth District, forty-four-year-old Fredericksburg delegate George C. Rawlings sought to create a coalition of Fairfax liberals together with large numbers of newly registered African Americans to square off against Howard W. Smith, the leader of the conservative coalition in the House of Representatives. To liberals, Smith was the symbol of a Congress that had bottled up progressive legislation.[30]

Age was also an issue, much to Judge Smith's dismay: "Newspapers always start their stories about me with 'Howard W. Smith, 83, . . .', as though my age were a title, like a PhD. Well, it is something of a badge, I guess."[31] But it was not so much the actual number of years that might cost Judge Smith the election. It was that he, like Willis Robertson, was from a different era and spoke for a different Virginia.

And Rawlings wasted no time in highlighting the difference. In a Fairfax County speech on May 6 he said, "It is important to Northern Virginia that we have a Representative who is sympathetic with the difficulties experienced by people in a rapidly growing urban area and who welcomes the idea of new people in Virginia."[32] He cited the critical importance of public transit and of long-range land use planning, topics that had never entered the list for Judge Smith.

Spong, Robertson, and the Democratic Primary of 1966

The line-ups were set for the Democratic primary to be held on July 12. The choices were clear-cut, both in policy and in manner and style. In the Spong-Robertson race and the Rawlings-Smith contest there was a generational choice that laid bare the philosophical, cultural, and stylistic differences. In the Byrd-Boothe race the philosophical differences were sharp, but both men belonged to the same generation and, in many ways, the same political culture.

Absalom Willis Robertson was born in 1887 in Martinsburg, West Virginia. He graduated from Richmond College (now the University of Richmond) in 1907, received his law degree, also from Richmond College, in 1908, and set up a law practice in Buena Vista, moving to Lexington in 1910. He called Lexington home for the rest of his life, dying there in 1971.[33] His law practice provided a living but was never financially successful, and Robertson talked often of having grown up poor and never having any money.

He was elected to the Virginia State Senate in 1915, the same year as Harry F. Byrd Sr. He was later elected commonwealth's attorney in Rockbridge County and to Congress in 1932. After six terms in the House of Representatives, he won the special election to the US Senate in 1946, filling the unexpired term of Senator Carter Glass, who had died in office. While he shared most of the conservative values of Harry Byrd Sr. and the organization, he was never close to the senior Byrd personally or politically. While Byrd maintained a "golden silence" in the presidential elections of 1948 through 1964, Robertson supported Truman and Stevenson actively and was a loyal Democrat in 1960 and 1964 as well. He never seemed to be the senior Byrd's choice for any office he sought. He considered himself passed over for a congressional seat in 1922 and was not able to win Byrd's endorsement for governor in either 1941 or 1945. When the Senate seat opened up in 1946, he quickly announced his candidacy but soon learned that both former governor Colgate Darden and Congressman Howard W. Smith also sought the seat. Byrd Sr. stayed neutral, and Robertson was chosen in a multiballot state convention.

In the Senate, as in the positions he had held prior to that, his interest focused on two areas: conservation and outdoor recreation and finance and banking. The former reflected both his western Virginia constituency and his personal love of the outdoors and the hunting and fishing that were such a central aspect of life in his part of rural Virginia. The latter was not a natural interest but grew out of his Senate committee assignments. He was not from Southside, and his area had few African Americans. He was not driven by issues of race and class in the same way as were other key members of the organization. Though he voted against civil rights bills and signed the infamous Southern Manifesto in 1956, he was not an outspoken supporter of the massive resistance movement.[34]

He was diligent in his Senate duties and slowly built up seniority and the expertise that came with it. In particular, his chairmanship of the Banking and Currency Committee and his seniority on the Appropriations Committee endeared him to the business community. He was for balanced budgets, against union influence, and for a strong military and an activist foreign policy. He supported the Truman Doctrine and the Marshall Plan, splitting with Byrd Sr. on both.

But he was clearly a politician of another era. And the contrast in policy and campaign styles between Robertson and his opponent, William B. Spong, would say much about both men and the changes overtaking Virginia.

William Belser Spong Jr. was born in 1920, four years after Willis Robertson entered the Virginia State Senate.[35] He was born and grew up in the city of Portsmouth, a part of the maritime-oriented urban complex of Hampton Roads. He went to the Hampden-Sydney College and the

University of Virginia School of Law and was admitted to the bar in 1947, his studies having been interrupted by service in Europe with the Army Air Corps from 1942 to 1945. He set up practice in Portsmouth and entered local politics, winning a seat in the House of Delegates in 1953. He came by both his politics and his lifelong interest in education naturally. His mother had been a member of the Portsmouth School Board for twenty-three years, and his father was an active Portsmouth Democrat. After a single term in the House of Delegates, he ran for and won a state senate seat in 1955, defeating a Byrd-backed businessman, and was reelected easily in 1959, 1963, and 1965, the last as a result of midterm redistricting.[36] He was one of several returning veterans who entered state politics in the early 1950s, sharing a belief that the generation that had stepped up for the country now needed to step forward in their local communities.

Upon arriving in the General Assembly in January 1954, Spong, a young (age thirty-three) father of two, was immediately thrown into the Young Turk struggle in the state legislature, joining the group of younger, more progressive members in the House of Delegates pushing unsuccessfully against a more conservative state senate for more funding for education. A year after the Young Turk revolt, Spong was himself a member of the senate and in 1958 was appointed chairman of the General Assembly's Commission on Public Education, raising his profile on the issue of greatest importance to the newer, younger families moving into Virginia, particularly those in Northern Virginia around Washington, DC, and in Hampton Roads, which had grown quickly as the nation's military grew.

Spong and Robertson were from different generations and different Virginias, further apart than even their ages would indicate. Robertson was true "old Virginia." Conservative in manner, dress, and personal habits, he fit naturally into a political system that was based in rural small-town Virginia and concerned itself principally with limiting government's intrusion. He was at home in the outdoors and on Main Street. He and Spong shared a seriousness of purpose and an affinity for substance, but little else.

Perhaps nothing better captured Robertson's attachment to an earlier political era than his reaction to modern personal campaigning. Though he was physically vigorous, he was unaccustomed to one-on-one campaigning, having come of political age when others did the individual politicking work for you and you presented yourself in set speeches to local business and civic organizations or you walked around rural courthouses, escorted by the local clerk of the court or sheriff, who vouched for you. He had not faced serious opposition since his elevation to the US Senate in 1946, and that fight had played out within the organization family at a state convention. He proudly boasted to a supporter that he had been reelected in 1960 "without ever having to give a speech to an audience or appear on TV or radio."[37] His frustrations with modern campaigning came through in letters he exchanged with his Richmond headquarters:[38]

> I frankly question the wisdom of asking me to wear myself out in the middle of the day shaking hands with Sperry Rand employees in their plant near Charlottesville. I would think that if I would merely make a call on the officials of that company, it would be enough.
>
> To tell you the truth, I have been making campaigns of one kind or another for fifty years and never yet have felt it necessary to engage in a general handshaking program at grocery stores, manufacturing plants, etc.—June 30, 1966
>
> Holidays [referring to July 4] are not conducive to good campaigning . . . so it would pay me to stay in Lexington and rest that day.—June 27, 1966

This same dichotomy in age and era played out in the Eighth District campaigns of Judge Howard W. Smith and George Rawlings. Like Robertson, Judge Smith was born in rural Virginia, in his case the Broad Run section of Fauquier County. Though he practiced law in Alexandria, he considered Broad Run his home throughout his career. Like Robertson, he was smart and substantive and focused his attention on limiting government, its spending, and its intrusion into business and personal life. He was conservative, even formal, in dress and manner and came from and spoke for the traditional Virginia.

Rawlings was a natural fit for the new, nontraditional parts of the Eighth District. He had been born in Fredericksburg in 1921, and when he received his law degree from the University of Virginia in 1947, Smith had already been in Congress for more than seventeen years. Outspoken on racial and other social issues, Rawlings defeated an incumbent Byrd organization candidate and was elected to the House of Delegates in 1963. He was soon recognized as one of the leaders of the small liberal group in the Democratic Party.[39] Volatile in temperament and flamboyant in manner, Rawlings was the antithesis of traditional Virginia. The contrast with Smith, in personality and policy, could not have been sharper.

The contrast in age and style was not as clear between Harry Byrd Jr. and Armistead Boothe. Similar in age (Boothe was born in 1907, Byrd in 1914), both attended the University of Virginia and spent the World War II years as naval officers, meeting each other for the first time. Both were from prominent families and were raised as part of the upper class in their communities, one the son of a prominent lawyer, the other of a governor, later senator. When Boothe was first elected to the House of Delegates in 1948, he was thought of as part of the organization of the senior Harry Byrd. It was not until the fight over education funding and the founding of the Young Turks in the mid-1950s that Boothe began to reflect the sharp differences in policies and politics of his home district of urban Alexandria as distinct from rural areas of the upper Shenandoah Valley represented by Byrd.

The fight over education funding and the repeal of the automatic tax refund weakened the organization by surfacing its generational split. But it was the five-year struggle over massive resistance and the state's response to the Supreme Court decision in *Brown v. Board of Education of Topeka* that defined the split most clearly. In the short run, the court decision gave the organization a tool to reassert its preeminence, at least temporarily. When Senator Byrd called for "massive resistance" to school desegregation, he set in motion a series of events that hardened positions on both sides, led to the defection of some suburbanites to the Republican Party, ultimately led to the creation of the Conservative Party in the rural areas of Southside, and, finally, became a determiner of where you stood in the election of 1966, based on where you had been in 1956. It was not happenstance that Boothe, Spong, and Rawlings had stood on one side and Byrd, Robertson, and Smith on the other side of the great divide over massive resistance.

During the years of Byrd-led dominance, the lines between the two camps—organization and anti-organization—had always been clear and direction for the organization had come from the top, from the handful of leaders that included Byrd, Congressmen Bill Tuck and Watkins Abbitt, and a small group of leaders in the General Assembly. For more than thirty years the leaders in local courthouses throughout rural Virginia and the business and professional communities, both rural and urban, had dutifully followed the "nod" as it was passed down from Senator Byrd through those local courthouse and business networks. They voted in the primaries for the organization candidate and in the fall for the Democrats, other than president.

A Political Vacuum and Emerging Demographic Changes

But in 1966, no one was passing the word; the organization had no recognized leader to give the nod. And by 1966 there were other attractive
choices. Both the Republican Party and the Virginia Conservative Party
benefited from the vacuum created by Harry Byrd Sr.'s retirement. Part
of the organization had broken away to follow the newly formed Conservative Party. The Conservative Party of Virginia had begun in earnest in
the 1965 governor's race. Stalwart members of the organization in Southside had been appalled by what they considered to be candidate Godwin's
apostasy as he sought and won support in 1965 from organized labor and
from the Independent Voters League and other Negro activist organizations. They had manned the barricades for massive resistance and could
not stomach the turnaround. In the general election in 1965, William B.
Storey Jr. became the candidate of the Conservative Party, which had been
founded only in July of that year. Storey warned that Virginia was moving
down the path to socialism, and was particularly incensed when Godwin
joined Lady Bird Johnson on her 1964 campaign train across Virginia.

As 1965 clicked over to 1966, national events provided the backdrop for
what would unfold in Virginia. Two topics led the news programs: the on-
going civil rights struggles vied for the headlines with the war in Vietnam
and the growing youth-led protests opposing it. What Walter Cronkite
(*CBS Evening News*) or Huntley and Brinkley (*NBC Nightly News Report*)
chose to highlight in their half-hour evening programs shaped attitudes in
millions of homes. And in the summer and fall of 1965 and the spring of
1966, viewers were bombarded with broadcasts from Alabama or Saigon.

The civil rights movement reached a high point in August 1965 with
passage of the Voting Rights Act, which prohibited racial discrimination
in voting and gave the US Department of Justice authority to review and
require changes in laws and practices affecting voting in those areas of
the country where fewer than 50 percent of the nonwhite population had
registered to vote (predominantly the thirteen states of the Old Confederacy). On their television screens, Americans had watched the events
taking place in Selma, Alabama, in the spring of that year and the riots in
the Watts section of Los Angeles in August. In Richmond, the Richmond
Crusade for Voters, founded in 1956 to increase the participation of African Americans in the civic and political life of the city, stepped up its registration efforts. In the decade from its founding to the spring of 1966, the
number of African Americans registered to vote in the city of Richmond
had quadrupled, from 8,500 in 1956 to more than 32,000.[40] The Crusade

for Voters, along with a comparable organization in Norfolk, would play a significant role in the politics of the 1966 Democratic primary.

In Virginia, the new governor took office in January 1966 and immediately presented the General Assembly with a series of far-reaching proposals, making that session one of the most active and progressive since the governorship of Harry F. Byrd Sr. in the late 1920s. The list of proposed legislation was, by conservative Virginia standards, dizzying: a new state sales tax, a newly created statewide system of community colleges, authorization by local option of the sale of liquor by the drink in publicly licensed restaurants and bars, and the start of annual sessions for the legislature.

Elections in Virginia and the campaigns that mark them seem to come and go quickly, in part because there is an election (state or federal) every year. Typically, a new political season kicked off with the close of the General Assembly in late February. This was certainly the case in 1966. While there had been considerable maneuvering behind the scenes, the formal campaigns got under way with the announcements of the principal players: Spong on March 16, Robertson on March 21, Boothe on March 3, Byrd on March 31, Smith on March 3, and Rawlings on March 26.

The fundamentals of any political campaign are pretty simple: figure out who your voters are and get them to the polls on Election Day, all within the finite human and financial resources your campaign assembles. For Harry Byrd and Army Boothe, figuring out who their supporters were was straightforward. For the past twenty years, Democrats had divided between those who supported the organization and those who did not. If one were to view the map of Virginia as a tricornered hat, the antiorganization forces were located mostly in the three corners, those parts of Virginia most remote from Richmond in geography, economic base, and culture. It was to those three corners that Boothe turned to find support.

His own home area of Northern Virginia was populated mostly by newcomers, many drawn to the Washington area by jobs with the federal government or federal contractors. They neither understood nor cared very much about Virginia traditions and history. They did care about the schools their children attended and were wary of anything that sounded like historic, segregationist Virginia. The southeastern corner of the state, comprising the cities in Hampton Roads, shared a reliance on the federal government, particularly the military, and a similar suspicion of Richmond. But unlike Northern Virginia, the cities of Hampton Roads had sizable African American populations, testing and stretching their political muscle in the mid-sixties and boosted by the national reforms consisting of the abolition of the poll tax and the passage of the 1965 Voting Rights

Act. It was the era of the Independent Voters League based in Nansemond County (today's city of Chesapeake) and surrounding jurisdictions, the Concerned Citizens for Political Education (Norfolk), and the Richmond Crusade for Voters.

The third corner, the Southwest, is unique in every respect other than its remoteness and suspicion of Richmond. Historically, it sided with the Union in the Civil War, had an economy based largely on mining, and was poor and predominantly white. It typically voted in overwhelming numbers for the antiorganization candidate.

In contrast, Byrd's base was the center of the state, the Central demographic region, which stretched from Fredericksburg south to the North Carolina line, from the western edges of Hampton Roads to the mountains and up into the Shenandoah Valley. Its only true urban area was Richmond, and the votes of the city itself were slipping away as its white population, many of them employees of the state government that Byrd had for so long dominated, moved to the suburban counties of Chesterfield, Henrico, and Hanover.

As the campaign got under way in the spring of 1966, Byrd and Robertson faced a challenge unusual for organization candidates. Supporters of their general philosophy had alternatives: both the Conservative Party and the Republican Party announced they would field candidates in the general election. Much of the dynamic of the Byrd and Robertson campaigns was driven by efforts to convince conservative, traditional supporters to remain faithful. Newspapers that were traditional supporters of the organization urged conservative voters to vote in the July primary and not to defect to either the Republicans or the Conservatives.[41] Regardless, in late May the Conservatives formally nominated candidates for each of the Senate seats in the fall election. By June the concern in the organization ranks was such that former governor Albertis Harrison was trotted out to make a direct appeal to voters who had supported the Conservative candidate for governor in 1965, saying, "[We will] leave a light in the window for any prodigal runaways who might wish to find their way home to the House of their Fathers."[42]

It was clear to the Boothe and Spong forces that every Conservative or Republican voter they could convince to stay out of the July primary was a vote lost to the organization.

Both Byrd and Robertson campaigned in traditional fashion, principally in set speeches opening local headquarters or before business and civic organizations, relying in large part on the courthouse-based local leadership that had always been the core of the organization in Southside and in the Shenandoah Valley. The newer, faster-growing parts of the commonwealth were more of a challenge, particularly to Robertson. In an early 1966 letter to a member of his finance committee, Robertson admitted, "Fairfax [is] . . . an area I expect to have some serious trouble, owing to the large number of people who live there from Northern states and work for the government."[43]

Byrd focused his speeches on the traditional verities of a balanced budget, limited government, and a strong stand against the outside threats of labor and other special interest groups. He relied on his name and the wide respect accorded his father. In the Senate only six months, he had little federal record to defend. His first speech as a newly appointed senator was in support of right-to-work laws and a commitment to preserve section 14(b) of the Taft-Hartley Act, which gave states the latitude to enact legislation prohibiting union membership as a condition of employment. Virginia had long prided itself on being a right-to-work state, and many in the business community considered the issue central to the economic success of the commonwealth.

Unlike Byrd, Robertson had been in Congress since 1932. "I am running for re-election of the basis of my past record of service to Virginia and the Nation and I believe that my seniority . . . puts me in a unique position to assure that Virginia's needs will continue to have strong and effective support in the Senate in the critical years ahead," he said in correspondence to business leaders.[44]

Spong was more than willing to make the campaign about Robertson's record. In a widely reported Fairfax County speech on June 6, Spong pointed out that Robertson had opposed

- the Higher Education Act of 1965 (all Virginia House members had supported it);
- the Vocational Education Act of 1965 (which included critical impact aid for Northern Virginia and Hampton Roads school systems);
- the Water Pollution Control Act of 1965; and
- the Urban Mass Transit Act in 1963 and 1964.

"Senator Robertson has fought every form of measure designed to cope with the problems that face a modern, urban society like Virginia today," one Northern Virginia editorial declared.[45]

That appeal to a new generation (and to new residents regardless of generation) on such issues as education that resonated with them was a constant theme of the Spong campaign. His campaign brochures, often headlined "The Man for Today," were designed to appeal to the younger generation by describing Spong as one of their own: "A man with a young family, his perspective on the issues of today reflects the thinking of a man whose children will grow up in the last third of the century."[46]

For Spong, support for education symbolized the divide and gave him opportunity to appeal to parents while staying above the traditional split of anti- and pro-organization. At every opportunity, he reminded voters of his chairmanship of the widely praised Commission on Education and his support for federal financial support for education at all levels. And he attacked Robertson for "blind opposition to education bills over a 20 year period."[47] Robertson always took the bait, attacking Spong for advocating federal aid to education and warning of federal control of public schools.[48]

For Byrd and Boothe, the dividing line was clear. Byrd was the organization, or at least its inheritor, and Boothe was a recognized leader of antiorganization efforts dating back to the days of the Young Turks and his 1961 race against Mills Godwin for lieutenant governor. And Boothe was willing to pursue the fight along those lines, believing that the population growth and increased voter registration in antiorganization areas would be enough to produce a win.

At every turn, Boothe attacked Byrd as unqualified but for his name, and repeatedly called on him to renounce his support in the 1950s for the policy of massive resistance, saying, "A man who could not face intelligently and courageously the greatest issue of his time in the State Senate cannot face intelligently and bravely the crucial issues of the future."[49] And in a speech in front of the Rockbridge County Courthouse on May 16, Boothe repeated the theme. "Virginia needs a man who looks forward, not backward. . . . This is our last chance for a generation to take Virginia from the hands of the 400 and turn it over to the care of the 4 million."[50]

Boothe understood his challenge. "I find I am a man running against a name, not against a record of another man."[51] Try as he might, he could not draw Byrd out into a direct confrontation. Byrd sought to stay above the fray. In a typical speech at a headquarters opening on May 2, Byrd said, "I make only one commitment . . . conscientiously, sincerely and wholeheartedly to study . . . and make the best decisions possible reflecting the best interests of the large majority of the people in our state."[52] For Byrd, the strategy was to ignore his opponent and rely on the organization to turn out its vote. That was the way the organization had always won its elections, from the courthouse to the governor's mansion and the US Senate.

And that was the way Howard W. "Judge" Smith had always won his re-election. But in the redrawn Eighth Congressional District much was new, including simply having to campaign.[53] Appearing for the first time in anyone's memory in Hanover County in late April, he greeted his supporters, saying, "You know, just ordinarily, I haven't bothered you folks. . . ."[54] He had not had to. Rawlings was the first serious opposition he had had in thirty years, since then president Roosevelt had tried to purge him in 1938.[55] And Rawlings was attacking at every opportunity: "In his 32 years of service he [Smith] has attempted to block almost all progressive legislation that has come before him. He argues that seniority can help the Eighth District, but his type of action has not helped us in the past, so why should it do so in the future?"[56]

And Rawlings continued to attack at every turn, concentrating his efforts in the parts of the Eighth District new to Smith, particularly Fairfax County, and in those rural counties where increased African American voter registration threatened to erode Smith's base. By 1966, African Americans made up more than 40 percent of the registrants in nine of the twenty counties of the Eighth District. Four of the nine were new to the district as a result of the 1965 redistricting.[57]

For Byrd and Boothe, Smith and Rawlings, the dividing lines were clear. Each would seek maximum participation from his wing of the Democratic Party. The organization versus antiorganization fights had drawn similar lines in elections going back to the early 1930s, and the organization had always prevailed. It relied on a predictable turnout from the courthouses and rural areas across the Southside, on the Northern Neck and Middle Peninsula, and up and down the Shenandoah Valley. That vote, along with that of the business and professional interests centered in Richmond, had produced reliable majorities in low-turnout primaries for more than fifty years.[58]

But Virginia had changed. And the change was dramatic and fell unevenly across the state. Large parts of the state had experienced population loss, while the number of new residents in the growing areas of Northern Virginia and Hampton Roads had exploded. Alexandria, Arlington, and Fairfax grew from 131,492 in 1940 to 539,618 in 1960; the industrial cities of Hampton Roads more than doubled in population, to 780,000, in that same period. Even in those sections of the state where the total remained steady, the population shifted from rural to urban and suburban. In the Northwest Piedmont section (defined as Albemarle, Culpeper, Greene, Madison, Nelson, Orange, and Rappahannock Counties and the City of Charlottesville), the net population increase from 1950 to 1960 was

6.8 percent. But Charlottesville and its two suburban counties grew by 16 percent, while every other county lost population.[59]

While the political divide in the Byrd-Boothe and Rawlings-Smith races was clear, that was not the case for Robertson and Spong. Robertson believed that the combination of his seniority and ability to deliver for the business community, plus his support for the conservative principles that animated the rural organization constituency, would be enough to prevail. It always had been. A campaign strategy document prepared for him in April 1966 urged him to emphasize his seniority and to promote himself as "progressively conservative." Pursing this strategy, he styled himself as "Virginia's Bread and Butter Senator," able to use his position on the Senate Appropriations Committee to get results for Virginia.[60]

While Spong had been a Young Turk, splitting with the organization over education funding, he had never been lumped in with the "liberals" like Boothe, Congressman Pat Jennings, or state senator Henry Howell of Norfolk. Part of the difference was temperament, part policy. Even the organization-stalwart editorial page of the *Richmond Times-Dispatch* noted Spong's competence and dedication while reaffirming its previously stated support for Robertson.[61] But it was acceptable in organization circles to be for Spong, especially if you lived in Hampton Roads or Northern Virginia or were part of the World War II generation. Hence Spong's speeches and materials did not have the sharp antiorganization rhetoric used by Boothe and Rawlings. He took issue with Robertson, of course, but not with the organization. He accused Robertson of having lost touch with Virginia, noting in one speech that "he [Robertson] has been in Tidewater more in the past three weeks than in the past two decades," and in Northern Virginia accused him of failing to vote for six major pay-raise bills for federal workers between 1957 and 1964.[62]

Spong understood he needed the enthusiasm generated by the Boothe and Rawlings campaigns to turn out the vote on July 12. On May 22 the Committee on Political Education of the state AFL-CIO endorsed Boothe, Rawlings, and Spong,[63] an essential step but one that would open Spong to attack because attacking organized labor had long been an organization staple. Byrd was the first to comment on the COPE action, noting the labor endorsement of Boothe and saying, "I'm not subservient enough. They are absolutely right about that."[64]

On June 7, state senator Ed Willey, Robertson's campaign manager, attacked Spong, alleging he supported the repeal of section 14(b) of the federal Taft-Hartley Act, which permits states to enact right-to-work laws prohibiting closed union shops. Virginia is a right-to-work state, and the organization had always made its support of right-to-work laws and its opposition to the repeal of section 14(b) a key part of its campaigns. Bill Battle, Spong's campaign manager, quickly responded, stating unequivo-cally Spong's opposition to the repeal of section 14(b).[65] It was recognized to be an issue that threatened to lump Spong in with the liberals and to scare off younger business and professional men and women who might otherwise be attracted to Spong's message. Robertson followed up the ini-tial attack on June 12, saying Spong was obligated to the AFL-CIO and to the Kennedys (Bill Battle had been a key Kennedy supporter in 1960 and his ambassador to Australia).[66] The threat of damage to the Spong effort was considerable.

Fortunately for Spong, this issue was pushed off the front pages almost immediately by an accusation, raised by a Byrd organization businessman (who supported Bill Spong, his friend and fellow Portsmouth resident), that Virginia banking interests were using coercion and arm-twisting tac-tics to raise money for the Robertson campaign. Dr. Russell M. Cox, a Portsmouth physician and secretary of the State Board of Medical Exam-iners, disclosed that he had resigned from the board of the Bank of Vir-ginia's Portsmouth branch to protest the fundraising drive. He contended that the Virginia Bankers Association had established a quota system for dollar contributions based on a particular bank's assets. He claimed that a bank executive had informed the Advisory Board on which he sat that each bank was assigned such a quota, that each Advisory Board member was expected to give money to and work for Senator Robertson, that the bank's quota was $2,500, and that he would twist the arms of bank officers to raise those funds.[67]

The *Washington Post* followed with a story that Manufacturers Han-over Trust of New York was asking its Virginia shareholders to "thank" Robertson for his support for critical banking legislation. (Robertson legislation protecting bank mergers from the antitrust laws had passed the Senate on February 9.) The story ran for multiple days, pushing everything else to the side. Charges were leveled that Robertson had a bank lobbyist working for his campaign. He's only doing research, was the response. The banks claimed all their fundraising was voluntary.[68]

Other issues, notably the labor issues that had threatened Spong, were smothered under the statewide media coverage of the banking controversy.

As the campaign entered its final weeks, Byrd and Robertson carefully watched the activity of the Conservative Party, which had nominated

John W. Carter of Danville for the seat held by Byrd and F. Lee Haw-thorne of Chesterfield for the Robertson seat. Leaders of the Conservative Party urged their members not to participate in the Democratic primary, echoing an earlier statement from A. Linwood Holton, the 1965 Republican candidate for governor, urging Republicans not to vote in the primary.

In prior years, the organization had sometimes called on Republican voters to participate in Democratic primaries when it felt threatened. For the Republican voter, this made sense. In most parts of the state the Republicans did not offer candidates for state or local office, and the organization was able to appeal to self-described conservative Republicans. Also, the organization maintained a close association with the business and professional men who formed the backbone of the Republican Party in most areas of the state. But 1966 was likely to be different: a new and younger group had taken control of the Republican Party, buoyed by victories in the presidential election years of 1956 and 1960. Led by F. Lee Potter of Arlington and A. Linwood Holton, a Roanoke attorney and the party's 1965 candidate for governor, these newer Republicans were intent on building a local precinct-by-precinct network separate from the organization.[69]

Worried that the Republican and Conservative voters might not show up for the July 12 primary, the Byrd campaign once more brought out former governor Albertis Harrison to say that the Democratic primary was open to Republicans and Conservatives, stating that it was up to the individual to decide.[70] On June 30, in Norfolk, Harry Byrd himself called for "a big turnout" to offset "organized pressure groups," saying, "I personally am not going to discourage anybody from voting."[71] Later that day he repeated the call in heavily Republican Roanoke: "I am in favor of every Virginian qualified to cast a vote to do so. I do not believe in restricting the electorate."[72] The call for Republican support was unmistakable. But the next day the state Republican Party, meeting in convention, nominated its own candidates: Mayor James P. Ould Jr. of Lynchburg, seeking the Robertson seat, and Lawrence M. Traylor of Heathsville, seeking the Byrd seat.

In the first week of July, Robertson traveled across Southside, wooing the Conservative vote in speeches emphasizing balanced budgets and attacking President Johnson's proposed anti-poverty program. Accompanied by former governor and current Fifth District congressman Bill Tuck, he campaigned from courthouse to courthouse, west to east along the North Carolina border, attacking "deficit spending" while touting his seniority in an obvious appeal to the potential followers of the Conservative

Party.[73] But that same week Carter and Hawthorne, the nominees of the Conservative Party, filed their official papers, using the occasion to urge their supporters to stay out of the Democratic primary.

During that week, an unsigned letter on Robertson headquarters stationery was widely circulated in Southside and in parts of the Richmond area. The letter called attention to three newspaper articles, which were attached. Each article contained references to Negroes involved in the Spong campaign, and those parts of the articles were circled. Spong promptly charged that Robertson was injecting race into the campaign, while reminding reporters that Robertson had unsuccessfully sought the endorsement of the Independent Voters League.[74]

Also in that week, state senator Ed Willey, Robertson's campaign manager, tried again to raise the specter of organized labor, charging that the national Committee on Political Education had funneled $13,000 to the state AFL-CIO for Spong. The state labor organization offered to open its books to refute the charge, and COPE stated that the $13,000 had, in fact, been sent, but that it was earmarked for Boothe and Rawlings, not for Spong.[75]

But once again, the labor story was overwhelmed by a more immediate issue, this time the reported serious illness of Harry F. Byrd Sr. Richard E. Byrd, the senior Byrd's youngest son, made his father's condition public, and Harry Jr. told the press he had no plans to return to the family home in Berryville unless his father's condition worsened. For the final week leading up to the July 12 primary, the story of the senior Byrd's health dominated the news. Byrd Jr. announced the suspension of his campaign on July 7 and returned to his father's bedside. Boothe had little choice but to follow suit, and suspended his campaign that same day. Robertson and Spong continued their campaigns, making clear their respect for the former senator and stating they would suspend all campaigning in the event of his death.[76]

Both sides focused on getting their key supporters to the polls. On the Sunday before the election, the Richmond Crusade for Voters, the group that since the mid-1950s had led the political and civic activities of the city's African American population, circulated its crucial sample ballot endorsing Boothe and Spong.[77] A similar double endorsement occurred in Norfolk where Concerned Citizens for Political Education announced its endorsements and produced the "Goldenrod Ballot" endorsing Boothe and Spong. The Independent Voters League had previously endorsed both Boothe and Spong, though not without an internal fight that pitted the longtime leadership headed by Nansemond County supervisor Moses Riddick against a group of younger leaders from Portsmouth and Norfolk.[78]

In the final days of the campaign, the state's newspapers announced their endorsements. The editorial pages of Virginia's newspapers had, for the most part, shared the conservative, fiscally prudent philosophy of the senior Senator Byrd. And Byrd himself was a newspaper owner and publisher, owning the *Winchester Evening Star* and the *Harrisonburg Daily Record*, along with several weekly papers in Fairfax and Prince William Counties. During the senior senator's time in the Senate, the running of the family newspaper interests was in the hands of Harry Byrd Jr. And across the state, editors and publishers were the young Byrd's friends and professional colleagues.

Despite these associations, some of the state's newspapers split their endorsements. The Richmond papers, the *Times-Dispatch* and *News Leader*, had previously endorsed Byrd and Robertson and simply reiterated that position. The *Norfolk Virginian Pilot* had supported Spong and Boothe from the beginning and did so again. But others split their endorsements and, in doing so, singled out Spong as speaking to the new Virginia.

> Senator Spong's moderate approach to governmental affairs is more in keeping with the needs of Virginia and the Nation. . . .—*Fredericksburg Free Lance Star*, July 8, 1966, which endorsed Byrd in the same editorial

> Senator Spong represents the new Virginia and does so without deserting the basic principles to which most Virginians adhere. . . .—*Hopewell News*, July 11, 1966, which endorsed Byrd the same day

> Mr. Spong is speaking for the new Virginia in advocating a faster tempo of progress without sacrificing—or showing disrespect for—the traditions and principles Virginians have admired and endorsed throughout the years. He has not fought the Organization as such; he is just not part of it.—*Martinsville Bulletin*, July 11, 1966; the paper endorsed Byrd for the other seat

These three newspapers served communities of organization strength. And it was to the younger generation in these areas that Spong had made his pitch, not antiorganization but independent of it, making the case that Virginia had changed and its leadership needed to change as well. Spong had made the appeal openly at the outset of his campaign; had made "A Man for Today" the tagline of his campaign, and had returned to it as a theme time and again. He knew he would be the beneficiary of the anti-organization vote and could piggyback on the enthusiasm generated by Boothe and Rawlings. But he knew he needed more, and he pitched his entire campaign to secure that slender, added vote.

The returns would prove him right, but only barely.

The Richmond newspaper headlines on the morning of July 13 told the tale:

Spong Appears Nominated; Byrd Wins
Rawlings Beats Smith by Small Margin

The official canvass of votes three days after the primary set Spong's margin at 612 votes out of a total of 433,159 votes cast. Rawlings's margin was similarly narrow, at 645 out of 53,585 votes cast in the Eighth District. Byrd had won by 8,225 votes out of 434,217 cast, closer than anyone in the organization had expected.[79]

The Robertson camp considered a recount based on allegations from some local supporters that ineligible voters had participated. But on July 22, on receipt of the official canvass from the State Board of Elections, the senator released a statement congratulating Spong and promising his support in the general election. Judge Smith did not challenge the outcome in the Eighth District, but he pointedly did not offer either congratulations or support to Rawlings.[80]

What had happened?

Campaigns are contests between individuals, but they often reflect and are affected by larger societal changes. And the winning campaigns are usually those that capture the underlying changes and ride with them. The outcomes of the 1966 campaigns were very much driven by those changes affecting Virginia and the South generally. The outcome of the two statewide contests and, especially, the Eighth District finally reflected Virginia's changing demographics, first by reflecting the exploding growth in Northern Virginia and the slower but steady growth in Hampton Roads, and second, by taking advantage of the drive to increase African American registration and participation.

The two counties (Arlington and Fairfax) and the three cities of Northern Virginia (Alexandria, Falls Church, and Fairfax City) provided Spong with a margin of 20,815 and Boothe with one of 19,459 votes as they gathered 67.5 and 65.8 percent respectively of the vote in those jurisdictions (Northern Virginia was more narrowly defined in 1966; Loudoun and Prince William Counties were still largely rural and not considered to be a part of Northern Virginia). The six large Tidewater cities gave Spong a margin of 20,815 (61 percent) and Boothe a margin of 16,706 (59 percent). In the larger urban corridor stretching from Northern Virginia through Richmond to Hampton Roads, Spong received 56.2 percent of the vote and Boothe received 54.8 percent. And, most important, the urban corridor cast over 59 percent of the total primary vote.

Byrd and Robertson received strong support in the traditional areas of organization strength: Southside, the Shenandoah Valley, and the suburban and rural areas outside Richmond. Their percentages were impressive (more than 60 percent in most and upward of 70 percent in some counties), but the absolute numbers were not. As noted earlier, the population base in the areas of organization strength was shrinking. From 1950 to 1960, Virginia had been the seventh fastest-growing state in the nation, but the population of the Seventh Congressional District (the Shenandoah Valley) had increased less than 2 percent, and most of that was in the city of Charlottesville. The percentage of people living on farms in the Seventh District in 1960 was about half what it was in 1950. A similar pattern existed in the Fourth and Fifth Congressional Districts (roughly equating to Southside). The overall population had dropped 6 percent from 1950 to 1960, and the percentage of people living on farms in Southside counties had fallen from 55 percent to 36 percent. That shift in how many Virginians lived where was the decisive factor in the election.[81]

Rising Importance of the African American Vote

The returns also underscored the increasing importance of the African American vote. Antiorganization support increased in African American precincts in the cities and in some rural counties in Southside and in the Eighth District owing to significant increases in the number of individuals registered to vote. A decadelong effort by civil rights groups, the ending of the poll tax and other arbitrary limitations on registering, and a focused effort by the campaigns led to marked increases in registrations, with resulting increases in turnout. The number of Black registered voters in the city of Richmond alone increased from 11,569 in 1956 to 29,970 in 1965. Their percentage of total registration in the city went from 19.1 percent in 1956 to 35.5 percent in 1965.[82]

Ralph Eisenberg, assistant director of the Institute of Government at the University of Virginia, tracked closely the voting patterns in African American precincts in Virginia and produced the following statistics for the 1966 primary vote in thirty-seven "predominantly Negro precincts" in eight Virginia cities: Boothe had a 20,127 to 878 margin over Byrd, and Spong had a 19,684 to 1,778 margin over Robertson.[83] The same pattern appears to have held in the rural counties with large African American populations (housing patterns in most of the rural counties make even precinct-level statistics hard to interpret based on race). Charles City County stands out as the only jurisdiction where the African American population greatly outnumbered the white population (4,415 to 917 in the 1960 census). It gave Boothe a 748 to 210 margin, and there is no reason to think that the African American vote pattern was different in other rural areas in light of the concerted efforts of several local and national organizations actively working to register voters in the area. In the 1961 Democratic primary, the total vote in Charles City County had been 403. Armistead Boothe, running for lieutenant governor that year, received 268 votes, only one-third the number of votes he would receive five years later when he ran for the US Senate. A similar increase in African American registrations from 1961 to 1966 occurred in the cities and greatly benefited both Boothe and Spong. The fifteen predominantly Black precincts in Richmond cast 8,342 votes for Boothe in 1966 (Byrd received 295). In 1961 the margins had been similar but the total vote was significantly lower. Boothe had received 5,397 votes to Godwin's 506.[84] The 46 percent increase in turnout from 1961 to 1966 in the predominantly African American precincts was replicated in major cities across the commonwealth, providing the margins that the challengers needed.

Longer-term political and demographic trends explain why the overall primary turnout of 434,217 was lower than many in the organization had expected.[85] In addition to slow population growth in the traditional organization areas, the emergence of a defined Republican Party and the steadfastness of the Conservative Party faithful further depressed the turnout in areas where the organization could normally have counted on seven out of every ten votes cast. In the Shenandoah Valley, the Republican Party had established an identity, coming close to winning the Seventh District congressional seat in 1962.[86] Linwood Holton, the Republican nominee for governor in 1965, had won the Valley. And in December 1965, the organization was stunned when J. Kenneth Robinson, the Republican candidate, won a special election to fill the state senate seat in the upper part of the Valley that had been vacated by Byrd Jr. on his appointment to the US Senate.

In Southside, unhappiness with the perceived leftward drift of the Democrats gave the Conservatives an argument to have their supporters boycott the primary. In mid-March, its Executive Committee formally urged its members to stay out of the Democratic primary. The results make clear these appeals had an impact. Brunswick County lies in the heart of the Southside along the North Carolina border. Its population in 1960 was 17,779, down nearly 12 percent from 1950. In the 1961 primary for governor it had given Albertis Harrison, the organization candidate, 2,429 votes (86 percent) and his antiorganization opponent 410 votes. Five years later Brunswick County gave Byrd 1,793 votes and Boothe 1,180. Similar patterns could be found in other Southside counties.[87]

Reduced levels of organization support occurred in the Shenandoah Valley as well. Montgomery County is typical. In the 1961 Democratic primary it gave Harrison, the organization candidate, 68 percent of the vote, 1,161 votes to 539 for Stephens. In 1966, Byrd polled only 875 votes to 685 for Boothe, 55 percent of the vote. Reduced turnouts with resulting thinner margins for the organization was the pattern in county after county up and down the Valley where both Byrd and Robertson lived. The Republican Party's efforts to encourage its supporters to stay out of the primary was showing success. In the 1966 general election, Lawrence Traylor, the Republican candidate, carried Montgomery County over Byrd, 2,928 to 2,593. And Spong lost Montgomery to the mayor of nearby Lynchburg by an even larger margin.

If these three trends accounted for the strong showing by Spong, Boothe, and Rawlings, what accounted for Spong's win and Boothe's loss? Each of the four candidates had run his own campaign, though Byrd and Robertson had appealed to the same core organization constituency, just as Spong and Boothe had appealed to those who were traditionally outside the organization. Statewide, Spong received 3,889 more votes than did Boothe, even though 1,057 more votes were cast in the Boothe-Byrd race than in the Spong-Robertson race.

It appears that Boothe's vote was largely an anti-Byrd, antiorganization vote, and Spong received virtually every such vote that was cast. That is most true in the rural counties. If Fairfax and Arlington Counties (the only two urban counties in 1966) are excluded, Boothe received 77,467 votes and Spong 77,524 in the rural counties across the commonwealth. In the cities, plus Arlington and Fairfax Counties, Spong outpolled Boothe by 3,832 votes. Who were these additional Spong voters? Many were from Spong's hometown of Portsmouth (2,204 votes). But in virtually every one of the larger jurisdictions, Spong received votes that Boothe did not, from a couple of hundred each in Henrico, Danville, and Arlington to more than a thousand each in Portsmouth and Virginia Beach.

The margin between Spong and Robertson and the gap between the votes for Spong and for Boothe are so small, even jurisdiction by jurisdiction, that one hesitates to assign a universal reason. Spong's hometown margins in Portsmouth and Virginia Beach are a clear vote for the local favorite. But the consistent, small margins across all of the urban areas appear to be evidence of a group of voters willing to support Spong, a perceived moderate, but not the more liberal Boothe. Conversely, they were supporters of Byrd and the organization but willing to back a younger, more moderate alternative to Robertson. Spong had pitched much of his campaign to this group, speaking of a changing Virginia and portraying himself as "A Man for Today." He directed his appeal to voters like himself: younger, usually with children in the schools, veterans of World War II, and, most important, living in the growing urban and suburban areas of the state. As the *Bristol Herald-Courier* stated in its June 12 editorial, "Mr. Spong . . . speaks for the New Virginia and does it without sacrificing the basic principles that most Virginians endorse."[88]

Perhaps that factor was what made Spong a winner and Boothe not. It is what Sidney Kellam had identified a year before the primary in his unsuccessful effort to replace Robertson with the younger and more moderate congressman Tom Downing.

Whatever the reasons might have been, the 1966 Democratic Party found itself on July 13 without its longtime leader and with statewide candidates for the US Senate, Byrd and Spong, representing different factions of the party. However, with Robertson's quick endorsement of Spong and Boothe's endorsement of Byrd, the factions came together for their mutual benefit and were successful in defeating the Republican and Conservative candidates statewide in the general election. When the votes in the Senate races are compared with those in the six congressional districts that were contested, it is clear that the efforts by the Byrd and Spong forces to present something of a united front benefited both candidates.

Spong led the ticket with 429,855 against 245,681 for the Republican James Ould and 58,251 for the Conservative candidate, Lee Hawthorne. Byrd's total was 389,028 against 272,804 for the Republican Lawrence Traylor and 57,692 for the Conservative John W. Carter and 10,180 for an independent, J. B. Brayman, a self-described lunchroom counterman from Lynchburg and perennial candidate.

The total turnout of 733,849 was 60 percent higher than the turnout in 1958, the last previous nonpresidential-election year Senate election. Population increases, the end of the poll tax, dramatic increases in African American voter registration, spirited contests in several congressional districts, and the excitement created by the July primary combined to create the larger turnout. Once again, Spong's vote was based in the cities in the urban corridor (including the counties of Arlington and Fairfax) stretching from Northern Virginia to Richmond and then southeast to the cities in Hampton Roads. Spong captured 63.3 percent of the vote in the thirty-three counties and cities in the urban corridor.[89] Byrd too carried the corridor, but with only 53.4 percent. A large share of the difference was in the African American vote. In the thirty-nine predominantly African American precincts identified by Ralph Eisenberg in his series on Virginia elections, Spong garnered 23,156 votes (96 percent), while Byrd received only 2,535 (13.5 percent). Traylor, Byrd's Republican opponent, received 15,585 votes, while Spong's Republican opponent received only 688 votes.[90] Clearly, the appeals to unify the factions of the Democratic Party behind a Spong-Byrd ticket did not sway the African American leadership of the Richmond Crusade for Voters or the Independent Voters League. They had supported Mills Godwin in 1965, but support for the son of the longtime leader of the organization was a step too far.

The Beginnings of a Major Political Shift

But one can see the beginnings of a major political shift in the returns. The Conservative vote was small and limited to Southside. But the conservative (small "c") vote remained significant, and it needed a place to go. The Republican statewide vote disappointed its leaders, and its two candidates ran well in only a few jurisdictions of traditional Republican strength in parts of the lower Valley and the mountains (e.g., Montgomery, Carroll, Floyd, and Grayson Counties). But if one looks at the results in the races for the contested congressional seats one can, with the clear benefit of hindsight, see the opportunity for a realignment. This is most obvious in the Eighth Congressional District, where George Rawlings had upset Judge Smith in the primary.

The Republican candidate, William L. Scott, was a Fairfax County lawyer who had twice run unsuccessfully for the Virginia State Senate. Near the close of the primary campaign Rawlings had launched a series of personal attacks on Smith, charging him with a conflict of interest involving his blocking of bank-related legislation while simultaneously serving as chairman of the board of the Alexandria National Bank. Smith and his supporters deeply resented what they considered to be unwarranted attacks, and when Smith failed to endorse Rawlings after the primary, many of his supporters began considering the possibility of voting for a Republican, something many of them had never done. The theory was that they would let the Republican have the seat for a term and then take it back with a conservative two years later.[91] In late September Smith wrote friends expressing that outrage:

> This was the first time in all my campaigns that my reputation for integrity and honesty was ever questioned. This I can never forgive or forget, and I hope that the people of my District will see that, in the future, this gutter type of campaign will not become the method of seeking election to public office in Virginia.[92]

The letter was leaked to the Fredericksburg *Free Lance Star* and reprints were circulated widely by the Scott campaign.[93] The final returns make clear that significant numbers of Smith supporters voted for Scott. Rawlings's general election vote of 37,929 was only 70.8 percent of the 53,585 votes cast in the July Democratic primary, and his November vote was less than the combined Rawlings-Smith July vote in every city and county in the district. The numbers make clear that he failed to capture enough of the Smith vote to prevent the election of the Republican Scott.[94] That lesson was not lost on a group of conservative Republicans who, in the space of six years, would use the principle of a combined Byrd Democrat and conservative Republican vote to wrest control of the Republican Party and dominate Virginia politics for a generation.[95]

As the tumult of 1966 drew to a close, the several political groupings took stock and plotted paths forward. The organization licked its wounds, pined for the good old days, and sought to limit defections to the Republicans and the Conservatives. The Spong Democrats reveled in victory, but their man was virtually alone. He had no allies in the state's congressional delegation, a governor who was happy to send him to Washington and forget about him, and moderate Democratic allies in the legislature, who immediately began jockeying for the 1969 statewide races for governor, lieutenant governor, and attorney general. The liberal Democrats, who had supported Spong, focused closely on the governor's race in 1969, intent on having one of their own, Henry Howell, as the nominee. The Republicans immediately moved to consolidate their gains and looked ahead to the presidential election in 1968 and the governor's race in 1969. The Conservatives sulked, wishing a pox on all the other houses.

But the door to power for a conservative coalition between the Republicans and what was left of the organization was opened in 1969 by a rupture in the liberal plus moderate Democratic alliance that had elected Spong. At the outset of the 1969 campaign there were three aspirants for the governor's chair: Fred G. Pollard, the incumbent lieutenant governor, supported by most of the organization; state senator Henry E. Howell, the unabashed liberal from Norfolk; and William C. Battle, the Charlottesville lawyer who had managed Bill Spong's campaign and ran for governor under the slogan "Not Right or Left, But Forward." At that time, state law required the nominee to win an outright majority and mandated a runoff election if no candidate received a majority in the initial balloting. Pollard ran third and was eliminated in the first round. In the moderate versus liberal runoff, Governor Godwin weighed in heavily for Battle, giving many Howell supporters an excuse to abandon the Democrat in the fall and support the Mountain Valley Republican, whose rhetoric on race was gentle and reassuring to the liberals.

What had happened in the short three years between the cooperation between the factions that marked the lead-up to 1966 and the open split that led to the defeat in 1969? Policy differences, conflicting ambitions, and personality differences all contributed to the result. In the discussions that began immediately following the November 1966 general election, the Spong-Battle forces considered themselves as having the right to pick someone from their own ranks to face Lieutenant Governor Pollard, the candidate of what remained of the organization. They chose not to include Howell or the liberals in the discussion. Howell believed he had deferred long enough and that it was his turn. And Howell and the rest of the liberals were intent on the governorship, which had been the goal all along.

At the root of much of this was a cultural divide between the leaders of the moderate faction, many of whom were prominent and established civic and professional leaders in their local communities, and the liberal faction, which included African Americans and organized labor, as well as the activists from Northern Virginia. It is not too much of an overstatement to characterize it as a split between the country club and the union hall. The campaign slogan for Howell and the liberals was "Keep the Big

Boys Honest." Many of the moderates considered themselves to be among the Big Boys.

The business-conservative coalition first glimpsed in the Eighth Congressional District in 1966 bookended Bill Spong's US Senate career. That coalition, later operating as a group called "Virginians For . . . ,"[96] influenced Virginia politics for the next thirty years, supporting governors and senators of one political party or the other and having its final success in 2001 as part of a much broader effort that elected businessman Mark Warner governor. By that time, the coalition was a shadow of its former self, as time had diminished the ranks of the old Byrd organization, and the succeeding generation had become comfortable as Republicans. But Harry Byrd Sr. would have been comfortable with the coalition. His Democratic Party, having solidified its urban constituency, increasingly sought to appeal to the suburban vote that determines modern Virginia elections, leaving by default the rural areas that had been the organization's base to the reshaping Republican Party.

Following his one Senate term, Bill Spong had a distinguished career in law and education as dean of the law school at William & Mary University and president of Old Dominion University. Harry Byrd Jr.'s reelection in 1970 and 1976 as an independent encouraged many of his followers to seek local office either as independents or as Republicans. And Bill Scott, whose election in 1966 served as the template for the realignment that followed, served just one term following his election to the Senate in 1972 and was succeeded by Republican John Warner.[97] George Rawlings remained active in state and national Democratic Party politics after losing a race for the US Senate seat to Byrd in 1970, but never again sought public office. Armistead Boothe returned to Alexandria, remained somewhat active though never again sought public office, and spent most of his considerable energies raising money for the Virginia Theological Seminary.

Notes

1. V. O. Key, *Southern Politics in State and Nation* (New York: A. A. Knopf, 1949), 19.
2. *Brown v. Board of Education of Topeka*, 347 U.S. 483 (1954). The case was a consolidation of five separate lawsuits in different states, including *Davis v. County School Board of Prince Edward County*, a Virginia case in which Attorney General (later Governor) J. Lindsay Almond led the legal team for the state.

3. "If we can organize the Southern States for massive resistance to this order [the Brown decision], I think that in time the rest of the country will realize that racial integration is not going to be accepted in the South." See Benjamin Muse, *Virginia's Massive Resistance* (Bloomington: Indiana University Press, 1961), 22.

4. Even then Boothe was careful not to break openly with the organization. In a speech to the House of Delegates on December 2, 1955, he insisted the issue was not integration versus segregation but one of support for public schools. He supported public segregated schools, while those on the other side supported segregated schools whether public or private. See Armistead Boothe Papers, MS164, Alexandria Library, Local History and Special Collections, Alexandria, VA.

5. Margaret Edds, *We Face the Dawn* (Charlottesville: University of Virginia Press, 2018), 293–98.

6. Ben Beagle and Ozzie Osborne, *J. Lindsay Almond: Virginia's Reluctant Rebel* (Roanoke, VA: Full Court Press, 1984).

7. J. Harvie Wilkinson III, *Harry Byrd and the Changing Face of Virginia Politics, 1945–1966* (Charlottesville: University Press of Virginia, 1968), 240–43.

8. The placing of state and local elections in odd-numbered years separating those choices from federal elections in even-numbered years began as early as the Virginia Constitution of 1861 and was continued in successive constitutions, those of 1902 and 1971. *Report of the Commission on Constitutional Revision* (Charlottesville, VA: Michie Publishing Co., 1969).

9. Those parts of the state geographically most remote from the capital in Richmond and most removed from the rural lifestyle the organization embodied were the three corners of the state: Northern Virginia, Hampton Roads, and the far Southwest. The first two were fast-growing and the third had been alienated from Richmond since before the Civil War.

10. Ralph Eisenberg, "The 1964 Presidential Election in Virginia: A Political Omen?," *University of Virginia Newsletter* 41, no. 8 (April 1965).

11. Wilkinson, *Harry Byrd and the Changing Face of Virginia Politics, 1945–1966*, 258–59.

12. Frank B. Atkinson, *The Dynamic Dominion: Realignment and the Rise of Two-Party Competition in Virginia, 1945–1980*, rev. 2nd ed. (Lanham, MD: Rowman & Littlefield, 2006), 161.

13. Wilkinson, *Harry Byrd and the Changing Face of Virginia Politics, 1945–1966*, 270–72. See also Gerald Paul Gaidmore, "The Virginia Conservative Party, 1965–1969" (thesis, Old Dominion University, 1999).

14. The political confusion and the irony of former segregationist leader Godwin being supported by the Richmond Crusade for Voters is best summarized in a humorous October 31, 1965, column by *Richmond Times-Dispatch* correspondent Charles B. McDowell, excerpted in Wilkinson, *Harry Byrd and the Changing Face of Virginia Politics, 1945–1966*, 276–78.

15. Statement of Votes Cast for Governor, General Election, November 2, 1965, Commonwealth of Virginia, Division of Purchase and Printing (1966).

16. The case was *Wilkins v. Davis,* 208 Va. 803 (1965).

17. Barry J. Dierenfield, "Conservative Outrage: The Defeat in 1966 of Howard W. Smith," *Virginia Magazine of History and Biography* 89, no. 2 (April 1981). The counties removed from the Eighth District were Albemarle, Culpeper, Fluvanna, Greene, and Orange, plus the city of Charlottesville. The counties added were Charles City, Essex, King and Queen, and New Kent.

18. Harry Byrd Jr.'s appointment continued a pattern that had resulted in Virginia voters never having had the opportunity to select a US senator for his first term. Since the passage of the Seventeenth Amendment to the US Constitution in 1913, every Virginia senator had arrived in Washington initially through appointment or selection at a state party convention.

19. *Norfolk Virginian Pilot,* January 24, 1966. Downing, forty-seven years old and a World War II veteran, was in his fourth term in the House of Representatives.

20. Unattributed, "Bankers Urge Robertson to Run Again," *Richmond Times-Dispatch,* June 20, 1965, C-11.

21. There were persistent rumors of a meeting in New York at the time of the annual presentation by the governor to the bond rating agencies at which Governor Godwin, Albertis Harrison, his predecessor, Byrd Jr., and Kellam were said to have discussed finding an alternative to Robertson. Letter to W. Brooks George, Larus and Brother Company, Inc., November 23, 1965, Drawer 117, Folder 34, Papers of A. Willis Robertson (Williamsburg, VA: College of William & Mary, Swem Library, Special Collections) (hereafter Robertson Papers). The *Richmond Times-Dispatch* reporter James Latimer quoted Governor Harrison as "confirming the meeting and the participants" but "denying" there was talk of dumping Robertson. His article put the meeting in mid-November, at the time of the annual State Chamber of Commerce meeting at the Waldorf Astoria in New York. *Richmond Times-Dispatch,* December 1, 1965.

22. AP, "Howell Criticizes Other Democrats, Raps Robertson," *Richmond Times-Dispatch,* December 3, 1965, A-6

23. Unattributed, "Howell to Ponder U.S. Senate," *Norfolk Virginian Pilot,* December 6, 1965, 21.

24. AP, "Howell Out to Break Silence," *Norfolk Virginian Pilot,* February 16, 1966, 3.

25. Among the documents in the Howell papers at Old Dominion University are copies of the outline of a campaign plan and the memorandum from a late January meeting of Howell and three key supporters. That memorandum, titled "Consensus of Meeting and Actions to be Taken," makes clear that Howell's primary goal was to be elected governor in 1969. To that end, the memo lays out a strategy under which Howell would indicate

his intention to run for the Robertson's seat to force Spong or Jennings or both to make certain commitments regarding the 1969 governor's race in order to keep Howell from running for the Senate. Copies of a February 25 letter signed by Howell and addressed to "Fellow Democrat" declare his candidacy for the Robertson seat and state that Jennings, Spong, and former State Senator Armistead Boothe were interested in opposing Byrd. That letter was never sent. Box 39, Folder 9, Papers of Henry Evans Howell Jr., Special Collections and University Archives, Patricia W. and J. Douglas Perry Library, Old Dominion University, Norfolk, VA

26. Unsigned, "Spong to Run for Seat Held by Robertson," *Richmond Times-Dispatch*, February 26, 1966., A-1

27. James Latimer, "First Dual Primary since 1911 Looms in Virginia," *Richmond Times-Dispatch*, February 27, 1966, A-1.

28. James Latimer and Charles McDowell Jr., "Boothe Will Run for Byrd's Seat," *Richmond Times-Dispatch*, March 3, 1966, A-1.

29. James Latimer, "Pressure on Downing Apparently Growing," *Richmond Times-Dispatch*, March 4, 1966, A-1. Latimer, the longtime political correspondent for the *Richmond Times-Dispatch*, reported that Downing was reconsidering whether to enter the race and ally himself with Byrd in an effort to give the organization a more youthful cast.

30. Rawlings was first elected to the General Assembly from Fredericksburg and Spotsylvania in 1963, defeating Delegate Francis B. Gouldman, a twelve-year veteran and organization stalwart and winning 63 percent of the primary vote. Many of the organization conservatives then voted Republican in the fall, but Rawlings prevailed. A conservative challenge to him gathered 48 percent in the 1965 general election, with Rawlings again prevailing.

31. Hank Burchard, "Farley Says Rep Smith Saved Fairfax County from 3-Way Split," *Washington Post*, June 12, 1966, B-3.

32. Box 1, Papers of Howard W. Smith (Charlottesville: University of Virginia Library, Special Collections) (hereafter Smith Papers).

33. The biographical material here comes from a variety of sources, including Heinemann's and Wilkinson's biographies of Byrd Sr., Dierenfield's biography of Smith, and Heinemann's biography of Robertson in the *Encyclopedia Virginia* (Charlottesville: Virginia Foundation for the Humanities, 2014), as well as from the Robertson Papers.

34. The Southern Manifesto was a document developed in 1956 opposing integration of public places. It was signed by eighty-two members of the House of Representatives and nineteen senators, including all of the members of the Virginia congressional delegation.

35. The biographical material on Spong comes from a variety of sources, including Heinemann's and Wilkinson's biographies of Byrd Sr., Dierenfield's

biography of Smith, and Heinemann's biography of Spong in the *Encyclopedia Virginia*, as well as from the Papers of William B Spong Jr, Accession #9838, Special Collections Dept., University of Virginia Library, Charlottesville, VA.

36. In 1965, redistricting created a multimember state senate district that included the city of Portsmouth and parts of the cities of Chesapeake and Virginia Beach. In a six-candidate general election for three seats, Spong ran first in each of the three jurisdictions, broadening his political base and increasing his stature as a vote-getter.

37. Robertson, letter to Paul H. Schneider, President of the Bank of Madison Wisconsin, Drawer 116, Folder 75, Robertson Papers.

38. Robertson, letters to Louis G. Fields and to State Senator Ed Willey, June 25–30, 1966, Drawer 116, Folder 50, Robertson Papers.

39. Sometimes called the Airlie Group (named for the rural resort in Fauquier County where the "liberals" met), the membership varied from time to time. Its stalwarts included Gus Johnson, chairman of the Tenth District Democratic Committee; Rawlings; state senator Armistead Boothe; and one or more of the legislators or local Democratic leaders from Norfolk. Its "leader" and organizer beginning in 1964 was John Paul Carter, an Episcopal priest connected with the Airlie Foundation. Papers of John Paul Carter (Norfolk, VA: Old Dominion University, Special Collections and University Archives) (hereafter Carter Papers).

40. Kimberly A. Matthews, *The Richmond Crusade for Voters* (Mount Pleasant, SC: Arcadia, 2017), 40.

41. See, for example, an, editorial published in the *Richmond Times-Dispatch*, April 3, 1966.

42. *Norfolk Virginian Pilot*, June 26, 1966.

43. Robertson, letter to Bryant B. Lipscomb, Drawer 118, Folder 38, Robertson Papers.

44. Robertson, multiple letters to business leaders, Drawer 117, Folder 6, Robertson Papers.

45. *Northern Virginia Sun*, June 7, 1966.

46. Spong Papers, quoted from campaign brochure used in the primary election.

47. Charles McDowell Jr, "Pair Campaigning Hard," *Richmond Times-Dispatch*, May 26, 1966, A-1.

48. Robertson speech in Lynchburg at the dedication of a public library, published in *Richmond Times-Dispatch*, April 17, 1966.

49. Charles McDowell Jr, "Boothe Terms Byrd 'Negative, Destructive,'" *Richmond Times-Dispatch*, May 18, 1966, A-7.

50. Boothe, speech, at Rockbridge County Courthouse, May 16, 1961, Box 168, Folder 1A, Boothe Papers.

51. Boothe, speech to Norfolk Committee dinner, May 11, 1966, Box 168, Folder 1C, Boothe Papers.

52. James Latimer, "Byrd Opens Campaign Headquarters," *Richmond Times-Dispatch*, May 3, 1966, A-1.

53. Judge Smith may have brought about his own defeat. From 1950 on he had been renominated every two years by the Eighth District Democratic Party through a district convention. His advisers urged he follow the same path in 1966, but he chose instead to file for a primary, declaring, "If they don't like Judge Smith, well, I'll go back to my dairy" (quoted in Dierenfield, "Conservative Outrage," 210–11).

54. Ken Tomlinson, "Smith Urges Hanover Backers to Enlist Women and Youth," *Richmond Times-Dispatch*, April 30, 1966, A-2.

55. Dierenfield, "Conservative Outrage," 66–75. Smith had actively opposed many of Roosevelt's New Deal priorities, including the controversial "court reform," and union-backed legislation to shorten the workday and establish a minimum wage. In the spring of 1938 Roosevelt signaled his support for William E. Dodd, Smith's challenger, and was joined by leaders of organized labor in the form of the Non-Partisan League of the Congress of Industrial Organizations and its leader, John L. Lewis. Smith won handily, winning three out of every four votes. The mutual animosity with labor would linger.

56. RTD News Bureau, "Rawlings Pledges Constructive Action," *Richmond Times-Dispatch*, April 30, 1966, A-2.

57. The special session of the 1965 General Assembly added Charles City, Essex, King and Queen, and New Kent Counties to a district that already included Caroline, Goochland, King William, Lancaster, and Louisa Counties.

58. V. O. Key estimated that the organization had to win the support of only 5–7 percent of the adult population to nominate its candidate. Key, *Southern Politics in State and Nation*, 20.

59. Lorin A. Thompson, *Recent Population Changes in Virginia*, Bureau of Public Administration, University of Virginia, Departmental Newsletter 37, no. 6 (February 15, 1961).

60. Unattributed Robertson campaign strategy document, Drawer 116, Folder 50, Robertson Papers.

61. Editorial Board, "Sen Spong Announces," *Richmond Times-Dispatch*, February 26, 1966, A-14.

62. AP, "Spong, Speaking in Norfolk, Scores Votes By Robertson," *Richmond Times-Dispatch*, May 17, 1966, A-4.

63. Unattributed, "Spong, Boothe Backed by Virginia AFL-CIO," *Richmond Times-Dispatch*, May 22, 1966, B-1.

64. AP, "Conservative Ticket Appears No Worry to Byrd, Robertson," *Richmond Times-Dispatch*, May 24, 1966, A-4.

65. Unattributed, "Robertson, Spong Clash on Unions Aired," *Richmond Times-Dispatch,* June 8, 1966, A-4.

66. Unattributed, "Robertson, Spong Clash on 'Obligation,'" *Richmond Times-Dispatch,* June 12, 1966, A-1.

67. James Latimer and Allan Jones, "Coercion Charged for Robertson Fund," *Richmond Times-Dispatch,* June 13, 1966, A-1.

68. Helen Dewar, "Spong Lists Finances for Campaign," *Washington Post,* June 14 1966, B-1; Helen Dewar, "Banks Confirm Fund Raised for Robertson," June 16, 1966; Helen Dewar, "Robertson Says He Was Unaware Bankers Had Raised $30,000," June 17, 1966: Unattributed, "School Issue and Ethics Enliven Va Senate Race," June 18, 1966; Helen Dewar, "Bankers' Help Could Backfire," June 21, 1966; Unattributed, "Bankers for Robertson Puts Bite on Colleagues," June 21, 1966.

69. Atkinson, *The Dynamic Dominion,* 185–90.

70. James Latimer, "Harrison Forsees 'Open Door' Voting," *Richmond Times-Dispatch,* June 24, 1966.

71. Charles McDowell Jr, "Byrd Takes Campaign to 2 'Weakest' Areas," *Richmond Times-Dispatch,* July 1, 1966, A-4.

72. Unattributed, "Byrd Denies Campaign Merger," *Roanoke Times,* July 1, 1966, 20.

73. James Latimer, "Robertson Takes Swing Through Southside," *Richmond Times-Dispatch,* July 5, 1966, A-2

74. Helen Dewar, "Letter Said to Seek White Backlash Aid for Robertson," *Washington Post,* July 4, 1966, B-1.

75. Allan Jones, "Senatorial Races Enter Home Stretch," *Richmond Times-Dispatch,* July 3, 1966, A-1.

76. James Latimer, "John S. Battle Backs Spong for Senate; Boothe Cancels Speeches in Campaign Against Byrd," *Richmond Times-Dispatch,* July 9, 1966, A-1.

77. Unattributed, "Group Backs Spong, Boothe," *Richmond Times-Dispatch,* July 11, 1966, A-14.

78. Melverse Nicholson, "Voters League Rebuffs Brass, Endorses Spong," *Norfolk Journal and Guide,* June 25, 1966, A-1.

79. All vote statistics in this and subsequent sections are taken from the Official Records compiled by the Secretary of the State Board of Elections and published by the Commonwealth of Virginia as the *Statement of the Vote* for that given election.

80. Dierenfield, "Conservative Outrage," 220–22.

81. All population figures in this section are from official census records. US Bureau of the Census, *Eighteenth Census of the United States: 1960, Population, Vol II.*

82. Robert A. Rankin, "The Richmond Crusade for Voters: The Quest for Black Power," *University of Virginia Newsletter* 51, no. 1 (September 1974).

83. Ralph Eisenberg, "1966 Politics in Virginia: The Democratic Senatorial Primary," *University of Virginia Newsletter* 43, no. 5 (January 1967).

84. The 1961 results are from the precinct-level returns published after the election in the *Richmond Times-Dispatch*, July 12, 1961.

85. There had been predictions of a turnout as high as 500,000, though that would have been unprecedented. Based on figures compiled by Larry Sabato in *The Democratic Party Primary in Virginia*, 18.7 percent of the voting-age population cast ballots in the 1966 primary, the second highest percentage since 1905. The highest (20.1 percent) had been in the 1949 primary for governor.

86. J. Kenneth Robinson, a Frederick County orchardist running as a Republican, came within 600 votes of defeating Jack Marsh, the organization candidate for Byrd's home district. *Official Statement of the Vote, General Election 1962*, Richmond.

87. *Official Statement of the Vote, Democratic Primary Election, 1961*, Richmond.

88. *Bristol Herald-Courier*, June 12, 1966.

89. Ralph Eisenberg, "1966 Politics in Virginia: The Elections for U.S. Senators," *University of Virginia Newsletter* 43, no. 9 (May 15, 1967).

90. Ibid.

91. The conservative Democrats did put up a candidate in 1968, but he lost in the Eighth District Democratic nominating convention to Andrew McCutcheon, a moderate supporter of Senator Spong. McCutcheon failed to get sufficient conservative support in the fall, and Congressman Bill Scott was reelected. In 1970 the conservatives did not even try to offer a candidate, and Scott trounced the Democratic nominee Darrell Stearns.

92. Smith, letter to C. B. McDaniel, President, Hilldrup Transfer and Storage, September 12, 1966, Box 1, Smith Papers.

93. Dierenfield, "Conservative Outrage," 217–18.

94. Reflecting on his loss in a 1999 interview, Rawlings thought Scott had simply "caught the tide": "Everybody was mad at me for beating Judge Smith." *Oral History of George C. Rawlings, Jr.* (Fredericksburg, VA: Central Rappahannock Heritage Center, 1999).

95. The origins and success of that group of Republicans, led by Richard D. Obenshain, is extensively documented in Atkinson, *The Dynamic Dominion*.

96. While Richard Obenshain had died tragically in a plane crash in 1978, other early leaders, such as Judy Peachee Ford and J. Kenneth Klinge, continued to work with campaigns, rallying support from members of the coalition up to and through the Mark Warner 2001 campaign.

97. John Warner became the Republican nominee after the tragic death of Obenshain, whose leadership of the conservative coalition had led to him securing the Republican nomination to succeed Scott.

3

Virginia's "Armageddon" and Its Legacy of Partisan Competition

THE 1973 GUBERNATORIAL ELECTION

Frank B. Atkinson

On the twelfth day of January 1970, Democratic governor Mills Godwin turned over the keys to the Virginia Executive Mansion to a Republican, Linwood Holton—the first time a chief executive so affiliated had taken possession in nearly a century.[1] Four years later, that same Godwin, clad now in Republican garb himself, returned to reclaim the keys—the first time a Virginia governor had gained a second term since the Civil War, and the only time by successive votes of the people.[2] Those signal events reflected the unique, transitional character of the times. Between them unfolded a titanic struggle for control of the state's highest office that would affect the course of Virginia politics for many years.

Dubbed "Armageddon" at the time by a leading political journalist,[3] the 1973 gubernatorial election pitted conservative Democrat-turned-Republican Mills Godwin against populist Democrat-turned-independent Henry Howell. The contest between the state's immediate past governor and its sitting lieutenant governor indeed seemed like the definitive battle for the commonwealth's political soul. Yet even this supposed Armageddon was only one consequential clash among many, for this was the 1970s in Virginia, a decade in which the Old Dominion, long renowned for its near-moribund unflappability, was given to flapping about wildly as one unruly display of participatory democracy followed another as if in a chain reaction, leaving a thoroughly transformed landscape in its wake. In the parlance of political scientists, it was a period of extensive partisan dealignment and partial realignment, with the old political order's full collapse enabling the emergence of a dynamic new environment characterized by two-party competition and artful coalition building, along with some inevitable score settling. At the time, the change seemed convulsive and, to many a bemused Virginian, downright incomprehensible. The hits just kept coming, and the most unusual thing usually happened.

Among the decade's more jarring developments: unprecedented state-wide wins by independent candidates on the right (Harry Byrd Jr. for reelection to the US Senate in 1970) and left (Henry Howell in a special election for lieutenant governor in 1971); hostile takeovers of both state parties by their more ideological adherents in 1972 (progressives in the Democratic Party, conservatives in the GOP); a mass egress of conservatives from the state Democratic Party fueled by George McGovern's presidential candidacy in 1972 and their abortive ingress into the state Republican Party as a result of Richard Nixon's Watergate scandal in 1973–74; the tragic death of each party's most promising young leader on the apparent cusp of political triumph (Democratic lieutenant governor J. Sargeant Reynolds's due to a brain tumor in 1971 and GOP US Senate candidate Richard Obenshain's as a result of an airplane crash in 1978); the sudden emergence of celebrity figures who would go on to play highly important leadership roles (Democrat Charles Robb, son-in-law of President Lyndon Johnson, elected lieutenant governor in 1977, and Republican John Warner, husband of Oscar-winning actress Elizabeth Taylor, elected to the US Senate in 1978); and, perhaps strangest of all, the 1973 gubernatorial election, when the Virginia Democratic Party, the dominant political force in the commonwealth throughout the twentieth century, opted not to exercise the most prized prerogative of state political parties, the nomination of a candidate for governor.

At first blush, this partial litany of the political oddities from the 1970s might appear balanced, with both parties discombobulated in roughly equal measure. But such an appearance would be highly deceiving, for Republicans benefited decisively from the upheaval and transition, at least in the short term. Bookending the decade's lively chapters were two especially significant elections that went the GOP's way: the 1969 contest for governor, when Linwood Holton scored a crucial breakthrough for Republicans in statewide races, and the 1980 presidential election, when Ronald Reagan added blue-collar Democrats to the usual GOP base in rolling up lopsided majorities nationally, regionally, and in the commonwealth. In the brief span from the former contest to the latter, Virginia Republicans went on a tear. They entered the period having failed to win a single statewide election for governor or the US Senate since Reconstruction and exited it as the winningest state party, Republican or Democratic, anywhere in the country.

Democratic Division and the Holton Breakthrough

How this remarkable transformation took place is a story with more twists and turns than this chapter can fully chronicle, but the big events are not hard to spot. As described in the preceding chapters, the inverted political order that long had characterized twentieth-century Virginia politics—Democrats of the southern or "Byrd" variety as the dominant conservative party, Republicans as the more progressive alternative, at least in state elections—already was fast unraveling when Linwood Holton, encouraged by his decent showing in the 1965 gubernatorial race, saddled up to lead the Republican charge again four years later.

A talented campaigner who embraced diverse people and new ideas, the energetic Holton seemed to sweep across the state from his native Southwest and Roanoke home base in 1969 like a burst of cool, fresh air.[4] In a turnabout, two crucial advantages that Democrat Mills Godwin had enjoyed in the 1965 governor's race—positive energy from the preceding year's successful presidential campaign and a largely unified state party—were distinct assets for Republican Holton four years later. Former vice president Richard Nixon, then a popular moderate, handily carried Virginia in 1968 and then returned as president a year later to campaign enthusiastically for Holton. Nixon's appeal and Holton's smart ticket-building had a unifying effect on the sometimes disparate elements of the Virginia GOP. Democrats, meanwhile, served the Holton cause by blowing themselves apart.

With Godwin's 1965 win and moderate US senator William Spong Jr.'s 1966 election as models, Democratic leaders had hoped to surmount their yawning factional divisions by fielding an appealing centrist for governor in 1969. But each of the party's factions had ideas, and a candidate, of its own. Many Byrd conservatives preferred Godwin's number two, Lieutenant Governor Fred Pollard; moderates rallied around William Battle, former Kennedy administration ambassador to Australia and son of accomplished Virginia governor John Battle (1950–54); and the party's restive liberal wing passionately preferred the populist firebrand, state senator Henry Howell of Norfolk. Following a contentious primary campaign and especially bitter runoff contest, Battle became the party's wounded nominee, Howell emerged angry and aggrieved, and Holton reaped the harvest of disaffection in November.

"The Republican governor-elect was given his margin of victory by one or both of two dissident groups of former Democrats," wrote sage political reporter James Latimer in the election's wake. "A group from the conservative right was motivated by hopes of [promoting] a realignment of parties along conservative versus liberal lines. A group from the liberal left . . . turned to the GOP gubernatorial candidate in hopes of stomping out the last trace of the Byrd organization."[5] Holton received crucial financial and political support from conservative Democrats and a group of business and professional leaders who declared themselves "New Republicans."[6] But with the Democratic Party having moved perceptibly leftward during much of the 1960s, the conservative defections were not nearly as surprising as the support Holton garnered from Democratic progressives. Howell publicly labeled his supporters "free spirits," providing thinly veiled encouragement for them to turn their backs on Battle.[7] But outgoing governor Godwin, who backed Battle forcefully in the runoff, generated the most intense progressive ire. African American and organized labor leaders, who in 1965 had taken a leap of faith in backing the erstwhile champion of resistance to school desegregation, alleged that Godwin had reneged on his promises of inclusion. Declaring that "a vote for Battle would be a vote for the Byrd machine," the state's most influential African American political organization overtly endorsed Holton in the fall campaign.[8]

An unusually broad coalition thus swept the moderate new Republican governor into office, and he was joined in the winner's circle by two Democrats who largely shared his centrist predilections, Lieutenant Governor J. Sargeant "Sarge" Reynolds and Attorney General Andrew Miller.[9] For a brief time in the election's wake, the state actually seemed poised for a continued, orderly transition from the stern, tight-fisted conservatism of the Byrd era to a less stingy and more inclusive, yet still buttoned-down and pro-business, moderate brand of Democratic leadership. Holton, the Republican interloper, had exploited the momentary chaos in the court to gain the throne in the traditionally Democratic domain, but Reynolds—youthful, wealthy, and "Kennedyesque"—seemed like the most compelling of crown princes. Less noticed, and of little apparent significance to those who did notice, was the seething antipathy that the election had engendered between Howell and Godwin. Few then imagined that either man, let alone both, would be on the ballot for governor in 1973.

As chronicled by the University of Virginia's then new political analyst, Larry Sabato, the state's Democratic primary had been "tantamount to election" during the golden days of the Byrd organization.[10] But in the wake of the fractious nominating contest in 1969, almost everyone who mattered came to the same conclusion about Democratic primaries: *avoid them at all cost.* Indeed, Senator Harry Byrd Jr., facing his first reelection campaign in 1970, saw greater risk in running for the Democratic nomination than in presenting his case directly to the general electorate.[11] Taking the road less traveled (and rarely with success) in American politics, Byrd stood for reelection as an independent candidate and rolled up a sizable majority of the vote against little-known nominees from both major parties.[12] When, a year later, another Democrat from the opposite end of the political spectrum largely duplicated Byrd's feat, it was clear that things were not about to settle down anytime soon.

Virginians were stunned by the announcement in August 1970 that Lieutenant Governor Reynolds was suffering from an inoperable brain tumor, and they watched with a keen sense of sadness and admiration as the stricken young leader courageously battled his illness for months, succumbing in June 1971 at age thirty-four.[13] His loss occasioned a special statewide election in November to fill the vacant post, one that Henry Howell, running as an independent, won with a plurality of the vote over Republican and Democratic foes.[14] Suddenly, the populist gadfly whose "Keep the Big Boys Honest" slogan set teeth on edge in corner offices and boardrooms across the commonwealth, could no longer be ignored or diminished by the establishment. He had won a statewide prize and claimed the pole position in the next race for governor. That race would be about various things but none more ominous to some and enchanting to others than the persona of Howell himself. "Virginia," observed then senator Douglas Wilder presciently on Reynolds's passing, "has lost more than she presently realizes."[15]

Party Takeovers Boost Realignment

It was during this time that two consequential movements, one national in scope and one indigenous to Virginia, set in motion events that would alter the trajectory of Virginia politics.

The presidential campaign of US senator George McGovern of South Dakota, a leading dove on defense and champion of the Democratic left, had only the combined seventeen electoral votes of Massachusetts and the District of Columbia to show for its efforts at the end of the day. But on the way to that landslide 1972 defeat, the McGovern juggernaut and its grassroots army rumbled through Democratic primaries and conventions, unceremoniously dispatching conservative hangers-on, squelching centrist aspirations, and replacing moderate apparatchiks with new party leaders who embraced the South Dakotan's unapologetically ideological brand of politics. In Virginia, this meant the ouster of the state Democratic Party's moderate and conservative officials, including the party chairman and national committee representatives, in favor of avowed liberals who generally were aligned with Howell. Godwin, the party's most recent governor, was even denied a delegate seat at the state convention. Recalled Andrew Miller,

> You had people in leadership positions in the party in previous years—and I am not talking about people who were obviously [Byrd] organization types; I am talking about people who were involved in Bill Battle's campaign, Sarge Reynolds's campaign, my campaign in 1969—who were just tossed out of any party position they might have held. It was done in such a way that you had literally thousands of Virginians saying, as a consequence of what occurred at the Roanoke convention in 1972, that [they] might never be involved in the Democratic Party again. And they haven't been, by and large.[16]

Henry Howell, unsurprisingly, had a different take. It was a great victory, he recalled years later, for the Democrats "who believed in life after birth and did not like this decadent Democratic Party [in Virginia] that really had a Republican philosophy."[17]

Virginia Republicans, at least its most active leaders, eyed the Howell and McGovern advances with unconcealed glee. They saw in Howell a polarizing figure whose gubernatorial candidacy promised to drive not only Byrd conservatives but moderate business leaders and independent-minded suburban voters into the GOP's arms. But the McGovern forces' takeover of the Democratic Party as an institution suggested the possibility of something more permanent. For more than a decade, Richard Obenshain had advocated a GOP party-building strategy focused on getting "conservatives to unite in the Republican party, the only national party which can be returned to the basic tenets of constitutional government and individual freedom."[18] As leader of the state's Young Republicans, then as a congressional candidate in Central Virginia, and most recently as the candidate for attorney general on Holton's 1969 ticket, the hard-charging young Richmond lawyer had been avidly promoting this realignment concept, winning adherents if not elections and hoping for just the kind of leftward lurch in the Democratic Party that could make his vision a reality.[19] Now the stars had aligned, with one very bright exception: Linwood Holton, the incumbent governor and leader of his party, disagreed.

Holton's views on the realignment opportunity actually were nuanced. He had spent most of his career fighting the Byrd organization and its lieutenants, nearly all of whom, until Godwin championed a burst of education spending in the late 1960s, had adhered to racial, social, and fiscal tenets that Holton regarded as repressive, regressive, and wrong. Though he saw the practical value of winning over Democratic conservatives and had welcomed their indispensable donations and votes in his own 1969 campaign, the new governor had little appetite for embracing Democrats like Byrd and Godwin whom he long had battled. And, such personal feelings aside, there was the contrary thematic thrust of Holton's administration, which stressed a new openness and inclusion, especially regarding matters of race. An "aristocracy of ability" had been the clarion call in his inaugural address, a plain contrast with the discriminatory attitudes and policies that had held Virginians back under his predecessors.[20] Holton wanted to take Virginia forward into a promising new era, not aid and abet politicians of the past in perpetuating their power.

When Byrd left the Democratic Party to run for the Senate as an independent, Holton resisted President Nixon's pressure to have the Virginia GOP endorse the Byrd candidacy as a catalyst for other southern Democratic switchovers. Having long touted the virtues of vigorous two-party democracy as an antidote to Virginia's suffocating one-party stasis, Holton believed it was the foremost duty of a political party to nominate candidates and offer voters a choice. Defying Nixon and GOP conservatives, he personally appealed for nomination of a Byrd opponent by the state Republican convention, a move that succeeded, ironically, because of Byrd's own refusal to publicly embrace the endorsement idea. The result was an embarrassing defeat for Republicans in the fall. The GOP Senate nominee finished a distant third to Byrd in the three-way race, a dismal performance that was essentially repeated a year later when another little-known, Holton-backed moderate placed last in the special election for lieutenant governor won by Howell. In the years following his promising 1969 breakthrough, Holton had succeeded in setting his party's course; the problem was, the direction was downward.

Obenshain shared Holton's Southwest Virginia roots and his progressive views on race, but what stirred the younger partisan's political passion was the cause of individual freedom and the overarching struggle between free markets and socialism he saw playing out not only on the world stage but in domestic politics. Where Holton viewed men like Byrd and Godwin chiefly through a backward-looking lens focused on their segregation-era sins, Obenshain looked forward to the advantage a consolidation of conservatives in the GOP could yield in coming races for the national soul, like the one Ronald Reagan was preparing to wage. From the moment Henry Howell won election as lieutenant governor in 1971, putting a bona fide liberal on the brink of the governorship, one notion dominated Obenshain's thinking: the imperative of recruiting Mills Godwin to defeat Howell and, in the process, dramatically realigning the Virginia political parties. But that could never happen unless the Virginia Republican Party rolled out the welcome mat for Godwin and his Democratic friends. And, far from inviting them in, Holton seemed to have locked the doors and turned out the lights.

Obenshain had been thinking about challenging popular incumbent senator William Spong Jr., who was up for reelection in 1972, but the Republican's coterie of party confidants argued that the only way to extend a welcome to Godwin and lay the foundation for future GOP wins was for Obenshain himself to capture the party chairmanship at the 1972 Republican state convention. Once the reluctant leader acceded to his friends' collective wisdom, Governor Holton and the incumbent party chair were duly advised of the challenge, campaign operations were assembled, partisans took sides, and the spirited contest played out in hundreds of Republican mass meetings and caucuses across the state. In the end, delegates gave the Obenshain insurgency a comfortable victory at the party's state conclave in June. The takeover had been a hostile one in fact but not so much in tone, and it left comparatively little of the collateral damage inflicted by the leadership fights on the Democratic side. The result was a seminal development in Virginia's realignment. In the wake of the two state conventions in 1972, the leadership of the Virginia parties for the first time was fully aligned with their respective national party organizations.

The fall elections looked so predictable—incumbents President Nixon and Senator Spong were deemed prohibitive favorites—that most of political Virginia cast its gaze forward a year to the looming gubernatorial showdown. Only Obenshain, it seemed, and a little-known three-term congressman from Fairfax named William Scott had other ideas. Nixon's coattails in the commonwealth proved long and strong enough to pull Scott in, making him the first Republican senator elected from Virginia in the twentieth century.[21] A determined Obenshain had ably managed the difficult Republican candidate and campaign, and he received due credit for the monumental upset. But the overwhelmingly adverse environment created by McGovern's doomed candidacy and the steady Spong's surprising campaign missteps also had contributed to the shocker. For Democratic moderates, so evidently on the rise just a few years earlier, the Spong defeat was especially deflating. For Republicans, the Senate bout proved to be a very useful preliminary to the main event in 1973. Not only had the upstart GOP captured the Senate seat and elected seven of ten members from the state's newly reapportioned US House of Representatives districts; it also had shown Mills Godwin that a conservative candidate running with the Republican label could win statewide in Virginia. And Godwin needed convincing.

Jockeying for Position: The 1973 Preliminaries

As 1973 approached, what puzzled Godwin was not whether to run for governor again but under what banner. Though not eager for a return to public life after his highly successful 1966–70 tenure, the former governor understood that he was the political figure best positioned to head off a Howell victory, which he deemed a dire threat to the state's continued progress and favorable business climate. Republicans, at least those newly at the helm of the state party, emphatically wanted Godwin to accept their nomination and their party label. But the former governor was more sanguine about a possible independent candidacy. A native of Nansemond County in rural southeastern Virginia, he had been a conservative "Byrd Democrat" throughout his lengthy career; Democrats had bestowed on him many honors, including their highest, the governorship, and Godwin abhorred ingratitude. By running as an independent in the manner of his close friend Senator Byrd, Godwin merely would be absenting himself from the Democratic Party; if he were actually to join the GOP, he would be *repudiating* it. Worse, he would be under pressure as a Republican to support all the nominees of his new party, including those who ran against his Democratic allies. Godwin valued his many friends in the Democratic courthouses and state legislature, and he meant to preserve those friendships.

On the practical side, however, the former governor understood that he had to walk a tightrope to win the election. It would have been difficult enough to bring longtime Republican and Democratic antagonists together for concerted action against a conventional liberal foe, but Henry Howell posed special problems. Howell's populist appeal cut across the usual philosophical lines; he had garnered backing in previous races not only from African Americans, labor, and liberals but also from a significant number of rural conservatives who had supported Byrd in 1970 and former Alabama governor George Wallace's independent presidential candidacy in 1968. Against such an opponent, Godwin could hope to amass a majority only by retaining as much of his old moderate and conservative Democratic support as possible while adding to it the traditional and suburban Republican base. He was uneasy about the prospects for getting die-hard Republicans to support an old nemesis, and he knew that moving all the way into the GOP camp would alienate many of his past supporters in the Democratic Party. The best resolution of those competing considerations, it seemed to Godwin, was for him to run as an independent and for Republicans to forgo fielding a candidate.[22]

There was only one problem with that approach. Nobody in a position of leadership in the Virginia Republican Party—not Richard Obenshain, not the group of conservative party leaders who had helped Obenshain oust the Holton-backed party chairman, and certainly not Governor Holton himself—was willing to go before the GOP convention in 1973 and ask the delegates to do what Godwin wanted. When Obenshain and his allies huddled in the summer of 1972 to discuss Godwin and the upcoming gubernatorial race, one influential voice stood out. Emporia attorney Dortch Warriner, an Obenshain ally, conservative Republican leader, and the party's 1965 nominee for attorney general, declared that the former governor should seek the GOP nomination and "run as a Republican" or the party should offer another candidate. The issue of whether the Republican Party was going to nominate candidates had been settled at the 1970 convention, Warriner insisted, and that battle should not be fought again.[23] Some of the assembled, including Obenshain, bristled at the idea of giving the proud Godwin any sort of ultimatum, and the new party chairman argued for a more flexible approach. But all agreed that a formal Godwin affiliation with the GOP was essential for the arrangement to succeed.

Warriner had helped wrest control of the party machinery from Governor Holton, but his reaction to Godwin's reluctance to embrace the GOP mirrored Holton's and the feelings of many partisans in traditionally Republican areas. "It seemed to me that he was putting us down," Warriner explained, "and I had worked too dad-blamed hard for something that I was proud of to have this man put it down." Having endured social slights and all manner of indignity over the years for his partisan affiliation,

Warriner was in no mood to accept Godwin on Godwin's terms. "He wanted our endorsement but he didn't want to call himself a Republican," Warriner said. "It was as though we were good enough for him to go to bed with but not good enough to marry." Having Godwin adopt the Republican label became an intense matter of principle as well as pride for Warriner. He pressed the case forcefully during discussions with and about the former governor and even threatened to launch his own gubernatorial bid if Godwin failed to move forthrightly into the GOP.[24]

During the fall of 1972 and ensuing winter, the deliberating former chief executive received a steady stream of political luminaries and friends at his home on Cedar Point near Suffolk. Obenshain, whose influence Godwin later credited as decisive, was among the most frequent visitors. He stressed the former governor's ability to advance realignment, the difficulty of rallying Republicans without his wholehearted embrace of the GOP, and the importance of the Republican precinct organization in the campaign against Howell. Obenshain was accompanied on the various pilgrimages by a mix of GOP activists and Republican lawmakers who sought to assure Godwin that he would be supported actively by local party workers if he joined the GOP. A parade of Democratic officials made the same trek. While some urged Godwin to maximize his Democratic support by following Byrd's independent course, others stressed the need to avoid a perilous three-way contest and assured the former governor that a Republican affiliation would not cause erosion of his support among their Democratic colleagues. The path forward was clear to Smith Ferebee, a key Godwin friend, fundraiser, and pillar of the Richmond business community. "[We had] to be united, and you couldn't get united with the Republicans if you didn't embrace them," he said.[25]

Godwin's embrace initially had all the warmth of a pandemic-inspired air hug. In publicly launching his campaign in early March 1973, he planned to say only that he would accept a Republican endorsement or nomination if offered. But at the last minute he added a promise to "run as a Republican," a concession to Warriner that only the irascible Ferebee likely could have extracted. The incantation was sufficient to head off the murder-suicide that would have resulted from a rival GOP candidacy like the one threatened by Warriner, but Godwin had trouble repeating it or anything like it in the months leading to the state Republican convention. He told reporters thereafter that he "[did] not consider [himself] to be a Republican at this time," that such a self-description would depend on the action of the convention, and that he would accept, but was not seeking, the GOP nomination for governor. Even uttering the "R" word seemed to challenge Godwin, who took to referring to Republicans as "you people" and to himself as "your nominee" as he trudged through the obligatory party caucuses, prompting some resentful convention delegates to don "I'm proud to be a 'you people'" buttons even as they prepared to nominate him.[26]

For many at the GOP state convention, only the presence of a lifelong Republican on the Godwin ticket—the nominee for lieutenant governor was state senator John Dalton of Radford, son of two-time GOP gubernatorial candidate and revered elder statesman Theodore Roosevelt "Ted" Dalton—made the whole business palatable. "The delegates understand and accept, in their heads, the political strategy involved in recruiting Godwin into their party at the very top of it," wrote columnist Charles McDowell. "They seem to believe in the concept of a conservative coalition and realignment of the parties in Virginia. But there is no mistaking that nominating an old Democratic foe is still a joyless business for most of these Republicans."[27]

The arranged marriage nevertheless was consummated. Obenshain had brought his party and his candidate to the altar, and he and his team labored mightily to make sure nothing marred the carefully choreographed ceremony. The decisive moment did not disappoint. Before they mounted the stage, Godwin showed Warriner the opening line of his remarks and suggested that an ovation following the salutation would help convey the enthusiastic acceptance of the former Democrat by the GOP partisans. Delighted by what he read, Warriner instantly concurred and spread the word to others on the platform. "*As one of you,*" Godwin intoned emphatically in beginning his remarks, and with that all on stage leapt to their feet, spurring the delegates to a loud ovation.

Henry Howell needed no such affirming send-off. A contrarian by nature as well as by design, the populist crusader found that the "independent" label not only matched his persona but served his cross-party appeal and coalition-building stratagem quite well. It also would be helpful in avoiding the "McGovernite" epithet that had dogged Democrats throughout 1972. So, rather than return officially to the Democratic fold, Howell opted for what Godwin had coveted but could not get: the blessing of his independent candidacy by a party willing to endorse him ("commend" was the official word used by the convention) and forgo fielding its own nominee. It was a remarkable action—abstaining from offering a candidate for the state's top office—for a Democratic Party whose dominance of state government had been a foregone conclusion for much of the century. Yet, after many decades in which the Democratic primary had been tantamount to election, the situation was familiar in one sense. Despite the contenders' labels of convenience, Virginia voters would once again choose between two lifelong Democrats in selecting their next governor.

The Crusader and the Citadel

What had no precedent in a Virginia governor's race was the personal, political, and philosophical chasm between the candidates. Their rhetoric made the stark divergence obvious. Though Howell sought to temper somewhat the strident language that had characterized his 1969 bid and to take advantage of his enhanced stature as lieutenant governor, he did not depart from his trademark anti-establishment themes. "Buckle up your armor and join a people's crusade," he beckoned in April. "We must restore power to the people of Virginia!"[28] Howell relished verbal blasts at the conspiratorial elites who, he charged, had anointed Godwin "behind the closed doors of the Commonwealth Club."[29] The lieutenant governor's populist platform centered on opposition to the sales tax on food and non-prescription drugs that had been enacted during Godwin's first term as governor, and to rates charged by the state's electrical and telephone utilities. Like former vice president Hubert Humphrey, the 1968 Democratic presidential nominee whom Howell had admired and supported, the lieutenant governor was a happy warrior whose often electrifying personality on the campaign trail energized his supporters.

Godwin responded to Howell's affronts to the business community and the affluent with apocalyptic warnings of radical change. "Unless we all face up to what is at stake," he declared in late May, "we must be prepared for drastic change in the kind of responsible, stable government to which we have become accustomed."[30] An unapologetic spokesman for the establishment, Godwin was serious, even austere, on the stump. His dark business suits seemed to match the clouds his dour speeches discerned on Virginia's horizon. Despite his progressive record as a Democratic governor, Godwin was cast in 1973 in the untenable political role of naysayer. That he needed to sound the alarm to defeat Howell was plain, but the difficulty Godwin faced was in defining just what about Henry Howell was so alarming. With the effervescent Howell campaigning for "the people," and with Godwin seeming to carry water for powerful business interests, the GOP watched its candidate's early lead in the polls transformed into a deficit by Labor Day.

As the general election campaign began in earnest, many Virginians viewed the contest as little more than a grudge match between old adversaries, a perception rooted in reality. The two men had been at cross-purposes, and often bitterly so, throughout their careers. Howell had begun his involvement in politics a quarter century earlier when he supported an anti-Byrd crusader for governor, while Godwin had been a Byrd organization stalwart since the 1950s. During the first Godwin administration, Howell had sued the governor successfully over the state's use of federal education funds. The two had clashed sharply in the 1969 gubernatorial race; Godwin helped engineer Howell's loss in the runoff, then the two traded charges of culpability for the Democrats' historic general election defeat. And, although Godwin had no interest in attending the 1972 state Democratic convention, it was Howell's forces who had inflicted the indignity of denying the former governor the option. The personal hostility between the two candidates was palpable in 1973, and the departure from Virginia's traditionally genteel political ways seemed to repel many voters.[31]

The motivational problems were most acute, however, among the Republicans. In his postelection comments on the race, GOP chief Obenshain explained that the Nixon administration's deepening Watergate scandal had sapped much of the usual Republican enthusiasm. "The campaign in some ways was almost like walking through a mine field because every two or three weeks another explosion at the national level would take place," he said.[32] In the summer there was the disheartening (for Republicans) spectacle of the Senate hearings on the Watergate break-in and related issues, during which the existence of the secret Oval Office tape recordings was first disclosed. As Senate investigators and the special prosecutor thereafter attempted to obtain the tapes, the Nixon White House stonewalled. In the campaign's closing weeks, the country was rocked by the resignation of Vice President Agnew as part of a tax evasion plea, followed by Nixon's firing of Watergate special prosecutor Archibald Cox in what became known as the Saturday Night Massacre. It was a traumatic time for Americans generally, and it was especially distracting and demoralizing for Republican activists.

The Watergate developments served to worsen the already widespread lethargy in Virginia GOP ranks. Mixed feelings about the nomination of the former Democrat Godwin did not disappear overnight for many old-line Republicans. While the recently converted Godwin enjoyed the unanimous bipartisan support of the state's congressional delegation, the backing of incumbent governor Holton and a large majority of state legislators, editorial support from every major state newspaper, and the active campaign efforts of the state Republican Party leadership, the grassroots GOP workers whose efforts would be needed to turn out the Godwin vote were slow to stir. Godwin's campaign organization contributed to the difficulty. Carter Lowance, a remarkable man who had served ably at the right hand of a succession of Virginia Democratic governors, chaired the Godwin campaign and staffed it with veteran Byrd organization operatives. The courthouse-based, "pass-the-word" style of campaigning had served the Byrd men well for decades, but by 1973 it had become hopelessly outdated. The electorate had expanded tremendously, many new people had come to the state, the urban corridor now held the key to elections, and targeted voter identification and turnout operations had displaced the pass-the-word technique.

The Godwin campaign's problems went beyond the Republican grassroots. Despite the magnitude of the Howell threat in the eyes of political insiders, much of the conservative business community initially failed to take the race seriously. Godwin's support seemed so broad and the GOP–Byrd Democrat alliance so formidable that few gave the liberal Howell much of a chance. The overconfidence proved highly damaging to the Godwin campaign's fundraising program, and that in turn constricted its organizational efforts and media advertising. The Republican nominee also had problems retaining his conservative Democratic base. Partisan Democrats, especially in Southwest Virginia, could not brook his party switch. In the rural Southside, where Godwin had been viewed with a measure of suspicion since his 1964 embrace of the Lyndon Johnson–led national ticket and his progressive program as governor, Howell's populist appeals seemed to be making substantial inroads among low-income White voters who previously had backed Wallace in 1968 and Byrd in 1970.

The situation looked bleak for Godwin and rosy for Howell, at least in the estimation of knowledgeable insiders, until late September, when Howell released an internal poll showing he had a nine percentage point lead. He thought release of the encouraging data would contribute to his campaign's growing momentum, but it had the opposite effect. Republican regulars, Democratic conservatives, and the business community were jolted out of their complacency. Dollars flowed into the Godwin campaign's coffers, precinct organizational activity picked up, and the Republican National Committee dispatched a team of veteran politicos to join a campaign salvage operation spearheaded by Obenshain.

For months, Howell had been on the offensive, and now it was the GOP's turn to seize the initiative. Obenshain's handpicked state party manager, Kenneth Klinge, assembled a field staff of experienced campaign operatives, established seven regional telephone banks, hired callers to canvass voters in targeted pro-Republican precincts, and saw to it that more than 250,000 calls were made to identify favorable voters. Campaign literature was mailed to the undecided respondents, and more than 100,000 voters who indicated support for Godwin were called again in the forty-eight-hour period preceding the close of the polls on November 6. The extensive program was made possible through innovations by the State Board of Elections—lists of registered voters had been computerized for the first time and made available to the public in 1972—under the leadership of the Holton-appointed election agency head, Joan S. Mahan. Telephone banks had been mainstays in previous Republican and Democratic campaigns, but the GOP's use of the new voter data, precinct targeting, paid callers, and direct mail in 1973 dwarfed all earlier efforts. It gave a boost to Republican turnout in targeted areas that was evident in the election returns, and it yielded a technological advantage that the GOP would continue to exploit until state Democrats finally countered and developed similar capabilities in the 1980s.

Obenshain was widely credited with masterful mechanics in the election's wake, but his personal impact on the Godwin campaign's public communications was even greater. He mobilized a bevy of vocal conservative surrogates for Godwin—Republicans and Byrd Democrats—who bashed Howell's issue positions daily for weeks. No one was more constantly on the attack than Obenshain himself. In the campaign's closing stretch he assailed Howell relentlessly for a variety of supposed heresies, including his ties to organized labor, opposition to the state's right-to-work law, embrace of McGovern's candidacy in 1972, support for gun control measures, and seemingly sympathetic statements concerning mandatory court-ordered busing to achieve school desegregation. The target of the attacks later pointed to Obenshain's efforts in explaining the election outcome. Citing the Republican chairman's "instinct for the jugular," Howell commented that "Obenshain turned defeat into victory by his last-minute attacks on me in 1973."[33]

The populist crusader later conceded, however, that his own campaign missteps had sealed his fate. Opposition to the sales tax on food had been his most potent political issue, but a Howell initiative announced in mid-October allowed Godwin and the Republicans to turn the tables. To replace the revenue that would be lost through repeal of the unpopular tax on food sales, Howell proposed a hike in the tax on alcoholic beverages, a new levy on bank and corporate stock dividends, an increase in the corporate income tax, and a ceiling on state spending. It was "as simple as ABC," the lieutenant governor said, referring to his plan to target *a*lcohol, *b*anks, and *c*orporations with new levies. But Godwin and W. Roy Smith, chairman of the House of Delegates Appropriations Committee, immediately denounced the Howell "ABC" plan as irresponsible and unworkable. Godwin warned that its enactment would "stymie the growth of the state," and at Republican headquarters fliers assailing the proposal as a "tax on jobs" were quickly prepared and distributed.[34]

The Godwin campaign surged in the closing days of the climactic contest. Howell's ammunition seemed to have been spent by early October, along with the lion's share of his campaign money. Reversing an early fundraising deficit, Godwin was able to outspend his opponent heavily on television and radio advertising in the campaign's critical final weeks.[35] While Obenshain, conservative heavyweights in both parties, and television ads pummeled Howell, Godwin touted his own accomplishments and positive prescription for Virginia's future. Displays of youthful support from well-organized college GOP activists helped give the former governor a more forward-looking image, and his handlers even managed to persuade Godwin to exchange his dark suits and ominous exhortations for more colorful attire and upbeat rhetoric. A powerful orator, the former governor proved highly effective on the stump during the stage of the contest when it mattered most.

Howell, by contrast, seemed stuck between strategies. He had established his unique brand in Virginia politics through years of joyfully unapologetic, no-holds-barred attacks on key moneyed interests and other large institutions in the state. His often clever, always scathing rhetoric endeared him to his followers, infuriated his foes, delighted reporters seeking good copy, and always seemed authentic. His efforts in 1973 to tone it down, strike a more statesmanlike pose, and avoid the liberal label may have backfired.

"In the end," commented Obenshain after the election, "our strongest weapon was the difference between Henry Howell during the campaign and Henry Howell during his previous political career."[36] In presenting himself as a populist rather than a liberal, Howell downplayed the litmus test issues that had earned him the fervent support of African Americans, organized labor, and Democratic liberals. His efforts to move to the middle met with initial success, but by October the GOP campaign was dramatically calling attention to issues that had long motivated Virginia's largely conservative electorate. Howell's attempts to dodge those criticisms were branded flip-flops by the Godwin camp, and for Virginia voters familiar with Howell from his several recent campaigns, the GOP's charge of inconsistency had the ring of truth to it.

Not surprisingly, Howell viewed the GOP's negative blitz differently. It injected phony issues into the campaign, he argued, and he saw the scare tactics in historical perspective:

> The organization always turns up the burner when you get close to November, just like when [Ted] Dalton was almost beating [Thomas] Stanley [for governor in 1953]. . . . They wait and turn on the busing situation towards the end. They take the gun issue and they begin to move it in October during hunting season. And that's when they get out all the ghosts and start scaring people—direct mail, television spots, [popular Washington Redskins football star] Sonny Jurgensen on the radio in Northern Virginia saying, "One of the candidates wants to send my son to school in the District of Columbia. . . ." That's their tradition. They like to be the gentle plantation owners as long as they can, but when it gets close they get mean. They are going to slug; they are going to kick; they are going to do anything to win the fight.[37]

Howell's complaints about the GOP–Byrd organization fusillade in the closing weeks of the 1973 campaign had merit, but the coalition arrayed against him included leading Republican and Democratic moderates as well. Governor Holton warmly embraced Godwin in the campaign's final days as "the man I want to succeed me,"[38] and the man Holton defeated in 1969 with Howell's help, Democrat William Battle, also endorsed the Republican nominee. "The fact of the matter is that in order to win a statewide campaign in Virginia, you have to appeal to significant segments of the Virginia community," commented Andrew Miller, who easily won reelection as the Democratic candidate for attorney general in 1973. "If you decide, as Howell did very early in his career, that you are going to run against substantial segments of the community and create a confrontation with them, you're not going to be elected."[39]

Close by Every Measure

Howell almost defied Miller's axiom. Opposed by nearly every major political figure in the state, all the major newspapers, and the vast resources
of the Virginia business community, Howell came within 15,000 votes of
defeating a popular former governor with ties to both parties. Voter turnout exceeded more than one million for the first time in a Virginia gubernatorial election, and nearly every statistical comparison reflected the
closeness of the contest. Godwin received 50.7 percent of the total tally
to Howell's 49.3 percent. The Republican carried forty-nine counties,
and Howell won in forty-six. Twenty cities gave majorities to Godwin,
while Howell received the most votes in nineteen. Godwin carried six
congressional districts (though both Northern Virginia districts turned
in razor-thin Godwin majorities), while Howell polled majorities in the
three southeastern Virginia congressional districts and in the southwestern "Fighting Ninth." In the critical urban corridor from Northern
Virginia through Richmond down to Hampton Roads, the candidates divided the vote almost evenly—Godwin's 55 percent suburban advantage
approximately offset Howell's 57 percent of the central city vote—while
Godwin managed a slim 51-percent majority in rural areas.[40]

Though voting tendencies in Virginia had been in transition for several
years, the 1973 results reflected a wholesale departure from the usual patterns. Godwin's party switch and reaction to Watergate were contributing
factors. But it was Howell's populist appeal and the resulting division of
the Virginia electorate largely along economic lines that created the most
upheaval and accounted for his strong showing. "I have always said the
[1968] Humphrey and Wallace precincts were joined together, and that's
why I came so close [in 1973]," Howell said later.[41] A postelection analysis
by the University of Virginia's Larry Sabato tended to corroborate the candidate's claim. Howell managed to poll well over 90 percent of the African
American vote while also improving on his previous showings in precincts
carried by erstwhile segregationist George Wallace in the 1968 presidential
race. Howell's tally even exceeded Harry Byrd's 1970 share of the Wallace
vote in some places, an impressive feat in light of the Godwin campaign's
emphasis on the racially fraught busing issue. Howell's vote in some urban
Wallace precincts exceeded 60 percent, and Godwin outpolled him only
narrowly in rural precincts that Wallace had carried.[42]

The unusual nature of the 1973 voting was apparent also in the other two
statewide races. Ticket splitting was rampant, and though Virginians only

narrowly rejected Howell's assault on the state's conservative orthodoxy, they gave large majorities to sons of the two most formidable Byrd organization challengers of the previous generation, Ted Dalton and Francis Pickens Miller. Neither Republican John Dalton nor Democrat Andrew Miller exhibited the crusading spirit that had been a trademark of his father, and it could be argued on behalf of each that a crusade no longer was warranted. The moderate and measured approach of both men in 1973 seemed to reflect Virginia's gradual transition from the staunch conservatism of their fathers' day to a more progressive or pragmatic period.

John Dalton polled 54 percent of the vote and carried every congressional district on his way to becoming Virginia's first Republican lieutenant governor.[43] He amassed his biggest margins in the traditionally Republican areas of the Sixth, Seventh, and Ninth Congressional Districts and clearly helped running mate Godwin in those regions, while he was the beneficiary of the former governor's coattails in the conservative and largely Democratic Southside region of the state. The Godwin-Dalton duo proved to be a potent combination. Courthouse Democrats rewarded Dalton's assistance to Godwin on the Republican ticket by including the GOP nominee for lieutenant governor on the informal but highly influential "Southside ticket." Meanwhile, Dalton's affable and well-regarded opponent, state senator J. Harry Michael Jr. of Charlottesville, was left to fend for himself as the down-ballot nominee of a leaderless Democratic ticket.

Incumbent attorney general Andrew Miller's reelection victory was the most impressive. The Democrat carried every city and county in the state, a feat not accomplished even by President Nixon in his landslide victory the preceding year.[44] In most localities the Miller margins were huge. Miller's GOP opponent, former state senator M. Patton "Pat" Echols Jr. of Arlington, entertained little or no hope of winning from the beginning, but his 29 percent showing was worse than it could have been. Concerned that association with Echols might hurt them among Miller partisans, Godwin and Dalton excluded their running mate from most campaign appearances other than those in Northern Virginia and in some partisan Republican strongholds. Echols's totals likely were depressed further by his prominent participation in the GOP's anti-Howell onslaught in the campaign's closing weeks. Ever the dedicated partisan, Echols had done his duty, but in the process the incumbent Democratic attorney general was awarded a landslide victory that made him appear the giant on the state political scene.

Watergate: Realignment Reassessed

The Godwin-Dalton victory made 1973 another GOP year, but the returns fell short of the rosy predictions offered by Republicans just months earlier. Godwin's narrow win prompted more sighs of relief than shouts of joy, and the legislative elections brought real disappointment to the Republican camp. During the previous year and into early 1973, there had been confident talk of impending party switches by a number of prominent Democratic state legislators, enough to flip control of one or both houses of the General Assembly. Two dozen of the Democratic lawmakers were personally courted by President Nixon at a secret Oval Office huddle in July 1972, an event Godwin later called "the high water mark for the realignment effort in Virginia." He explained, "If we could have gotten that group to switch, it would have brought a lot of other people over quickly. But then Watergate intervened. I had many people tell me that the stigma from Watergate was the reason they did not want to take on the Republican label."[45] By the time Godwin formally joined the GOP in June 1973, most of his friends on the Democratic side of the aisle already were seeking reelection as independents or Democrats. In November, voters elected only twenty Republicans to the hundred-member House of Delegates, a net *loss* of five seats for the GOP, even as Godwin and Dalton were claiming statewide wins.

The scandal's impact on Virginia's legislature became even more apparent after the fall elections. Fifteen independents won House of Delegates races, including a number of senior lawmakers who had chaired committees as Democrats during the previous legislative session. But when the General Assembly reconvened in January 1974, several of the legislators successfully sought readmission to the Democratic caucus. The new governor, hardly a stickler for party labels in the best of times, recognized that Watergate was making Republican affiliation a serious political liability, and he did not encourage his Democratic friends in the General Assembly to switch parties. To the contrary, Godwin urged them to stay where they were, lest their forfeiture of key committee chairmanships impede passage of his legislative initiatives. With no realistic prospect of achieving GOP legislative majorities in the foreseeable future, party switches by Godwin's powerful Democratic friends would only serve to diminish their influence and hasten the elevation of more junior, and more liberal, Democratic legislators.[46]

As Nixon's Watergate problems worsened in the months leading up to his resignation in August 1974, public sentiment toward the Republican

Party soured nationally. The 1972 break-in at the Democratic National Committee headquarters by operatives linked to Nixon's reelection committee was only a small part of the myriad disclosures and charges that streamed out in late 1973 and the first half of 1974. New allegations of partisan "dirty tricks," campaign finance abuses, misuse of public office, and obstruction of justice at the highest levels of the Nixon administration were daily fare for months. The damage to Republican officeholders and to the GOP was compounded many times over by the vigorous, long-running partisan defense of the president. With the revelations of clear presidential culpability in the summer of 1974, many of Richard Nixon's staunch Republican defenders were perceived by voters as gullible or even corrupt. A month after the Nixon resignation, the already widespread hostility toward Republicans was sharply exacerbated by the decision of the new president, Gerald Ford, to grant his disgraced predecessor a full pardon.

The 1974 congressional elections brought decisive Democratic gains nationwide: a net increase of forty-eight seats in the US House of Representatives, including two from Virginia. Republican malfeasance was blamed not only for the nation's debilitating immersion in scandal but also for a deepening recession that defied conventional economic theories by inflicting high inflation and high unemployment at the same time. The strong anti-GOP tide continued to flow throughout 1975 in Virginia, where off-year state legislative elections produced a further drop in GOP representation—to just twenty-two seats in the entire 140-member General Assembly. The fortification of the Democratic legislative bastion, coupled with the party's congressional advances in 1974, forestalled Virginia Democrats' further decline and signaled the return of stability to the state's political scene.

Nearly a decade of preoccupation with the leftward shift of the national Democrats and the ascendancy of unabashed liberals within the state Democratic Party supplied a powerful impetus for partisan realignment in Virginia, an opportunity state Republicans moved decisively to seize in 1972 and 1973. But the pressures for philosophical realignment and the resultant downward spiral of Democratic fortunes in Virginia were largely arrested beginning in 1974. The "specter of Watergate overshadowed all other issues," Larry Sabato wrote at the time, and the new focus "permitted the state Democratic Party to shed the millstone of McGovernism."[47] Conservative Democrats, so recently the dominant party's dominant faction, had exited the political home of their fathers in droves, if not by public declaration then at least in the privacy of the voting booth. This was the dealignment part of the Virginia transition story. But Watergate had intervened just in time to prevent an influential body of Democratic conservatives, including many elected officials and prominent business leaders, from formally affiliating with the GOP. This was the decelerated and delayed realignment part of the transition story. The net result was that the balance of political power in Virginia would be held by neither party but instead by independent voters, whose center-right views would produce more continuity than change in the Old Dominion. Republican statewide candidates would continue to benefit during the 1970s—basically, for as long as the warring titans, Godwin and Howell, and Godwin's protégé Obenshain still loomed large on the scene—but in the failure of a more complete realignment in the mid-1970s lay the ingredients for a centrist Democratic rebound in the 1980s.

Conservative Coalition and Two-Party Competition

It was easy for observers to mistake the Republican winning streak of the 1970s for a newfound dominance. Even at mid-decade, and especially after the GOP racked up additional statewide wins for governor in 1977 and the US Senate in 1978, commentators routinely suggested that the Byrd organization, or at least its conservative icons and maxims, had packed up and moved over into the state GOP. Such characterizations were not wholly groundless, but they tended to misconstrue the nature, extent, and durability of the newly acquired GOP strength. The commonwealth, which had been a uniquely one-party, one-faction state as recently as the 1960s, experienced a full flowering of two-party competition as the 1970s unfolded. Republicans succeeded in this newly competitive environment because of four main elements: conservatism, coalition, suburbanization, and organization.

The commonwealth's cultural, social, and political traditions long had been distinctly, even uniquely, conservative. And, from 1972–73 through the end of the decade, the Virginia GOP gained sole custody of the important "symbols of conservatism,"[48] familiar conservative themes and leaders to which a majority of the state electorate regularly would respond. That the GOP should have such a monopoly was a reflection of leading Republicans' strategic consensus and unity of purpose, but it also reflected the state Democratic Party's continual inability to muzzle or modulate the resolutely liberal voices within its ranks.

Because neither major party since the mid-1960s had commanded the allegiance of a majority (or even a clear plurality) of the commonwealth's voters, the name of the game in Virginia politics had become coalition building. Following the collapse of the Byrd organization in the 1960s, Democrats forged a winning coalition by combining liberals, African Americans, the weak organized labor elements in the state, White Democratic moderates, and a significant number of conservatives who were willing to embrace left-of-center Democratic candidates out of long-standing party loyalty and the hope that the party eventually would move back toward the center. In the early 1970s, beginning with Obenshain's installation as GOP chairman, Godwin's acceptance of the Republican label, and the Godwin-Dalton ticket's election in 1973, Republicans were able to assemble a philosophically oriented coalition of conservative and conservative-leaning Virginians of both parties. Suburban Republican regulars, "mountain and valley" GOP moderates, former Byrd Democrats, and conservative business interests practiced successful coalition politics, aided from time to time by factional infighting among the divergent elements of the state Democratic Party.[49]

Demographic changes in Virginia worked to enhance the GOP's advantage. The state's population increased more than 10 percent in the 1970s, and most of that increase was in the suburbs. The once rural Old Dominion had experienced rapid suburban growth for several decades, and the conservative proclivities of suburban voters combined with their burgeoning numbers to significantly expand the Republican base. While GOP candidates found the prosperous suburbs squarely in their corner during most of the 1970s, mostly because of the primacy of economic and national security issues, the largest suburban bloc consisted of independent-minded voters for whom social issues such as education, public safety, race relations, and abortion rights also could weigh heavily in voting. Depending on the circumstances, issues, and candidates, these suburban swing voters could side with either party—and over time they would.

The GOP wins during the 1970s also were a product of superior political organization. Under the leadership of Obenshain and his successor as party chairman, Delegate George McMath,[50] the Republican Party and successive GOP campaigns cultivated an effective precinct-level organization and complemented it through the development and use of modern technology for raising campaign funds, targeting precincts, identifying favorable voters, communicating with the undecided, and getting to the polls those willing to cast Republican ballots. The Republican Party's financial, technological, and organizational edge was only a temporary one, but the GOP used its window of opportunity to full advantage before Democrats were able to close the gap in the 1980s.

Even with these various advantages, Republican victories did not come easily in the second half of the 1970s. All of the contests either began or ended as close ones. And, as developments in the early 1980s would confirm, even at the height of its winning streak the GOP was only a misstep or two away from defeat. Virginia's political environment was a truly competitive one. Though voting tendencies were becoming significantly more Republican, the balance of political power remained in the hands of a large bloc of nonaligned voters, many of whom had considered themselves Democrats at some point in their lives. If there remained after Watergate an opportunity for a more immediate and complete realignment of Virginia's conservative majority with the GOP, it vanished with developments in the late 1970s—most notably the quiet arrival of Charles Robb on the state political scene in 1977 and the tragic departure of Richard Obenshain from it in 1978.

Armageddon's Aftershocks

Democrats approached the 1977 race for governor with optimism even though their setbacks in recent years had far outnumbered their successes. To the former category was added their failure to carry Virginia for southerner Jimmy Carter in the 1976 presidential race. Carter put a solid South in his winning presidential column except for Virginia, where incumbent president Gerald Ford eked out a narrow victory. Various factors contributed to Ford's thin win, including the state GOP's organizational prowess, Virginia Republicans' resolve to reunify after the fractious nomination fight between Ford and former governor Ronald Reagan, and Carter's anti-Washington rhetoric, which went over like a lead balloon in Northern Virginia suburbs, where many families earned their living across the Potomac River.[51] Carter's Virginia allies also came up well short in their 1976 challenge to incumbent senator Harry Byrd Jr., who again ran for reelection as an independent, this time without Republican opposition.[52] Still, Virginia Democrats were buoyed by the prospect of an imminent reversal of fortune, and with good reason. Their party had just recaptured the White House, and their presumptive gubernatorial nominee, Attorney General Andrew Miller, enjoyed unusually broad appeal, which had been on full display in his landslide reelection victory in 1973.

His personal ambitions long since sated, Mills Godwin was more than ready to reexit the governor's office after his often arduous second term. His nemesis, Henry Howell, who had come excruciatingly close to claiming the prize in 1973, possessed no such peace. The irrepressible populist resolved to take another shot, and he thought his best chance this time would be as the Democratic Party's nominee. But as winter gave way to spring and the primary voting approached, Howell was so far behind Miller in fundraising and opinion polls that few gave him much of a chance. The Howell camp was not alone in viewing this conventional wisdom as flawed. An internal poll conducted for the campaign of the Republican candidate, Lieutenant Governor John Dalton, revealed that despite Miller's large lead among all Democrats, Howell actually enjoyed an advantage among those who felt most strongly about voting in the primary. This was good news for the Republican strategists, who preferred a fall matchup against the polarizing Howell over a nonideological popularity contest with the moderate Miller. But the poll also contained this sobering news for the Dalton gang: anti-Howell feeling among conservative voters was running so strong that they might enter the Democratic primary and vote for Miller as a way of ending the Howell menace once and for all.

For Dalton, the conservative establishment's preoccupation with the Howell threat initially posed a serious problem. "The business community was just determined to beat Henry Howell," Dalton later recalled,

and my problem early on in that campaign was the fact that Andrew Miller was perceived as the strongest person to keep Virginia from going to Henry Howell. Along in the '76 and early '77 period, Miller had worked the business community. He had been to see many of the people on Main Street that finance conservative-type campaigns and was getting commitments from a lot of those people on the basis that he was the savior to keep Henry Howell from being governor. And his track record looked good. He carried every city and county in 1973, and I don't recall anybody doing that even in Harry Byrd's heyday.[53]

Dalton and his team worried that, once on board with Miller in the primary, many moderate and conservative business leaders, independent-minded public officials, and swing voters were likely to stick with the Democrat in the fall contest.

During much of the spring, Howell's campaign appeared outwardly to be on the verge of collapse for lack of funds. The two Democrats engaged in a lengthy series of debates and joint appearances that primarily served to convey the visceral nature of their mutual dislike. Howell made campaign finances and alleged "dirty tricks" by the Miller camp a principal issue, and he also attacked Miller's spending record as attorney general.[54] Miller countered with volleys aimed at Howell's past disloyalty to the Democratic Party and also at his liberal legislative record, including his support for collective bargaining for public employees. The labor-related attacks may well have backfired on Miller because it was the strong and active backing from the state AFL-CIO and Virginia Education Association that enabled Howell to offset much of Miller's financial advantage. With organized labor and the Crusade for Voters, the preeminent African American political organization in the state, handling the get-out-the-vote effort for his campaign, Howell did not need a large campaign war chest to produce a strong turnout by his supporters on primary day.

The possibility of Republican crossover voting in the Democrats' open primary—a common occurrence during the years of Byrd hegemony and outcome-determinative Democratic primaries—was a much-discussed topic throughout the primary campaign. Speculation focused not only on how many would cross over but for whom they would vote. Despite polling data suggesting that interloping conservative Republicans likely would vote against the liberal Howell, the widespread belief that Howell would be a weaker foe for Dalton led to much talk about possible GOP voting to boost the Howell candidacy. Six weeks before the primary election, Miller publicly charged that an "unholy alliance" had been formed between the Dalton and Howell camps to that end.[55] Dalton's campaign fired back, calling Miller's remarks "those of a desperate man whose attempts to be all things to all people have cost him the support of committed conservatives."[56] A few days later, Dalton leveled a charge of his own; he told reporters that Miller was "scared to death" and "want[ed] Republicans and conservatives to go into that primary and bail him out."[57] For the record, Dalton reiterated his request that his supporters stay away from the polls on June 14.

The Howell camp received some direct help from Republicans. Smith Ferebee, the conservative fundraiser and Godwin intimate, was so doubtful of Dalton's ability to rally conservatives against Miller in the fall that he secretly raised funds for the Howell campaign.[58] The Democrat's campaign also received ad hoc assistance from individuals on Dalton's staff, mostly in the form of technical advice and voter lists.[59] Dalton campaign chief William Royall and Howell manager Paul Goldman had a number of conversations prior to the primary voting, but suggestions from Miller that there was high-level collusion were baseless, according to Royall. The Republican operative said that an active conspiracy was unnecessary because the two camps independently had obtained reliable polling data showing that the moderate Miller could be squeezed from the left by Howell and from the right by Dalton.[60] What Howell needed was for Dalton to rally conservatives, and the Republican gladly obliged during the ten days between the GOP convention and the Democratic primary.

The "Ten Days in June" campaign was an idea conceived by Dalton organization director Judy Peachee as a means of decreasing Democratic primary turnout by focusing the attention of conservative voters on Dalton and the November election rather than on the imminent primary election. Immediately after the Republican convention nominated Dalton and a pair of state senators, Joe Canada and Marshall Coleman, as his running mates in early June, the GOP ticket went on the road for a high-profile, ten-day campaign tour of the state. Coinciding with the trio's much-ballyhooed jaunt was a statewide media buy that featured Mills Godwin, a popular figure among many Miller supporters, urging voters to "save" their votes until November, when John Dalton would be on the ballot. The widespread airing of Godwin's praise for his lieutenant governor sent a clear message to conservative political leaders and the business community: November would be soon enough to save Virginia from Henry Howell.

The primary election turnout confirmed the worst fears of the Miller camp. Many moderate and conservative voters who preferred Miller stayed away from the polls, leaving the Democratic Party business to the dedicated "Howell people," who handed their liberal hero a dramatic upset victory. Statewide, slightly fewer than 25 percent of all registered voters (fewer than 14 percent of the voting-age population) went to the polls. The urban corridor, which Howell carried with a 55-percent majority, accounted for nearly two-thirds of the total vote. Rural areas, where Miller prevailed by a similar margin, turned in less than a third of the statewide ballots. Turnout was lowest in the suburbs, and Howell had a slim advantage there. The strong vote for Howell in the cities, especially in his native Tidewater, was the result of his lopsided victory among African American voters—he polled better than 85 percent of the vote in selected African American precincts—as well as his lingering support among blue-collar Whites. Only in the rural areas did Howell's populist appeal among low-income Whites show signs of wearing thin.[61]

The impact of Republican voting in the primary was difficult to measure. Though Miller found in the results "significant signs that there was an organized effort among the Republicans" for Howell,[62] a study by several William & Mary political scientists concluded that a majority of the GOP interlopers had cast ballots for the more conservative Miller.[63] Moreover, the turnout was so low as to preclude the existence of extensive Republican crossover voting. The impact, if any, of GOP efforts was reflected in the widespread abstinence of would-be conservative voters on primary day. The Dalton handlers had succeeded in giving their candidate a high profile at a critical time, and that reinforced the disposition of all but the most active Democratic partisans to forgo participation in nominating contests. As Dalton had urged, Virginia's vast moderate-conservative majority left the June 14 primary to "the liberal-thinking people of the state who consider themselves Democrats."[64]

In his postelection analysis of the Miller-Howell contest, Larry Sabato put the primary turnout and outcome in historical perspective:

> While many factors contributed to [Howell's upset win], the underlying structural reason is clearly the unique nature of the primary electorate. With the growth of the Republican party and the development of a mass electorate in Virginia, the Democratic party primary has ceased to be tantamount to election. The average voter, less party oriented and more independent in political outlook than ever before, has begun to look upon the primary as a preliminary procedure, reserved for party activists; he prefers to delay his electoral participation until the November general election, when the "real" decision is made. . . . This change in voter attitude toward the primary has had a significant effect on turnout. A low participation rate in the primary has allowed the Democratic party activists (liberals, organized labor, African Americans and urban voters) to dominate the party nominating process to a degree far surpassing their strength in the electorate as a whole. These activist groups are the most important components of the Howell coalition, a fact that makes Howell's 1977 triumph less surprising.[65]

In retrospect, the only truly surprising thing about the 1977 Democratic primary outcome is that so many people found it surprising at the time. The growing progressive domination of Democratic Party nominating processes had been a more than decade-long trend by 1977. It had derailed the nomination and renomination bids of numerous center-right

Democrats and had been the chief reason for Senator Harry Byrd Jr.'s decision to run for reelection as an independent in 1970 and again in 1976. By failing to heed those lessons and, in their overconfidence, neglecting to mount a massive get-out-the-vote drive, Miller and his strategists had squandered the candidate's immense popularity and irreparably damaged his very promising political career. While the 1973 general election has no rival as the watershed political race of the decade, if there were a second-place award for pivotal impact it would go to the 1977 Democratic primary that robbed Miller's star of its luster and sent a doomed Howell into the fall fray with Dalton.

While the general election contest appeared close at the start, the disciplined Dalton romped to victory in the fall, aided by a technically proficient campaign organization, fully mobilized conservative coalition, plenty of Democrats sore at Howell, and the mercurial Howell's rhetorical excess. The Democratic primary had yielded what supporters dubbed a "rainbow ticket," ranging from Howell at the liberal reach of the spectrum to a Byrd organization stalwart at the conservative end. Situated rather benignly between those polar opposites for governor and attorney general, respectively, was the centrist Charles "Chuck" Robb, son-in-law of the late president Lyndon Johnson, who won the race for lieutenant governor. Robb was the only one on his ticket to win in 1977, and the victory threw his party a lifeline. He would give Democrats an appealing and increasingly formidable figure around which to rally four years later in a showdown with the other 1977 down-ballot winner, Marshall Coleman, who became the first Republican to gain the Virginia attorney general's post since Reconstruction. In the meantime, 1977's winning moderate-conservative trio—Dalton, Robb, and Coleman—and the split-ticket voting that elected them pretty much said it all about where Virginia politics had settled after the tumult earlier in the decade: two-party competitive, comfortably right of center, steady as she goes.[66]

The Great Indoor Primary

The 1970s card still had one heavyweight fight on it, and that was for the US Senate seat held by Republican William Scott, who had gained an upset win over incumbent William Spong in the 1972 Nixon landslide. Scott had done little to endear himself to Virginia voters in the intervening years, and his announcement that he would retire at the end of his term surprised no one. Seeing a chance to reclaim the seat of his friend and ally

Spong and in the process secure a quick bounce-back win for himself, Andrew Miller jumped into the contest. Both parties decided to choose their nominees by convention, and Miller, standing out in a crowded field of lesser-known figures, won the Democratic nomination easily. The selection of his GOP opponent a week earlier was anything but easy.

Republicans gathered the first weekend in June for a convention that broke all existing records for attendance at such affairs. So large was the assemblage (more than nine thousand delegates and alternates) and so extended were the proceedings (voting continued through six ballots over twelve hours) that *Richmond Times-Dispatch* columnist Charles McDowell, dubbed it the "Great Indoor Primary," a moniker that—like his "Armageddon" label for the 1973 governor's race—would stick.[67] That Richard Obenshain emerged the nominee hardly was puzzling to anyone who had watched his well-organized forces march to victories in prior Republican conventions and who understood the intense personal appeal of the man among the conservative faithful who dominated Virginia GOP processes. The more unexpected thing was the difficulty of Obenshain's feat and, especially, the seriousness of the challenge posed by a relative newcomer, John Warner of Middleburg.

The well-heeled Warner had been Nixon's Navy secretary and head of the American Revolution Bicentennial in 1976, and all agreed he looked the part of a senator, but it was his celebrity wife, actress Elizabeth Taylor, who attracted the interest and generated the crowds. Warner's canny operatives converted many of the star-gazers into convention delegates, where they joined Republican faithful who thought Warner more "electable" than the ideological Obenshain. Warner's hustling campaign, moderate positioning, and cash advantage squeezed out Linwood Holton, the still popular former governor who had his own credible claim to electability. Once Holton and a fourth contender, state senator Nathan Miller of Rockingham, bowed out after multiple rounds of balloting, Obenshain got his one-on-one showdown with Warner and emerged on top. It was the most hard-fought of victories in a massive convention that played to a national and international audience, and it propelled the twice-defeated Obenshain into the general election contest looking very much like a winner.

Two months later the Republican nominee died in an airplane crash on the way home late in the evening after a day of political events. Obenshain's campaign by now had the momentum and, in the estimation of observers in both parties, was poised to win.[68] His successor's candidacy would pose a greater challenge.

As the convention's second-place finisher, with resources to bankroll an abbreviated campaign, John Warner was the logical stand-in. Disconsolate conservative activists grumbled, but an endorsement by Governor Dalton and a compelling appeal from Helen Obenshain, the candidate's widow, ensured the nod was Warner's by consensus. Most of the fallen standard bearer's campaign staff stayed on to work for the new nominee, assuring continuity. And the Godwin-led conservative coalition and business donors, having cast their lot with Obenshain against Miller, now remained largely on board with the substitute Republican nominee. But Warner was no Obenshain; while the newcomer was indefatigable on the campaign trail, his lack of experience in the spotlight showed repeatedly in campaign gaffes. Miller, by contrast, was a solid if diminished political figure broadly familiar to Virginians. It was a sign, then, of how strong the Virginia GOP had become, especially when allied with the conservative lions who still gathered around Godwin, that Warner emerged the winner in a November squeaker.[69] Though the margin was less than five thousand votes, the Democratic loss also reflected how fast the Miller star had faded and how unpopular the presidential administration of Jimmy Carter was becoming in the commonwealth.

The following year, Democrats held GOP gains in the Virginia General Assembly to a handful of seats, but the modest Republican wins still lifted the party's representation in the state legislature to a modern high.[70] Back on federal election turf in 1980, Republicans resumed their surge, capturing nine of the state's ten US House of Representatives seats and delivering the commonwealth's electoral votes to presidential candidate Ronald Reagan by a thirteen-point statewide margin.[71]

The Virginia GOP's string of statewide victories in the 1970s, enabled by the coalescing of Democratic conservatives with moderate and conservative Republicans, presaged the emergence of a similar combination nationally. Aided by rural and blue-collar "Reagan Democrats," Republican nominees would defeat their Democratic opponents by an aggregate of 133 states to seventeen, and 1,440 electoral votes to 174, in the three presidential elections during the 1980s.[72] But while the nation seemed to be following the Virginia script as it turned the page on the 1970s, Virginians were moving on to a new chapter. Each of those Republican presidential wins in the next decade would be followed by a Democratic victory in the ensuing year's contest for Virginia's governorship.

Though he barely gained the Senate seat, John Warner would go on to become an institution esteemed by Virginians across the political spectrum, a national leader on defense policy, and the commonwealth's second-longest-serving senator.[73] What he would not do is guide his party. Just as Harry Byrd Jr. had eschewed the organization leadership role in succeeding his formidable father in the mid-1960s,[74] John Warner had neither the inclination nor the insight to lead his party in Obenshain's absence. Virginia Republicans' sudden loss of their master strategist and philosophical leader in the 1978 plane crash would unleash factional rivalries and intraparty strife that would continue for several election cycles. Like the Democratic discord that assisted Linwood Holton's 1969 gubernatorial breakthrough and helped inaugurate a Republican decade in the 1970s, the GOP factional fights in the aftermath of Obenshain's death would help Charles Robb win back the governorship for Democrats in 1981 and set the stage for a Democratic decade.

Conclusion

The 1970s in Virginia brought tumult and transition, chaos and competition without parallel before or since. But the decade was remarkable not only for what happened but for what might have been. Two tragedies had the most profound impact. The sudden death of young Lieutenant Governor J. Sargeant Reynolds in 1971 deprived Virginia Democrats of a Kennedy-esque moderate who almost certainly would have won the governorship in 1973, put his party on a winning course in Virginia, and gone on to make his mark in national affairs, perhaps in the White House. Then, in 1978, Republicans' loss of Richard Obenshain denied them the Reaganesque champion who likely would have aligned Virginia with the ascendant national GOP, strengthened the Republican hold on the state, and played his own major role on the national stage, perhaps as Reaganism's next act. Both parties also saw their other key leaders' promise fade prematurely. The narrowest of defeats—Howell's in 1973 and Miller's in 1978—derailed the political careers of the state's two most prominent Democratic politicians, and none of the decade's three Republican governors was ever on the ballot again.[75] Thus did unexpected twists and tragedies conspire with discernible trends and tides to produce a dizzying decade of change in Virginia, the main effect of which was to usher in a sustained period of intense two-party competition and closely contested state elections.

The major realignment trend of the second half of the twentieth century—Virginia's evolution from a staunchly conservative, rural-dominated, one-party Democratic state to a center-right, swing-voting, suburban, two-party competitive commonwealth—had been unfolding since World War II, the all-encompassing event that had catalyzed economic, social, and cultural change in the once staid Old Dominion. The trend had received some big shoves forward before the 1970s, notable among them Republican Dwight Eisenhower's 1952 presidential win, the cascading legal rulings and reforms that rapidly expanded Virginia's electorate in the 1960s, and the occasional appearance of attractive statewide GOP candidates like Ted Dalton and Linwood Holton. The trend had been impeded at times, too, as when "massive resistance" to school desegregation threw a lifeline, ultimately untethered, to the Byrd organization. The 1970s saw this emergent realignment rapidly reach its consummation, first in chaos, then in coalition, and ultimately in durable two-party competition. If the realignment tide did not come in as far in as it might have absent Watergate's blowback and Obenshain's passing, it came in farther and faster than it would have absent Reynolds's passing and McGovern's movement. The decade's chief combatants, Mills Godwin and Henry Howell, embodied the fundamental forces—conservative and progressive ideas and impulses—that would continue to clash even as times and labels changed.

Armageddon, of course, never was. Virginians' political chasing after the wind never really deserves comparison with the transcendent struggle for the soul. But the events of 1972–73 did prove to be a watershed in Virginia's modern political evolution. It was to be—for at least four decades—the high-water mark of anti-establishment populism and McGovern-style progressivism in the commonwealth.[76] Voters thereafter turned the state toward the familiar and the safe, fortifying the centrist tendencies of their venerable commonwealth even as its insularity yielded to pluralism and tradition gave way to innovation. Those voters would keep choosing convincing candidates with mainstream views in both parties from decade to decade, ensuring a continual duel for leadership of the competitive state as it gradually transitioned from center-right to center-left . . . and from there to who-knows-where.

Notes

This chapter draws from the author's *The Dynamic Dominion: Realignment and the Rise of Two-Party Competition in Virginia, 1945–1980*, rev. 2nd ed. (Lanham, MD: Rowman & Littlefield; Charlottesville: University of Virginia Center for Politics, 2006).

1. William Cameron was elected governor in 1881 as the candidate of the Readjuster-Republican coalition, which formally adopted the name Republican Party of Virginia in 1884, during Cameron's gubernatorial tenure. The party did not experience success in another gubernatorial contest until Governor Linwood Holton's election in 1969. See James Tice Moore, "William E. Cameron (1842–1927)," in *Encyclopedia Virginia* (Charlottesville: Virginia Humanities, November 2, 2015), online, and Frank B. Atkinson, "Republican Party of Virginia," in *Encyclopedia Virginia* (Charlottesville: Virginia Humanities, August 31, 2016), online.

2. Patrick Henry, the first governor of the Commonwealth of Virginia, and several of his early successors were chosen by the General Assembly and served multiple one-year terms. Prior to Godwin, the most recent governor to hold the office for more than a single term was William "Extra Billy" Smith, who was chosen as governor by the General Assembly in 1845, held the office during 1846–49, regained it by popular election in 1863, and served until the end of the Civil War. See Emily J. Salmon and Edward D. C. Campbell Jr., *The Hornbook of Virginia History*, 4th ed. (Richmond: Library of Virginia, 1994), 101–13.

3. See Charles McDowell Jr., "When the Experts Are Undecided," *Richmond Times-Dispatch*, October 28, 1973, quoted in Larry J. Sabato, *Aftermath of "Armageddon": An Analysis of the 1973 Gubernatorial Election* (Charlottesville: University of Virginia, Institute of Government, 1975), x.

4. See J. Harvie Wilkinson III, "Linwood Holton," in *The Governors of Virginia, 1860–1978*, ed. Edward Younger and James Tice Moore (Charlottesville: University Press of Virginia, 1982), 393–96.

5. James Latimer, "The Coming Decade: A Political Sphinx," *Richmond Times-Dispatch*, December 21, 1969, reprinted in *Virginia Government and Politics: Readings and Comments*, ed. Weldon Cooper and Thomas R. Morris (Charlottesville: University Press of Virginia, 1976), 115.

6. See Atkinson, *The Dynamic Dominion*, 214–15.

7. Jack Bass and Walter DeVries, *The Transformation of Southern Politics* (New York: Basic Books, 1976), 353.

8. The quoted statement was by the Crusade for Voters, a predominantly African American political action group based in Richmond. Jack R. Hunter, "Linwood Holton's Long Quest for the Governorship of Virginia and Its Impact on the Growth of the Republican Party" (thesis, University of Richmond, 1972), 64.

9. The major party vote totals in the 1969 general election for governor, lieutenant governor, and attorney general were: for governor: Linwood Holton (R)—480,869 (52.5 percent), William C. Battle (D)—415,695 (45.4 percent); for lieutenant governor: J. Sargeant Reynolds (D)—472,853 (54.0 percent), H. Dunlop Dawbarn (R)—371,246 (42.4 percent); for attorney general:

Andrew P. Miller (D)—455,264 (52.1 percent), Richard D. Obenshain (R)—402,382 (46.1 percent). Larry Sabato, *Virginia Votes 1969–1974* (Charlottesville: University of Virginia, Institute of Government, 1976), 142–53.

10. See Larry J. Sabato, *The Democratic Party Primary in Virginia: Tantamount to Election No Longer* (Charlottesville: University Press of Virginia, 1977). The author is indebted to Dr. Sabato, the preeminent political chronicler of the period covered by this chapter, and to the University of Virginia Center for Politics for the resources referenced herein, including the successive *Virginia Votes* volumes in which the pertinent elections are analyzed in depth.

11. See Harry F. Byrd Jr., *Defying the Odds: An Independent Senator's Historic Campaign* (Harrisonburg, VA: R. R. Donnelly and Sons, 1998).

12. The vote totals in the general election for US Senate were: Harry F. Byrd Jr. (I)—506,633 (53.5 percent), George C. Rawlings Jr. (D)—295,057 (31.2 percent), Ray L. Garland (R)—145,031 (15.3 percent). Sabato, *Virginia Votes 1969–1974*, 158–61.

13. See generally C. Matthew West, *A Time for Moderation: J. Sargeant Reynolds and Virginia's New Democrats, 1960–1971* (Richmond: Virginia Historical Society, 2019); Andy McCutcheon and Michael P. Gleason, *Sarge Reynolds: In the Time of His Life* (Richmond: Gleason Publishing Co., 1996).

14. The vote totals in the special election for lieutenant governor were: Henry E. Howell Jr. (I)—362,371 (40.0 percent), George J. Kostel (D)—334,580 (36.9 percent), George P. Shafran (R)—209,861 (23.1 percent). Sabato, *Virginia Votes 1969–1974*, 162–65.

15. Donald P. Baker, *Wilder: Hold Fast to Dreams* (Cabin John, MD: Seven Locks Press, 1989), 78. Following Reynolds's election as lieutenant governor in 1969, Wilder won a special election to succeed him as one of the City of Richmond's two representatives in the state senate.

16. Author's interview with Andrew P. Miller, July 24, 1980.

17. Author's interview with Henry E. Howell Jr., June 12, 1980.

18. Richard Obenshain, Letter to the Editor, *Richmond Times-Dispatch*, March 10, 1963.

19. See generally John Stanley Virkler, "Richard Obenshain: Architect of the Republican Triumph in Virginia" (thesis, Auburn University, 1987); Joel L. Hensley, *Richard Obenshain: A Spirit of Fire* (self-published manuscript, 2019).

20. See Linwood Holton, *Opportunity Time* (Charlottesville: University of Virginia Press, 2008), 225.

21. The major party vote totals in the 1972 Virginia general election for US president and senator were: for president: Richard M. Nixon (R)—988,493 (67.8 percent), George McGovern (D)—438,887 (30.1 percent); for US senator: William L. Scott (R)—718,337 (51.5 percent); William B. Spong Jr. (D)—643,963 (46.1 percent). Sabato, *Virginia Votes 1969–1974*, 166–73.

22. Mills E. Godwin Jr., *Some Recollections* (self-published manuscript, 1992), 61–68.
23. Author's interviews with D. Dortch Warriner, October 26, 1979, and August 30, 1984.
24. Ibid.
25. Author's interviews with J. Smith Ferebee, June 4, 1980, and August 30, 1984.
26. See Atkinson, *The Dynamic Dominion*, 301–4.
27. Charles McDowell, *Richmond Times-Dispatch*, June 10, 1973.
28. Sabato, *Aftermath of "Armageddon,"* x.
29. "State GOP Will Hear Holton," *Richmond Times-Dispatch*, May 31, 1973.
30. Sabato, *Aftermath of "Armageddon,"* x.
31. For a description of the mutual disdain exhibited by Howell and Godwin, its origins, and its manifestation in campaign attacks, see James R. Sweeney, "Armageddon Revisited: The 1973 Gubernatorial Election in Virginia," *Virginia Magazine of History and Biography* 130 (2022), 292–97, 302, 333. Sweeney's well-researched article includes the observation that the 1973 contest's uncommon bitterness, including the extensive use of harshly negative messages in campaign advertising, set a negative campaigning precedent that would influence subsequent Virginia races.
32. Guy Friddell, "Obenshain Talks Politics," *Virginian-Pilot*, February 10, 1974.
33. Virkler, "Richard Obenshain," 72.
34. Sabato, *Aftermath of "Armageddon,"* 20.
35. See Melville Carico, "'73 Campaign Floated on a Sea of Cash," *Roanoke Times*, February 10, 1974, reprinted in *Virginia Government and Politics*, 145–49.
36. Friddell, "Obenshain Talks Politics."
37. Author's interview with Henry E. Howell Jr., June 12, 1980.
38. James Latimer, "Holton Lauds Godwin," *Richmond Times-Dispatch*, October 24, 1973.
39. Author's interview with Andrew P. Miller, July 24, 1980.
40. See Sabato, *Virginia Votes 1969–1974*, 82–91. The vote totals in the general election for governor were: Mills E. Godwin Jr. (R)—525,075 (50.7 percent), Henry E. Howell Jr. (I)—510,103 (49.3 percent). Sabato, *Virginia Votes 1969–1974*, 174–77.
41. Author's interview with Henry E. Howell Jr., June 12, 1980.
42. Sabato, *Virginia Votes 1969–1974*, 88–95. Howell gained the votes of Wallace supporters without a nod from Wallace himself, though some influential Howell backers actively sought such an endorsement for their candidate. See Sweeney, "Armageddon Revisited," 313–15.

43. The vote totals in the general election for lieutenant governor were: John N. Dalton (R)—505,729 (54.0 percent), J. Harry Michael Jr. (D)—332,990 (35.5 percent), Flora Crater (independent; endorsed by the Virginia Women's Political Caucus)—98,508 (10.5 percent). Sabato, *Virginia Votes 1969–1974*, 178–81.

44. The vote totals in the general election for attorney general were: Andrew P. Miller (D)—662,568 (70.6 percent), M. Patton Echols Jr. (R)—276,383 (29.4 percent). Sabato, *Virginia Votes 1969–1974*, 182–85.

45. Author's interviews with Mills E. Godwin Jr., September 9, 1979, September 18, 1984, and May 8, 1990.

46. One delegate who ran as an independent in 1973 and retained that status was Eva Scott of Amelia. In 1979, Delegate Scott affiliated with the Republican Party and successfully sought a seat in the Virginia Senate, becoming the first woman to serve in that body.

47. Sabato, *Virginia Votes 1969–1974*, 118.

48. See Larry Sabato, *Virginia Votes 1975–1978* (Charlottesville: University of Virginia, Institute of Government, 1979), 1.

49. In the 1970s and continuing into the 1980s, former Byrd Democrats and other independent conservatives perennially organized themselves under the "Virginians for" banner, such as "Virginians for Godwin" in 1973. The groups predominantly supported Republicans in the 1970s but eventually splintered into competing "Virginians" groups as Democratic moderates regained the upper hand in their party in the early 1980s.

50. McMath, a conservative businessman from Virginia's Eastern Shore and the only Democratic incumbent to switch parties and gain reelection to the House of Delegates in 1973, became Republican state chairman following Richard Obenshain's selection as cochairman of the Republican National Committee in 1974. McMath held the post until 1979.

51. The major party vote totals in the Virginia general election for president were: Gerald R. Ford (R)—836,554 (49.3 percent), Jimmy Carter (D)—813,896 (48.0 percent). Sabato, *Virginia Votes 1975–1978*, 114–21.

52. The vote totals in the general election for US senator were: Harry F. Byrd Jr. (I)—890,778 (57.2 percent), Elmo R. Zumwalt (D)—596,009 (38.3 percent), Martin H. Perper (I)—70,559 (4.5 percent). Sabato, *Virginia Votes 1975–1978*, 122–25.

53. Author's interviews with John N. Dalton, July 1, 1980, and September 10, 1984.

54. The extensive changes in the organization of the attorney general's office during Andrew Miller's tenure are described in Thomas R. Morris, "The Office of Attorney General in Virginia," *University of Virginia Newsletter* (Charlottesville: University of Virginia, Institute of Government), April 1980.

55. "Dalton Sees Democratic 'Alliance,'" *Richmond News Leader*, May 5, 1977.

56. Ibid.
57. "Miller Hit on Two Fronts," *Richmond Times-Dispatch,* May 8, 1977.
58. Author's interviews with J. Smith Ferebee, June 4, 1980, and August 30, 1984.
59. Author's interview with William Bayliss, June 20, 1980.
60. Author's interview with William A. Royall, June 5, 1980.
61. The vote totals in the Democratic primary for governor were: Henry E. Howell Jr.—253,373 (51.4 percent), Andrew P. Miller—239,735 (48.6 percent). Sabato, *Virginia Votes 1975–1978,* 126–29.
62. Author's interview with Andrew P. Miller, July 24, 1980.
63. Alan Abramowitz, John McGlennon, and Ronald Rapoport, "Voting in the Democratic Primary: The 1977 Virginia Gubernatorial Race," in *Party Politics in the South,* ed. Robert Steed, Laurence W. Moreland, and Ted Baker (New York: Praeger, 1981), 89–91.
64. James Latimer, "Dalton Plea on Primary Is Repeated," *Richmond Times-Dispatch,* June 3, 1977.
65. Sabato, *Virginia Votes 1975–1978,* 32, 36.
66. The major party vote totals in the 1977 general election for governor, lieutenant governor, and attorney general were: for governor: John N. Dalton (R)—699,302 (55.9 percent), Henry E. Howell Jr. (D)—541,319 (43.3 percent); for lieutenant governor: Charles S. Robb (D)—652,084 (54.2 percent), A. Joe Canada (R)—550,116 (45.8 percent); for attorney general: J. Marshall Coleman (R)—617,628 (53.6 percent), Edward E. Lane (D)—535,338 (46.4 percent). Sabato, *Virginia Votes 1975–1978,* 138–49.
67. McDowell's piece for the *Richmond Times-Dispatch,* filed before the convention outcome was known, began, "At the largest political convention in the history of the world, the Great Indoor Primary, it has been a long day—about a month and a half in the real world." Charles McDowell, "The Longest Day at the Coliseum," *Richmond Times-Dispatch,* June 4, 1978.
68. Atkinson, *The Dynamic Dominion,* 421–22.
69. The vote totals in the 1978 general election for US senator were: John W. Warner (R)—613,232 (50.2 percent), Andrew P. Miller (D)—608,511 (49.8 percent). Sabato, *Virginia Votes 1975–1978,* 150–53.
70. Republicans in 1979 won twenty-five seats in the one hundred-member House of Delegates and nine seats in the forty-member Senate. Democrats captured seventy-four House seats and twenty-one Senate seats. The other House seat was held by an independent.
71. The vote totals in the 1980 Virginia general election for president were: Ronald Reagan—989,609 (53.0 percent), Jimmy Carter (D)—752,174 (40.3 percent), John Anderson (I)—95,418 (5.1 percent), others—28,831

(1.6 percent). Larry Sabato, *Virginia Votes 1979–1982* (Charlottesville: University of Virginia, Institute of Government, 1983), 152–63.

72. Reagan defeated incumbent president Jimmy Carter in 1980 and former vice president Walter Mondale in 1984. Vice President George H. W. Bush defeated Massachusetts governor Michael S. Dukakis in 1988.

73. Warner served in the US Senate from 1979 until his retirement in 2009. The only Virginian to serve longer was Senator Harry F. Byrd Sr., who held the office from 1933 until 1965. See Frank B. Atkinson, "John W. Warner (1927–2021)," *Encyclopedia Virginia*, Virginia Humanities (May 12, 2023), https://encyclopediavirginia.org/entries/warner-John-w-1927-2021/.

74. See Atkinson, *The Dynamic Dominion*, 193–94.

75. Former governor John Dalton was considering a second run for governor in 1985 when he suffered a recurrence of lung cancer, and he died in 1986 at age fifty-five. See Frank B. Atkinson, *Virginia in the Vanguard: Political Leadership in the 400-Year-Old Cradle of American Democracy, 1981–2006* (Lanham, MD: Rowman & Littlefield; Charlottesville: University of Virginia Center for Politics, 2006), 14.

76. For an engaging fictional adaptation of the Virginia political story in the 1970s, see Garrett Epps, *The Shad Treatment* (Charlottesville: University Press of Virginia, 1997; first published in 1977 by G. P. Putnam's Sons).

4

Chuck Robb's 1981 Gubernatorial Campaign and the Democratic Realignment

Stephen J. Farnsworth, Stephen P. Hanna, and Sally Burkley

Charles S. "Chuck" Robb's 1981 campaign for governor of Virginia took place during a difficult era for the commonwealth's Democratic Party. After decades of partisan domination, the conservative Virginia Democrats who had ruled both the party and the government for generations faced a profound identity crisis. The federal voting rights reforms of the 1960s created a far more diverse Virginia electorate, and the resulting expanded population of Democratic primary voters showed far less interest in the conservative orientation of the long-dominant Byrd organization. As the more liberal Virginia Democratic Party that emerged from the tumult of the 1960s struggled to find a winning electoral strategy, Robb offered a more moderate vision of the party that sought to bring together urban liberal communities, African Americans, the conservative business community, and some longtime Byrd Democratic voters, who wondered whether the rapidly changing party still had much to offer them.[1]

Robb's gubernatorial victory in 1981 marked the revival, at least temporarily, of Democratic fortunes in the commonwealth.[2] The Robb-led Democratic sweep of the three statewide elected offices that year marked the first of three successful Democratic gubernatorial campaigns during the 1980s. Even decades later, the victorious Democratic gubernatorial trifecta of Chuck Robb (1981), Gerald Baliles (1985), and Doug Wilder (1989) represented an exceptionally successful time for the party.[3] Those elections marked the only string of three consecutive Democratic gubernatorial victories since the splintering of the Byrd organization in the late 1960s. After Wilder, Republican candidates won the next two contests for the commonwealth's top office, in 1993 and 1997.[4]

The Robb centrist pivot for the party was one of the more successful models for Democratic candidates running statewide in the conservative Virginia that existed during the final third of the twentieth century.[5] In addition to redefining the Democratic Party in a way that assisted his immediate successors, Robb's centrist political formula also helped him win his 1988 and 1994 US Senate elections. The centrist image Robb pioneered helped pave the way for many other moderate Virginia Democrats who ran successfully over the past several decades, including Mark Warner, who won elections for governor (2001) and for the US Senate (2008, 2014, and 2020), Jim Webb, elected to the US Senate in 2006, and Ralph Northam, elected governor in 2017.[6]

Robb's political perspective also shaped national politics as he sought to move the national Democratic Party away from its liberal orientation.[7] As Robb said after the party's forty-nine-state defeat in the 1984 presidential contest, "The national party is so much heavy baggage."[8] Robb went on to help organize the Democratic Leadership Council (DLC), a movement dominated by southern and midwestern Democrats and designed to promote centrist voices in the party.[9] This national effort had some successes in the 1990s as another prominent figure in the DLC, Arkansas governor Bill Clinton, was elected president in 1992.[10]

While Democratic statewide electoral victories have become much more common in Virginia's far more diverse electorate of the early twenty-first century, the commonwealth's political environment and geography were quite different when Robb first ran for office.[11] Democratic campaigns waged following the end of the Byrd era had to stitch together their own tenuous coalitions to win statewide. In those days, Virginia Democratic candidates had to win a larger share of the vote beyond the cities and the suburbs than is necessary for Democratic candidates to win statewide elections today. Many Democratic candidates of that era were not up to that challenge.[12]

This chapter examines the pivotal Robb 1981 campaign by comparing that election with the failed 1977 campaign of Democrat Henry Howell. We examine the different results of these two campaigns across Virginia, paying particular attention to the jurisdictions where Robb did significantly better and worse than Howell did four years earlier. Before delving into the election data, we first discuss the political environment Virginia Democratic candidates faced following the splintering of what had been an extremely powerful rural political machine, one that had elected generations of conservative Democrats across the commonwealth.[13]

The Conservative Foundations of Virginia Politics

From the state's colonial roots, the influence of conservative Virginians on state politics has been immense. At times, conservative interests in Virginia diverged, as they did during the early nineteenth century. Those differences declined over time as a result of the political and economic transformations brought about by the Civil War and its aftermath. Taken together, the end of slavery, the departure of the mountain counties that became West Virginia, and the postwar US military occupation reduced the salience of previous policy disputes among White conservative Virginians.[14]

As Virginia industrialized and the population centers of Hampton Roads, Northern Virginia, and Richmond continued to grow and prosper, urban and suburban voters remained less influential than their growing populations might suggest, given the continuing control of Virginia by a conservative White rural elite.

While more urbanized states, including New York, Massachusetts, Illinois, and Missouri, had powerful urban political organizations that wielded statewide and sometimes national influence, rural voices dominated Virginia's most influential political machine. The so-called organization began to dominate the state in the late nineteenth century and rose to greatest prominence during the twentieth century under Harry F. Byrd Sr. of Clarke County, a newspaper publisher, apple baron, governor, and highly influential US senator.[15] Byrd, a conservative Democrat, regularly feuded with a series of Democratic presidents (Harry Truman, John F. Kennedy, Lyndon Johnson) and with northern liberals in Congress over racial matters. Byrd was one of the leading national voices of "massive resistance," the effort to block US Supreme Court orders in *Brown v. Board of Education of Topeka* (1954) that public schools be racially integrated.[16]

Virginia's opposition to desegregation was particularly intense, as some public schools closed in defiance of the courts, and state lawmakers threatened to eliminate state financial support for any school district that complied with the *Brown* ruling on its own.[17] When the elder Byrd resigned from office in 1965 because of failing health, his son Harry F. Byrd Jr. took over the Senate seat and the family political machine. "Young Harry," as he was known, continued his father's tradition of racial and economic conservativism.[18] Throughout his career and into retirement, he never apologized for his role in Virginia's racial history during his years as a state lawmaker and as a US senator, saying that his approach was designed to prevent violence.[19]

As the national Democratic Party realigned itself in a more liberal direction to take account of the very different electorate that emerged following passage of the Civil Rights Act and the Voting Rights Act in the 1960s, the Byrd organization had little interest in an inclusive approach and suffered politically as a result.[20] During this era, organization-backed candidates increasingly faced primary threats from within the Democratic Party, which attracted a far more diverse pool of voters in the wake of new federal civil rights and voting rights laws, as well as the elimination of the Virginia poll tax.[21] A massive increase in the Democratic primary electorate in 1966 triggered the twin renomination defeats of two key organization-backed candidates, US senator A. Willis Robertson of Rockbridge County and US representative Howard W. Smith of Fauquier County, who had blocked congressional consideration of civil rights legislation as chair of the House Rules Committee.[22]

Byrd Jr., who barely survived a 1966 renomination challenge of his own in a special election for the remainder of his father's Senate term, subsequently campaigned as an independent during his successful Senate reelection campaigns in 1970 and 1976. Many of the Byrd organization's candidates and voters migrated to the Republican Party during this era, while others remained conservative Democratic legislators who represented rural districts that generally turned to Republican candidates once the conservative Democratic incumbents left office.[23]

The previously tiny Republican Party of Virginia, which had fought the Byrd organization without success for decades, managed to elect the state's first Republican governor of the twentieth century in 1969. That reform-oriented governor, Linwood Holton, favored school desegregation and opposed welcoming members of the Byrd organization into the GOP, but Holton's moderate vision of Republicanism fell out of favor as White rural conservative voters and Byrd organization politicians increasingly made the Republican Party their new home.[24] Mills Godwin, who served from 1966 to 1970 as the Byrd organization's last Democratic governor, won election for a second (nonconsecutive) term as a Republican in 1973.[25] His campaign was buoyed by the growing number of Byrd Democrats who became Republicans or independents supporting Republican candidates, a trend that reduced the influence of the Virginia GOP's once dominant reformist elements. (Virginia law allows former governors to run for a second term after being out of office for at least four years, and Godwin was the commonwealth's only two-term governor of the twentieth century.) As many of the conservative Democrats aligned with the Byrd organization left the party's ranks, Virginia Democrats of the 1970s saw their opportunities to win statewide elections considerably diminished.

The Political Rise of Chuck Robb

Chuck Robb, elected Virginia's lieutenant governor in 1977, governor in 1981, US senator in 1988, and reelected as senator in 1994, provided the blueprint for a Democratic reversal of these partisan declines. Robb argued that the party should respond to the loss of many Byrd organization voters by using a centrist strategy. From the start of his political career, Robb focused on his background as a US Marine, aggressively seeking to present himself as a moderate voice on key issues such as national defense and fiscal prudence, particularly when compared to national figures in the Democratic Party.[26]

From the start, some of his moderate policy positions rankled Democratic activists, particularly those from urban areas of the state. Robb focused on fiscal prudence, and his tight budgets irritated some other Democratic lawmakers in Richmond.[27] Robb was more supportive of the death penalty than many other Democratic elected officials, for example, and he was a cofounder of the DLC, created explicitly to challenge the leftward movement of the Democratic Party nationally.[28]

But on other issues Robb was a conventional Democrat. On racial matters, for example, Robb was the opposite of those organization candidates who promoted massive resistance to civil rights. Robb was particularly aggressive in appointing African Americans and women to positions in government. Robb also encouraged voters to support the party's very diverse 1985 statewide ticket, which included candidates who became Virginia's first African American lieutenant governor and its first woman elected attorney general.[29] Like many other Virginia Democratic candidates who followed him, Robb's political success throughout his career depended on a biracial coalition that, starting with Robb, became the cornerstone of Democratic statewide victories in Virginia.[30]

Robb had first drawn national attention as a Marine Corps officer who married Lynda Johnson, the daughter of then US president Lyndon B. Johnson, in the first White House wedding in more than six decades. The wedding received front-page treatment in the *New York Times*.[31] Then came military service in Vietnam and law school at the University of Virginia. With his law degree in hand, Robb started working for a Washington-area law firm and became active on Democratic Party committees in Fairfax County and statewide. Robb's connection to the former president, and his access to the Johnson family's wealth, proved a double-edged sword. Robb's connections and his wealth eased his way into Democratic politics but generated some resentment from other Democrats, who felt themselves pushed aside despite their seniority in politics and fidelity to a larger range of liberal causes.[32]

In part, some of the in-party frustrations with Robb stemmed from unrealistic expectations. From the start, White liberals and African American voters expected more progressive politics from the son-in-law of the creator of the Great Society than Robb ever had in mind.[33]

The 1970s, the decade when Robb launched his political career, represented a bleak time for Virginia Democrats. In addition to the party's defeats in recent statewide elections—and the splintering of the Virginia Democratic organization—the party faced further frustration at the hands of the national Democratic Party, which offered Senator George McGovern as the party's 1972 presidential candidate—a choice that led to a forty-nine-state victory by Richard Nixon and redefined the party in a way immensely unhelpful to Democratic fortunes in Virginia.

Robb became the Democratic lieutenant governor nominee in 1977 after defeating two more liberal Democratic candidates in a primary.[34] In that primary, some political observers thought Robb's centrism was a canny political strategy for a first-time candidate in a three-way nomination race with liberal alternatives. As one of Robb's 1977 campaign aides noted, "We realized there was a lot of room to the right and we were trying to move him that way. We never dreamed that was where he wanted to be."[35]

Robb won the general election for lieutenant governor in 1977 after securing 54 percent of the vote against A. Joe Canada, a state senator who lost ten of Virginia's eleven congressional districts.[36] Robb's success that year was in sharp contrast to the fate of the party's gubernatorial nominee. Henry Howell, a progressive populist Democratic activist at the top of the ticket, lost by more than 150,000 votes.

Howell had previously served as a Virginia lieutenant governor and as a state senator and delegate from Norfolk, but he never won the state's top office. Throughout his career Howell had offered a very liberal policy portfolio for the Virginia of his day, including battling the conservative trifecta of segregation, the Byrd organization, and Virginia's poll tax law, a voting fee that discouraged voting by African Americans and by poor Whites.[37] Throughout his professional life, Howell championed African American voters, urban liberals, and union voters in a state famous for its right-to-work laws, its aggressive efforts at massive resistance to desegregated schooling, and its longtime dominance by White rural interests.[38] As his obituary noted,

> As much as anything, Howell's career reflected the changing patterns of Virginia politics. His election as lieutenant governor in 1971—when he ran as an independent to complete the term of J. Sargeant Reynolds, who died that year—would have been unthinkable during the era of the Byrd organization. It was described in newspaper editorials as a final indicator that little more was to be gained from the race issue that had figured so prominently in the state's politics during the era of Massive Resistance.[39]

Virginia lieutenant governors serve part-time, and they are not required to do much more than preside over the Senate of Virginia, break ties when they occur in the upper chamber, and stand ready to serve if the governor's office becomes vacant. Even with this modest list of responsibilities, Robb's position as the only Democratic candidate elected statewide in 1977 made him the obvious choice for the party's gubernatorial nomination four years later.[40]

Even so, Robb's electoral success in 1977 did not settle the argument about whether the party should nominate liberals for statewide campaigns, nor did it end the high volume of in-fighting among Virginia Democrats. As then lieutenant governor, Robb remarked with irritation in 1978 regarding his fellow Virginia Democrats: "To execute our party plan, we request a firing squad and line up in a circle."[41]

Even after he secured his party's gubernatorial nomination in 1981, Robb continued to face intraparty disapproval over his centrist ideology. Howell, the party's liberal conscience and the defeated gubernatorial candidate in 1977, expressed little interest in supporting Robb in the 1981 gubernatorial election, saying that Robb had undermined liberal Democrats in the state party.[42] The less than warm feelings went both ways. Robb's team did not appear to desire Howell's help, in part because of concerns that a Howell endorsement might hurt Robb with more moderate voters in Virginia.[43] Even without much assistance from the previous nominee, voters in 1981 elected Robb the first Democratic governor in the wake of the splintering of the Byrd machine.

At the time, reporters speculated that J. Marshall Coleman, Robb's Republican opponent, may have made an error by focusing on the fact that Robb was not a Virginia native (he was born in Arizona). Coleman might have done better had he focused on Robb's long-term ties to Fairfax County, an affluent suburban enclave, which might have generated more ill will among many Virginians than campaign attacks that focused on Robb's out-of-state birth.[44] Before Robb's election, there had only been two governors from Northern Virginia: the first was Confederate general Robert E. Lee's nephew Fitzhugh Lee, who spent most of his life in Alexandria but won the office in 1885 after moving to Stafford County; the second was Westmoreland Davis, a Loudoun County resident elected in 1917.[45] Of course, neither Stafford nor Loudoun would have qualified, in a cultural sense, as part of Northern Virginia at the time of those earlier electoral victories.

Coleman's campaign faced other challenges as well. He worried about appearing too conservative for suburban voters, and so he did not pursue Virginia's Christian conservative voters as aggressively as he might have.[46] When it appeared the election was slipping away, Coleman sought to pivot to the ideological right, organizing a last-minute campaign rally with President Reagan and former governor Godwin, a leading voice in the Byrd organization. L. Douglas Wilder, a state senator and future governor, said that Coleman's decision to do so "galvanized" African American voters to support Robb more enthusiastically than might otherwise have been the case.[47]

Other analysts believed that Robb's victory benefited from the framework built by previous Democratic candidates, including the failed campaigns that preceded him. In a comparison of the 1977 and 1981 gubernatorial elections, Knickrehm and colleagues wrote that Robb was a beneficiary of a period of realignment in Virginia that took place over several gubernatorial elections, starting with Holton's 1969 victory and continuing through the 1981 contest.[48] Several years later, Coleman offered a similar line of argument about the man who beat him in 1981, saying that former Republican governor Holton, among others, helped set the stage for Robb's centrist brand of politics in Virginia.[49]

The 1977 and 1981 Gubernatorial Elections Compared

The effectiveness of Robb's redesign of the Democratic electoral coalition can be seen in a comparison of the 1977 and 1981 gubernatorial elections. In 1977, Republican John Dalton was elected governor over Democrat Henry Howell by 56 percent to 43 percent of votes cast, a roughly 158,000-vote advantage out of 1.25 million ballots cast. Four years later, Robb defeated Republican J. Marshall Coleman by a 53.5 percent to 46 percent margin, a roughly 101,000-vote advantage out of 1.42 million votes cast. A total of 760,357 votes were cast for Robb, as compared to 541,319 for Howell four years earlier. Howell's margin of defeat and Robb's margin of victory represented a net swing of more than a quarter million votes to the Democratic candidate during this four-year period.[50]

Table 4.1 shows the fifteen political jurisdictions where Robb lost ground or gained the least compared to the percentage of votes cast for Howell four years earlier. Of those fifteen comparatively poor-performing political jurisdictions for Robb, only five showed a percentage decline in support for the Democratic gubernatorial candidate between 1977 and 1981. Stafford County, just north of Fredericksburg, ranked as the least favorable jurisdiction for Robb compared to Howell, with a 6.8 percent decline in Democratic votes over that four-year period, while the City of Manassas Park registered a 5.1 percent decline (though one might note the city's tiny electorate—fewer than 900 votes were cast there in the 1981 gubernatorial election). Election-to-election percentage declines in those locales listed in table 4.1 also emerged in Scott County, in the state's rural southwestern corner, and in Spotsylvania and King George Counties, which, along with Stafford, are jurisdictions located near Fredericksburg.

Two of the fifteen jurisdictions on this "lost the most/gained the least" list—Stafford and Scott Counties—backed the Democratic candidate for governor in 1977 and favored the Republican four years later. One of these relatively poor-performing counties for Democrats in 1981, Prince William, flipped in the opposite direction, voting Republican in 1977 and Democratic in 1981.

Among the other unfavorable/less favorable jurisdictions for Democrats over this period listed in table 4.1, the Democratic candidate won in both gubernatorial elections in Manassas Park, Spotsylvania, Greensville (a largely rural county located at the intersection of Interstate 95 and the North Carolina border), Dickenson, Fredericksburg city, and Russell. Both Dickenson and Russell are rural counties in Southwest Virginia.

TABLE 4.1. Fifteen jurisdictions with least increase in support for Democratic candidates, 1977–81

County	Votes (%) in 1977			Votes (%) in 1981			Change in Votes (%) for Democrat
	Democrat	Republican	Total	Democrat	Republican	Total	No. of Votes (%)
Stafford	4,069 (53.83)	3,415 (45.18)	7,559	4,625 (47.01)	5,214 (52.99)	9,839	556 (−6.82)
Manassas Park (City)	478 (58.01)	338 (41.02)	824	468 (52.88)	417 (47.12)	885	−10 (−5.13)
Scott†	3,228 (51.44)	3,018 (48.10)	6,275	3,264 (48.80)	3,424 (51.20)	6,688	36 (−2.64)
Spotsylvania	3,018 (55.35)	2,355 (43.19)	5,453	4,088 (54.21)	3,453 (45.79)	7,541	1,070 (−1.14)
King George	1,051 (49.23)	1,047 (49.04)	2,135	1,172 (48.91)	1,224 (51.09)	2,396	121 (−0.31)
Greene	614 (41.15)	872 (58.45)	1,492	763 (41.72)	1,066 (58.28)	1,829	149 (0.56)
Poquoson (City)	799 (37.76)	1,305 (61.67)	2,116	1,044 (38.71)	1,653 (61.29)	2,697	245 (0.95)
Prince George	1,709 (46.15)	1,929 (52.09)	3,703	2,302 (49.06)	2,389 (50.92)	4,692	593 (2.91)
Greensville	1,642 (55.16)	1,216 (40.85)	2,977	1,790 (59.08)	1,240 (40.92)	3,030	148 (3.92)
Lancaster	1,296 (36.25)	2,250 (62.94)	3,575	1,474 (40.59)	2,156 (59.38)	3,631	178 (4.34)
Dickenson	3,326 (56.32)	2,502 (42.36)	5,906	3,977 (60.76)	2,566 (39.21)	6,545	651 (4.45)
Fredericksburg (City)	1,916 (50.45)	1,841 (48.47)	3,798	2,226 (55.19)	1,807 (44.81)	4,033	310 (4.75)
Russell	3,928 (55.87)	3,062 (43.56)	7,030	4,753 (60.64)	3,085 (39.36)	7,838	825 (4.77)
New Kent	936 (44.89)	1,114 (53.43)	2,085	1,227 (49.84)	1,235 (50.16)	2,462	291 (4.95)
Prince William*	8,700 (46.18)	10,014 (53.15)	18,841	13,387 (51.41)	12,644 (48.56)	26,039	4,687 (5.24)
Virginia (statewide)	541,319 (40.50)	699,302 (40.50)	1,250,940	760,357 (51.76)	659,398 (46.42)	1,420,611	219,038

Note: Jurisdictions that flipped from Republican to Democrat are marked with an asterisk (*). Jurisdictions that flipped from Democrat to Republican are marked with a dagger (†).
Source: Virginia Department of Elections.

With the exception of Prince William County, these relatively poor-performing jurisdictions for Robb are relatively small. In fact, fourteen of the fifteen jurisdictions in Virginia where Democrats lost the most ground or gained the least ground between the 1977 and 1981 gubernatorial elections cast fewer than 10,000 votes in the 1981 contest for governor. They constituted a variety of mostly rural jurisdictions scattered around the state, including Southwest Virginia, the Tidewater, along the North Carolina border, and in the largely rural areas beyond what were then the suburbs of Washington. While one would call Manassas Park part of the Washington suburbs these days, the community was much smaller and far more culturally distant from Washington four decades ago. One could say that same thing about the Fredericksburg area of that era, although today many consider that area part of the Washington suburbs.

Table 4.2 lists the jurisdictions where Democratic fortunes improved the most between the Democratic gubernatorial elections of 1977 and 1981. As in table 4.1, many of the jurisdictions listed in table 4.2 as exhibiting the greatest change between those two gubernatorial elections were not major sources of votes in Virginia. Many of the communities appearing in table 4.2 were part of the conservative, rural heartland that had been key components of the Byrd organization where Robb was a more appealing choice than Howell had been. Only one of these political jurisdictions cast more than 15,000 votes in the 1981 gubernatorial election, Henrico County, which cast a total of 63,320 votes that year.

As shown in table 4.2, three jurisdictions increased their support for the Democratic gubernatorial candidate by over twenty percentage points between these elections: Appomattox and Buckingham Counties and the City of Bedford, all in Central Virginia. (At the time of these two elections Bedford was an independent city; it is now a town within Bedford County.) Another three had an election-to-election increase of between nineteen and twenty points for Robb over Howell: Montgomery County and the City of Radford in Southwest Virginia, and Lunenburg County, located in Southside Virginia.

Robb received between 54 percent and 69 percent of the vote in all six of these communities, all of which had backed the Republican candidate for governor in 1977. Montgomery County had the largest number of votes cast of these top six: 13,678. Robb also flipped the Southwest Virginia county of Wythe, which ranked eighth on the list of most improved jurisdictions for Democrats in 1981.

TABLE 4.2. Fifteen Virginia jurisdictions with greatest increase in support for Democratic candidates, 1977–81

County	No. of Votes (%) in 1977			No. of Votes (%) in 1981			Change in Votes (%) for Democrat
	Democrat	Republican	Total	Democrat	Republican	Total	No. of Votes (%)
Appomattox*	1,162 (35.37)	2,109 (64.20)	3,285	2,219 (59.89)	1,486 (40.11)	3,705	1057 (24.52)
Buckingham*	1,470 (47.87)	1,555 (50.63)	3,071	2,415 (69.26)	1,068 (30.63)	3,487	945 (21.39)
Bedford City*	720 (35.84)	1,281 (63.76)	2,009	1,141 (56.68)	872 (43.32)	2,013	421 (20.84)
Montgomery*	4,232 (34.57)	7,894 (64.48)	12,242	7,451 (54.47)	6,225 (45.51)	13,678	3219 (19.90)
Radford City*	1,427 (37.72)	2,321 (61.35)	3,783	2,070 (57.31)	1,542 (42.69)	3,612	643 (19.59)
Lunenberg*	1,072 (36.43)	1,854 (63.00)	2,943	1,875 (55.62)	1,492 (44.26)	3,371	803 (19.20)
Staunton City	1,859 (30.51)	4,210 (69.10)	6,093	3,138 (49.18)	3,241 (50.80)	6,380	1,279 (18.67)
Wythe*	2,056 (33.79)	4,005 (65.83)	6,084	3,898 (52.43)	3,537 (47.57)	7,435	1,842 (18.63)
Winchester City	1,319 (29.89)	3,069 (69.54)	4,413	2,522 (47.50)	2,787 (52.50)	5,309	1,203 (17.62)
Henrico	14,417 (25.65)	41,588 (73.98)	56,217	27,054 (42.73)	36,246 (57.24)	63,320	12,637 (17.08)
Campbell	2,361 (26.07)	6,644 (73.37)	9,056	4,650 (42.84)	6,202 (57.13)	10,855	2,289 (16.77)
Prince Edward	1,707 (38.92)	2,648 (60.37)	4,386	2,729 (55.66)	2,165 (44.16)	4,903	1,022 (16.74)
Patrick	1,757 (41.99)	2,398 (57.31)	4,184	2,847 (58.56)	2,014 (41.42)	4,862	1,090 (16.56)
Clarke	716 (33.52)	1,399 (65.50)	2,136	1,258 (49.88)	1,261 (50.00)	2,522	542 (16.36)
Martinsville City	2,199 (38.73)	3,449 (60.74)	5,678	3,100 (54.95)	2,537 (44.97)	5,642	901 (16.22)
Virginia (statewide)	541,319 (40.50)	699,302 (55.90)	1,250,940	760,357 (51.76)	659,398 (46.42)	1,420,611	219,038 (11.26)

Note: Jurisdictions that flipped from Republican to Democrat are marked with an asterisk (*).

Source: Virginia Department of Elections.

Robb narrowly lost the Interstate 81 communities of Staunton and Winchester, but he increased the Democratic vote share by more than seventeen points over that four-year period in both.

Robb also lost the then Republican stronghold of Henrico County, in the Richmond suburbs. Henrico, which ranked tenth in terms of the strongest Democratic gains between these two elections, cast 42.7 percent of its votes for Robb, another seventeen-point jump for Robb compared to the 1977 gubernatorial contest.

As shown in table 4.3, Robb flipped ten of fifteen of these "most improved for Democrats" jurisdictions. In addition to those named above, Robb also flipped Prince Edward and Patrick Counties and the City of Martinsville. All are located in Central and South-Central Virginia.

Of course, Robb's greatest electoral success took place in more populous parts of Virginia, starting a trend for Virginia Democrats that persists to this day. Table 4.3 lists Virginia's fifteen largest political jurisdictions as measured by votes cast in the 1981 contest. All fifteen showed a gain of at least five points for Robb compared to Howell's performance four years earlier; eight of them registered double-digit gains. Robb won twelve of these population centers in 1981. Among those top fifteen voting locations, Robb lost only Henrico and Chesterfield Counties in the Richmond area and Roanoke County in South-Central Virginia. In all three counties, though, Robb managed to secure a double-digit increase in the Democratic vote share compared to the votes Howell received there four years earlier. Losing by less in an unfriendly county is helpful to a candidate, as is winning by more in a friendly one. Robb consistently succeeded on both counts, as these county-by-county comparisons demonstrate.

Four years earlier, Republicans had won four of the top five voting jurisdictions on this list—Fairfax County, the City of Richmond, the City of Virginia Beach, and Arlington County. All of them flipped to Robb in 1981. Among the top fifteen vote-rich locales, Robb also flipped three others: the City of Newport News and Roanoke City and Prince William County.

These three tables demonstrate the success Chuck Robb had in building a Democratic coalition beyond the party's performance in 1977. Robb's campaign did worse than Howell's in only a handful of jurisdictions, all of them casting only a tiny portion of the total number of Virginia ballots cast. In other words, the "lost" Democratic votes (so to speak) between 1977 and 1981 in a few rural jurisdictions are not all that significant when compared to the huge increases in the percentages and in the raw numbers of votes that Robb secured from the electorates of Fairfax and Arlington Counties and the City of Richmond over that same period.

Table 4.3. Change in support for Democratic candidate in Virginia's fifteen largest jurisdictions, 1977–81

County	No. of Votes (%) in 1977			No. of Votes (%) in 1981			Change in Votes (%) for Democrat
	Democrat	Republican	Total	Democrat	Republican	Total	No. of Votes (%)
Fairfax*	51,754 (40.50)	75,216 (58.86)	127,790	85,818 (51.76)	79,909 (48.20)	165,800	34,064 (11.26)
Richmond City*	31,454 (48.63)	32,512 (50.26)	64,682	45,378 (64.48)	24,926 (35.42)	70,375	13,924 (15.85)
Virginia Beach City*	19,810 (42.26)	26,875 (57.33)	46,875	27,993 (50.83)	27,060 (49.14)	55,069	8,183 (8.57)
Norfolk City	32,420 (60.31)	21,022 (39.11)	53,753	34,780 (67.75)	16,526 (32.19)	51,336	2,360 (7.44)
Arlington*	19,495 (47.08)	21,589 (52.13)	41,412	27,472 (59.20)	18,870 (40.66)	46,404	7,977 (12.13)
Chesterfield	8,762 (26.33)	24,371 (73.23)	33,281	16,639 (38.09)	27,032 (61.89)	43,679	7,877 (11.77)
Henrico	14,417 (25.65)	41,588 (73.98)	56,217	27,054 (42.73)	36,246 (57.24)	63,320	12,637 (17.08)
Newport News City*	16,395 (49.17)	16,532 (49.58)	33,341	20,240 (57.70)	14,824 (42.26)	35,076	3,845 (8.53)
Hampton City	14,656 (54.07)	12,346 (45.55)	27,107	17,509 (61.18)	11,103 (38.80)	28,617	2,853 (7.12)
Portsmouth City	16,910 (61.00)	10,390 (37.48)	27,723	19,718 (70.03)	8,427 (29.93)	28,156	2,808 (9.03)
Roanoke City*	12,344 (46.74)	13,906 (52.65)	26,412	16,448 (61.33)	10,367 (38.65)	26,821	4,104 (14.59)
Chesapeake City	14,345 (55.28)	11,476 (44.23)	25,948	16,335 (60.99)	10,448 (39.01)	26,785	1,990 (5.70)
Alexandria City	11,536 (49.90)	11,417 (49.39)	23,118	15,892 (60.21)	10,487 (39.73)	26,393	4,356 (10.31)
Prince William*	8,700 (46.18)	10,014 (53.15)	18,841	13,387 (51.41)	12,644 (48.56)	26,039	4,687 (5.24)
Roanoke	6,994 (34.89)	12,964 (64.67)	20,047	12,038 (49.99)	12,040 (50.00)	24,080	5,044 (15.10)
Virginia (statewide)	541,319 (40.50)	699,302 (55.90)	1,250,940	760,357 (51.76)	659,398 (46.42)	1,420,611	219,038 (11.26)

Note: Jurisdictions that flipped from Republican to Democrat are marked with an asterisk (*).
Source: Virginia Department of Elections.

Even in highly Republican populous areas of this era, such as Chesterfield and Henrico Counties, Robb lost by a smaller percentage than Howell had four years earlier. Robb's strategy of reaching out to more moderate voters, including some historically Democratic voters in the Byrd organization's rural heartland, clearly paid off. Robb's effort to ramp up support among African American voters in both the cities and the rural Virginia counties with high African American populations likewise paid off. These two groups of voters would never have found much common cause with Democratic nominees during the Byrd era. But Robb brought them together.

Figure 4.1 is the first of three maps that allow us to take a more geographic perspective of the gains and losses for Democratic gubernatorial candidates in 1977 and 1981. This map shows the percentage of the votes Henry Howell received during his unsuccessful run for Virginia's top office in 1977. For a contemporary reader, these city and county results might seem to be inverse images of the current political environment. Howell won several of the struggling communities of Southwest Virginia, where decades later Republicans rarely lose. Mining was more influential in the politics of Southwest Virginia four decades ago, and the relatively strong presence of unions there helped Democrats be more successful in the region's "Fighting Ninth" congressional district back then.[51] In addition, the intensely Democratic regions of today's Northern Virginia were not so Democratic in 1977, and the Democratic-leaning suburbs of the Richmond area were solidly Republican in this election.

Other results from the 1977 gubernatorial election would not seem so odd to modern eyes. Howell performed poorly along the northern portion of the Interstate 81 corridor, where Democratic candidates often struggle today. Howell did well in his home region of Hampton Roads and in some of the areas near the North Carolina border that have above-average numbers of African American voters. Both areas continue to treat Democratic candidates favorably today.

Figure 4.2 shows the percentage of the vote Chuck Robb received during his successful run for Virginia's top office in 1981, four years after Howell's failed attempt. The 1981 results look more like what one would see in a contemporary Virginia election than the 1977 results did, though with some important differences.

At first glance, one can see how figure 4.2 demonstrates that Robb's success owed to a pervasive increase in Democratic vote share in nearly all parts of Virginia. As mentioned earlier in the chapter, Robb gained ground—either winning by more or losing by less—in the vast majority of cities and counties in the commonwealth. Most obviously evident is that

Robb won a majority of voters in more than ninety jurisdictions, while Howell's 1977 campaign earned majorities in only thirty-three. Like Howell, Robb did well in the Hampton Roads area in some of the southern Virginia counties with relatively large African American populations. Robb was also strong in the cities of Richmond and Alexandria. Even in places where Republicans almost always would win during this era, they won by less in 1981.

Compared to the Democratic performance in more recent elections, Robb's 1981 victory gained far more support in some of the rural counties of Southwest Virginia than Democrats would in the elections that followed. While Robb won many of the jurisdictions of Northern Virginia in 1981, he won them by far less than Democratic candidates did in subsequent elections.[52] Only the two lightest shades mark those places where Robb failed to obtain 50 percent of the vote.

Of course, traditional acreage-based election maps like those in figures 4.1 and 4.2 illustrate jurisdictions by physical size, not population. As such, compact places such as Arlington County are barely visible compared to large counties such as nearby Fauquier, which has a notably smaller population. To compensate for the fact that physical size may be misleading when talking about electoral influence, social scientists often employ a cartogram, which resizes political jurisdictions by the number of votes cast. This allows one to see an electorate as it really exists.[53] After all, people vote, acres do not. Cartograms are commonly employed, for example, in maps of the Electoral College, where the most populous

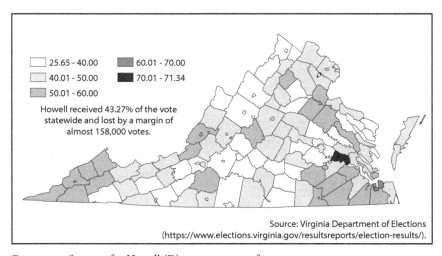

FIGURE 4.1. Support for Howell (D) as percentage of votes cast

states, such as California, expand in size and the most rural states, such as Wyoming or Alaska, shrink in accordance with the relatively few Electoral College votes allocated to states with smaller populations.

Figure 4.3 employs the cartogram technique for political jurisdictions in Virginia, adjusting the acreage-based image in previous figures to account for population. This image shows the relative importance of those jurisdiction in elections, as measured by the number of votes cast. For this image, we use a comparative metric for analyzing the results of these two elections. Rather than look at the Democratic vote percentage, as we did in figure 4.1 (1977) and figure 4.2 (1981), we examine in figure 4.3 the change in Democratic vote percentage between 1977 and 1981. The figure shows the darker counties and cities where Robb gained the greatest percentage of votes and the lighter ones are where he gained the smallest percentage of votes. The handful of jurisdictions where Robb did worse than Howell did are marked with diagonal lines. In other words, the shading here no longer represents the magnitudes of wins and losses; rather, figure 4.3 shows the relative change in percentage of Democratic votes cast in 1977 and 1981.

In a cartogram that represents electoral influence rather than acreage, Virginia looks like a pair of scissors, with the more populated counties and cities of the Interstate 95 and Interstate 64 corridors expanding to reflect the larger numbers of votes cast in those parts of the commonwealth. Many of the counties where Robb gained the most ground, such as those in Northern Virginia, Hampton Roads, and the Richmond area, had the

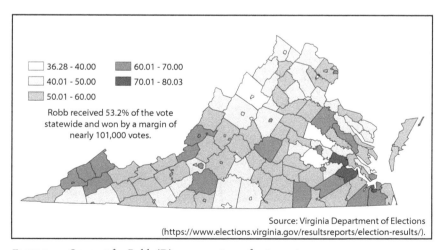

FIGURE 4.2. Support for Robb (D) as percentage of votes cast

largest numbers of voters and thus appear as the largest areas in figure 4.3. Other population centers where Robb did far better than Howell, including the independent cities of Winchester, Harrisonburg, and Staunton along Virginia's western edge, stand out on the cartogram as well.

More rural jurisdictions where Robb's support increased the least when compared to Howell's shrink in the cartogram, reflecting the relatively small number of ballots cast there. This is particularly noticeable in some counties in Southwest Virginia, where Robb's performance in 1981 lagged Robb's performance statewide.

Figure 4.3 also demonstrates the success of Robb's multipronged strategy to reach out to African Americans, to the business community, and to more conservative White voters who might have been Byrd Democrats a decade or two earlier. The near absence of jurisdictions where Robb lost ground underscores that all these aspects of his campaign fired effectively. While the 1977 election that is used as a comparison here may represent a low point for the Democratic Party in Virginia, figure 4.3 shows that Robb succeeded in creating a remarkable amount of change for a Democratic gubernatorial candidate over a short period of time.

Discussion

Electoral success is a definite but nevertheless an imprecise measure of the quality of political strategies employed in a political campaign. While each

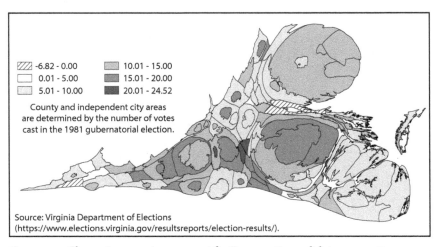

FIGURE 4.3. Change in percentage support for Democratic candidate, 1977–1981

campaign does everything it can to win, individual elections have a variety of idiosyncratic circumstances that can make a mess of campaign plans. Breaking news items and the actions of other candidates are two largely unpredictable matters that may affect the Election Day results as much as anything a campaign does or does not do.

As this chapter has demonstrated, Robb's 1981 electoral victory represented a powerful renewal for the Virginia Democratic Party, which had been discouraged and defeated in nearly all statewide elections after the splintering of the Byrd organization in the late 1960s. The combination of fiscal conservatism and social progressivism that marked the Robb years as governor did much to mend what had been broken in the party.[54] As the Democratic strategist H. Benson Dendy III has noted, Robb brought together a party that had been badly fractured before he appeared on the political scene.

> In the 1970s, there were two Democratic parties. There was the legislative Democratic Party that was very conservative [and] fiscally responsible. . . . And there was the [statewide] Democratic Party that had been so weak in 1973 that they fielded no candidate for governor, that even Henry Howell who, as the darling of the liberals, didn't want the Democratic nomination because he thought it would hurt him.[55]

Veteran Democratic legislator Hunter B. Andrews went even further in his assessment: "Democrats owe a tremendous debt of gratitude to Chuck Robb. He put it all together. It became respectable again to call yourself a Democrat."[56]

Chuck Robb's defeat for reelection to a third term in the US Senate in 2000, nearly two decades after his 1981 election as governor, was not a defeat for his vision of centrist politics in Virginia. One year later, centrist Mark Warner was elected governor in a campaign that featured significant outreach efforts to more conservative parts of Virginia, as Robb had done.[57] Throughout his time as governor, Warner kept to a largely moderate pattern of governing, and one that was rewarded with additional electoral victories in the years that followed.[58]

Six years after Robb's 2000 electoral defeat, Jim Webb won election to the US Senate as a centrist Democrat.[59] Like Robb before him, Webb sought to put daylight between himself and the national Democratic Party, a key part of securing White votes in rural regions that were becoming increasingly Republican. During his time in elected office, Webb frequently lamented that the Democratic Party seemed to be moving increasingly leftward and the Republican Party to be moving ever more right, a pattern that Webb felt doomed the Democratic Party's prospects with White working-class voters in Virginia.[60]

Webb, who did not seek reelection to the Senate in 2012, unsuccessfully ran for president as a Democrat in 2016. In that contest, Webb's ideological distance from national party activists became particularly obvious during that nomination cycle, and he dropped out after his centrist campaign generated little interest among Democratic loyalists.[61] Webb then discussed running as an independent but eventually decided against doing so.[62]

As the continued success of moderates like Warner, Webb, and recently Ralph Northam demonstrates, Robb's pioneering brand of centrist Democratic politics retains significant relevance in Virginia today. Decades after Robb paved the way as a centrist Democratic candidate in 1981, Democratic primary voters often select more moderate nominees for statewide office, as they did in the selection of moderate Ralph Northam over liberal Tom Perriello in the 2017 nomination for governor.

But Robb's moderate vision is no longer the only path to Democratic victory in statewide elections. After all, Virginia has changed a great deal since Robb's pivotal victory in 1981. The parties have become more polarized, both nationally and in Virginia, and that limits the effectiveness of appeals to the sliver of moderate voters who are generally undecided about the two parties. Even Mark Warner, one of the most successful Virginia Democrats at offering a moderate vision of the party, nearly lost his reelection bid in 2014 in the anti-Obama headwinds.[63] In addition, Warner fared far worse in rural counties in 2014 (and again in 2020) than he had during his 2001 gubernatorial campaign. The growing share of Virginia votes cast in urban and suburban jurisdictions gives Democratic candidates in recent elections more ideological latitude than was the case in 1981.[64]

Tim Kaine, a former governor, lieutenant governor, and mayor of Richmond, is one of those who campaigned on a less centrist path than Robb or Warner. Kaine was elected governor in 2005 and subsequently won the 2012 US Senate election to replace Webb. Kaine's gubernatorial record included a focus on environmental protection, greater restrictions on guns, and increased spending on mass transit, education, and health care, issues that demonstrated he was a far more liberal Democratic candidate than many others who had been running statewide as party nominees in previous election cycles.[65]

Kaine's more liberal politics found considerable success in his campaigns for office in a Virginia where a much higher proportion of votes were cast in the suburbs than during Robb's 1981 race. This trend accelerated in the most recent statewide elections, as many suburban voters did not embrace the combative vision of Republicanism personified by Donald Trump.[66] By the time the 2020 presidential campaign rolled around, Republicans barely campaigned for Trump's reelection in Virginia, which demonstrated how much the commonwealth's partisan ground had shifted since Robb's 1981 election.[67]

As Democratic fortunes have improved in today's Virginia, perhaps some Democratic liberals might be confident enough about their prospects that they believe the party now can abandon the centrist approach that marked Robb's political career and that of so many other successful Democratic candidates campaigning statewide in recent decades.[68] But when given a chance to abandon the Robb approach, Democratic primary electorates often hesitate to do so in statewide nomination contests. Perhaps the painful memories of the defeats of the past continue to push party activists more often than not in the practical, moderate direction favored by Robb decades ago.[69]

Whatever the reason, Robb's centrist vision remains influential within the party to this day, as moderate Democratic candidates continue to win contested nominations in Virginia. That may be for the best in terms of the party's prospects, as the commonwealth's electorate retains a certain level of skepticism if not hostility toward the federal government and toward liberal, big-government solutions.[70] As a result, Robb's vision of centrist Democratic politics remains a commonly played winning hand for the Virginia Democratic Party in statewide elections long after Robb's 1981 redefinition of what it means to be a Democratic statewide candidate in the Old Dominion.

Notes

Thanks to Kate Seltzer and Eden Shenal for research assistance and to the University of Mary Washington Center for Leadership and Media Studies for financial assistance.

1. Earl Black and Merle Black, *The Rise of Southern Republicans* (Cambridge, MA: Harvard University Press, 2002).

2. Tom Sherwood, "Robb: New Image for State: Va. Legacy of Moderation Seen Enduring," *Washington Post,* January 1, 1986; Tom Sherwood, "Robb:

Democratic Enigma: National Attention Follows Va. Governor," *Washington Post*, January 2, 1986.

3. Frank B. Atkinson, *Virginia in the Vanguard: Political Leadership in the 400-Year-Old Cradle of American Democracy, 1981–2006* (Lanham, MD: Rowman & Littlefield, 2006).

4. Stephen J. Farnsworth, "Campaigning against Government in the Old Dominion: State Taxation, State Power and Virginia's 1997 Gubernatorial Election," *Politics & Policy* 30, no. 3 (2002): 460–80.

5. Bob Lewis, "A Commonwealth Divided? Republican Rural Virginia loses Ground to Democrats' Suburban Strongholds," *Virginia Mercury*, November 11, 2019; Sabrina Tavernise and Robert Gebeloff, "How Voters Turned Virginia from Deep Red to Solid Blue," *New York Times*, November 9, 2019.

6. Stephen J. Farnsworth, "Virginia Politics, Washington-Style," *Washington Post*, October 23, 2005; Stephen J. Farnsworth, "The Yin and Yang of Virginia Politics," *Richmond Times-Dispatch*, February 17, 2008; Stephen J. Farnsworth and Stephen P. Hanna, "Virginia's Changing Party Dynamics," *Richmond Times-Dispatch*, November 12, 2017; Stephen J. Farnsworth and Stephen P. Hanna, "People Vote, Acres Don't: Virginia's 2017 Election in Perspective," *Virginia Capitol Connections*, Winter 2018.

7. David S. Broder, "Chuck Robb's 'Instant Credibility,'" *Washington Post*, October 26, 1986; Black and Black, *The Rise of Southern Republicans*; Tom Sherwood, "Robb Aids Democratic Party Revival: LBJ Son-in-Law Called Key Figure in Leadership Search," *Washington Post*, December 2, 1984.

8. Sherwood, "Robb Aids Democratic Party Revival."

9. Black and Black, *The Rise of Southern Republicans*; Sherwood, "Robb Aids Democratic Party Revival."

10. Black and Black, *The Rise of Southern Republicans*.

11. Virginius Dabney, *Virginia: The New Dominion* (Charlottesville: University Press of Virginia, 1971); Bruce J. Dierenfield, *Keeper of the Rules: Congressman Howard W. Smith of Virginia.* (Charlottesville: University Press of Virginia, 1987); Stephen J. Farnsworth, Stephen P. Hanna, and Kate Seltzer, "Declining Rural Influence in Virginia Politics: Comparing Mark Warner's 2001 and 2020 Elections," in *Vibrant Virginia: Engaging the Commonwealth to Expand Economic Vitality*, ed. Margaret Cowell and Sarah Lyon-Hill (Blacksburg: Virginia Tech Publishing, 2022), 41–58.

12. Atkinson, *Virginia in the Vanguard*.

13. V. O. Key Jr., *Southern Politics in State and Nation* (New York: Knopf, 1949).

14. Dabney, *Virginia*.

15. Stephen K. Medvic, "Forging 'Debatable Ground': The Transformation of Party Politics in Virginia," in *Government and Politics in Virginia: The Old Dominion at the 21st Century*, ed. Quentin Kidd (Needham Heights, MA: Simon & Schuster, 1999).

16. Black and Black, *The Rise of Southern Republicans*.
17. Dabney, *Virginia;* Kristen Green, *Something Must Be Done about Prince Edward County: A Family, a Virginia Town, a Civil Rights Battle* (New York: Harper, 2015).
18. J. Harvie Wilkinson III, *Harry Byrd and the Changing Face of Virginia Politics, 1945–1966* (Charlottesville: University Press of Virginia, 1968).
19. Donald Baker, "Why They Mattered: Harry F. Byrd Jr., 1914–2013," *Politico,* December 2013.
20. Larry J. Sabato, *The Democratic Party Primary in Virginia: Tantamount to Election No Longer* (Charlottesville: University Press of Virginia, 1977).
21. Dabney, *Virginia.*
22. Bruce J. Dierenfield, *Keeper of the Rules: Congressman Howard W. Smith of Virginia* (Charlottesville: University Press of Virginia, 1987); Wilkinson, *Harry Byrd and the Changing Face of Virginia Politics, 1945–1966.*
23. Black and Black, *The Rise of Southern Republicans;* Mark Rozell, "Virginia," in *The New Politics of the Old South,* 7th ed., ed. Charles S. Bullock III and Mark J. Rozell (Lanham, MD: Rowman & Littlefield, 2021).
24. Atkinson, *Virginia in the Vanguard.*
25. Ibid.
26. Chuck Robb, *In the Arena: A Memoir of Love, War and Politics* (Charlottesville: University of Virginia Press, 2021).
27. R. H. Melton, "Methodical Robb Proves Master at Art of Politics: Robb Described as Leader Who Turned Va. Democrats into a Version of GOP," *Washington Post,* October 28, 1988.
28. Black and Black, *The Rise of Southern Republicans.*
29. Sherwood, "Robb: New Image for State."
30. Atkinson, *Virginia in the Vanguard;* Black and Black, *The Rise of Southern Republicans.*
31. Nan Robertson, "Lynda Johnson Is Wed in White House; Reminders of War Touch Ceremony in East Room," *New York Times,* December 10, 1967.
32. Glenn Frankel and Donald P. Baker, "Robb's Political Baptism Slow, Painful," *Washington Post,* September 14, 1981.
33. Ibid.; Melton, "Methodical Robb Proves Master at Art of Politics."
34. Frankel and Baker, "Robb's Political Baptism Slow, Painful."
35. Ibid.
36. Ibid.
37. Bart Barnes, "Henry E. Howell Dies," *Washington Post,* July 8, 1997.
38. Ibid.
39. Ibid.
40. Atkinson, *Virginia in the Vanguard.*
41. Frankel and Baker, "Robb's Political Baptism Slow, Painful."

42. Sherwood, "Robb: New Image for State."

43. Barnes, "Henry E. Howell Dies."

44. Jack Eisen, "Robb vs. History: He Won: Robb's Breakthrough for Northern Virginia," *Washington Post*, November 5, 1981.

45. Ibid.

46. Atkinson, *Virginia in the Vanguard.*

47. Donald Baker, *Wilder: Hold Fast to Dreams* (Cabin John, MD: Seven Locks Press, 1989).

48. Kay Monaghan Knickrehm, B. Douglas Skelley, and Devin C. Bent, "Partisan Realignment and Decomposition: The Virginia Case," *Journal of Political Science* 11, no. 1 (1983): 31–39, 34.

49. Marshall J. Coleman, "Chuck Robb Didn't Do It All: And Not Everything Was Great during His Administration," *Washington Post*, January 7, 1986.

50. Virginia Department of Elections, *Historical Elections Database* (accessed May 21, 2021), https://historical.elections.virginia.gov/.

51. Gregory S. Schneider, "In Virginia's Coal Country, a Democratic Challenger Makes His Case to Trump Voters," *Washington Post*, October 31, 2018.

52. Gregory S. Schneider, "Democrats Wexton, Luria and Spanberger Unseat Republicans Comstock, Taylor and Brat, while Kaine Cruises in Virginia," *Washington Post*, November 6, 2018.

53. Stephen J. Farnsworth and Stephen P. Hanna, "Why Republicans Lost in Virginia—in Three Great Maps," *Washington Post*, November 12, 2013.

54. Sherwood, "Robb: New Image for State"; Sherwood, "Robb: Democratic Enigma."

55. Dendy quoted in Atkinson, *Virginia in the Vanguard*, 45.

56. Andrews quoted in Atkinson, *Virginia in the Vanguard*, 46.

57. Matt Bai, "Nascar-Lovin'," *New York Times*, September 15, 2002; David Beiler, "Mark Warner's Five-Year Plan," *Campaigns & Elections* 22, no. 10 (December 2001/2002): 34.

58. Katherine France, "Cultivating Effective Practices in Government and Policy-Making: Summary of an Interview with Virginia Governor Mark Warner," *Policy Perspectives* 12 (March 31, 2005); Garrett Graff, "Is Mark Warner the Next Bill Clinton?," *Washingtonian*, February 2006; Sara Hebel, "A Businessman Bridges the Political Aisle," *Chronicle of Higher Education*, February 25, 2005.

59. Copeland, "Don't Call Him Redneck"; Jim Webb, *A Time to Fight: Reclaiming a Fair and Just America* (New York: Broadway Books, 2008).

60. Webb, *A Time to Fight.*

61. Stephen J. Farnsworth, "How a Jim Webb Independent Presidential Bid Could Actually Matter (Hint: Virginia)," *The Fix* (blog), *Washington Post*, November 29, 2015.

62. Rachel Weiner, "Jim Webb Will Not Run for President as an Independent," *Washington Post,* February 11, 2016.
63. Stephen J. Farnsworth, Stephen P. Hanna, and Benjamin Hermerding, "Warner's Moderate Approach Is Falling Out of Favor," *Charlottesville Daily Progress.* November 23, 2014.
64. Stephen J. Farnsworth, Stephen P. Hanna, and Kate Seltzer, "Declining Rural Influence in Virginia Politics: Comparing Mark Warner's 2001 and 2020 Elections," in Cowell and Hill, *Vibrant Virginia,* 41–58.
65. Laura Vozzella, "No TV Ads, No Presidential Visits: Virginia's Era as a Swing State Appears to Be Over," *Washington Post,* September 18, 2020.
66. Norman Leahy, "Virginia Republicans Aren't Completely Out of the Picture," *Washington Post,* November 6, 2020; Bob Lewis, "A Commonwealth Divided? Republican Rural Virginia Loses Ground to Democrats' Suburban Strongholds," *Virginia Mercury,* November 11, 2019; Schneider, "Democrats Wexton, Luria and Spanberger Unseat Republicans"; Gregory S. Schneider and Laura Vozzella, "With Blue Cities and Red Rural Areas, the Suburbs Are the New Political Battleground," *Washington Post,* November 7, 2018.
67. Vozzella, "No TV Ads, No Presidential Visits."
68. Antonio Olivo, "After Fueling a Blue Tide, Democrats in Changing Virginia Suburb Aim High for More Influence," *Washington Post,* January 4, 2021.
69. Farnsworth, "Virginia Politics, Washington-Style"; Farnsworth, "The Yin and Yang of Virginia Politics"; Farnsworth, "Virginia Voters and Decentralized Governmental Power: Federal Frustration and State Satisfaction?," *Virginia Social Science Journal* 50 (Spring 2015): 81–90; Farnsworth, "How Gerrymandering Cost Virginia Its Medicaid Expansion," *Washington Post,* January 18, 2015.
70. Farnsworth, "Virginia Voters and Decentralized Governmental Power"; M. V. Hood, Quentin Kidd, and Irwin L. Morris, "Race and the Tea Party in the Old Dominion: Split-Ticket Voting in the 2013 Virginia Elections," *PS: Political Science & Politics* 48, no. 1 (2015): 107–14.

5

Breakthrough

THE RISE AND 1989 GUBERNATORIAL ELECTION OF L. DOUGLAS WILDER

Julian Hayter

> Not surprisingly, the ensuing pride in seeing our state climb in rank among our sister states in the nation and in pre-eminence among the Southern states, causes Virginians everywhere to feel good about our cause, our mission, and our success in forging Virginia's New Mainstream. That commitment to looking ahead rather than behind—of building rather than destroying, of bringing people together rather than pitting them against each other—also calls for me to address you with measured sobriety in facing conditions in the commonwealth today.
>
> —L. Douglas Wilder, "Inaugural Address of the General Assembly and to the People of Virginia," January 14, 1990

ON JANUARY 13, 1990, Supreme Court associate justice Lewis F. Powell, himself a native of Virginia, swore in a new governor of the commonwealth, Lawrence Douglas Wilder. Wilder, the grandson of enslaved peoples, became not merely the first African American governor in Virginia but also the first elected African American governor in US history. The nation, it seemed, had come to terms with its tortured racial history. Richmond's and Virginia's history are inextricably linked to race. By the mid-nineteenth century, the capital of the commonwealth had become the largest slave-trading center in the Upper South (experts estimate that Virginians sold millions of slaves to cotton producers in the Deep South).[1] It was also the final home of the Confederacy. In the very building where Wilder was to assume power, segregationists had passed some of the South's most draconian race laws, including the Racial Integrity Act of 1924.[2] After administering the oath of office, Justice Powell said, "It's a great day for Virginia."[3]

Powell recognized the historical gravity of the moment. So too did many Virginians and Americans more generally. An estimated 30,000 people

showed up to witness the ceremony in Capitol Square in Richmond—a record number. Nearly two-thirds of the crowd, the media presumed, were African American. That a Black man was now governor of what was once one
of the wealthiest slave-owning states in the South was not lost on the crowd.
It was not lost on Americans either. Reflecting on Wilder's victory, former
Texas congresswoman Barbara Jordan, herself an instrumental leader in the
civil rights movement, said, "I believe that the victory of L. Douglas Wilder
as governor of Virginia sends a loud signal across this country that the cof-
fin of segregation and discrimination has been nailed shut." Political scientist Merle Black was more cautious. He stated, "Wilder holds a singular
political position among Black politicians, especially in Southern states. He's
a Black politician but does not really have a Black agenda."[4] Both Jordan and
Black were right. The political symbolism of Wilder's election was undeni-
able, but the election had ominous undertones.

This chapter is not a biography of Doug Wilder's political career but
a barometer. Wilder, perhaps because of his success in statewide office,
epitomizes deeper trends in mid- to late twentieth-century Virginia politics (in some cases, American political development writ large). Much
has been made about the political importance of Wilder's gubernatorial
campaign and election. We also know a great deal about the forces of resistance that were deeply concerned about Wilder's election.[5] Very little,
however, has been written about the manner in which Black Virginians,
and Black Richmonders in particular, made Wilder's election possible.
For Wilder was a product of Richmond politics—he owed his political career to Black associationism. Much of his famed political shrewdness was
forged in the crucible of segregationist Richmond politics. Wilder crafted
his color-blind approach to campaigning for statewide office by watching
Black Richmonders change the complexion of city hall during the mid-
twentieth century. Though Wilder may have campaigned as a color-blind
candidate, he, much like his Richmond counterparts, staunchly defended
African American issues while in office. In time, however, his election to
the governorship came to symbolize a darker trend in American politics.
African Americans' electoral victories were often tempered by the continuity of White resistance to political parity.

Wilder's election in 1989 confirmed the clout of Black Democratic voters in Virginia. In the predominantly Black precincts, 96 percent voted for
Wilder over his Republican opponent, Marshall Coleman.[6] Yet these voters, and Wilder himself, did not emerge out of thin air. Virginia's and Richmond's African Americans had long since organized one of the South's

most successful voting constituencies, one that was indistinguishably connected, even if Wilder was not, to the civil rights movement. It is difficult, if not impossible, to understand Wilder's election without Richmond. It is even hard to grasp Wilder's political ascent without coming to terms with Virginia's brand of polite racism. In the end, it was Virginia's brand of racist civility that helped give rise to African American politics in the first place. Richmond's African Americans laid the foundation for Wilder's path to the governorship. During the 1950s and 1960s, Black Richmonders were already influencing local politics—they elected Oliver W. Hill to the city council in 1948, seventeen years before the federal government enacted the Voting Rights Act. They elected another African American councilperson, B. A. "Sonny" Cephas, in 1964. By 1966, Richmonders had elected three African Americans to the city council. Three years later, the very same voters elected Wilder to the state senate. Although Wilder was often peripheral to local political activism, his political career often mirrored the ways Black Richmonders aspired to elected office. They often took a race-neutral (antipartisan) approach to campaigning while remaining deeply committed to racial issues once in office.

Wilder was born and raised among hyperpoliticized Black Richmonders. On the one hand, Black Richmonders like Wilder took to the polls because White political powerbrokers knew they could pay lip service to limited Black political participation without conceding substantial political power. Tidewater Virginians used politics and poll taxes rather than violence to control the segregated system. During the mid-twentieth century, this meant that African Americans often challenged direct disenfranchisement free from the types of violence that characterized racial politics in the Deep South. Richmond's suffrage crusades of the 1960s, this chapter demonstrates, informed the type of politician Wilder became and the manner in which he campaigned for statewide office.[7] The continuity of White racist paternalism and the persistence of African Americans who rose to contest it informed the racial moderation that Wilder rode to the governorship. In fact, Wilder, who often refused to discuss race or answer questions with racial overtones while campaigning for statewide office, learned to negotiate Virginia's brand of regionally specific racial politics in 1960s Richmond.

White resistance to Black governance outlasted the civil rights era and Wilder's governorship. Virginians did not just elect Wilder by the narrowest margin of the twentieth century, Black turnout was eight percentage points higher than White turnout. On the one hand, Whites cast two-thirds of Wilder's votes, which was a stunning result for any African American politician.[8] One the other hand, Wilder purposefully moderated appeals to racial favoritism while on the campaign trail to garner White votes. In time, his election—and its muted appeals to racial politics—came to symbolize a generational shift in Black politics more generally. A generation of Black elected officials—Tom Bradley, Wilson Goode, Richmond's own Roy West—rose from the ashes of the civil rights era and moderated appeals to racial favoritism to get elected.[9] In the end, his election also failed to stop the tidal wave of White antipathy to African American ballots that had been building in the commonwealth since the 1960s, exemplified in the rise of the Republican Party. As African Americans moved into the Democratic Party after 1965, their White counterparts moved out. By 1993, Virginians had swung the pendulum of racial politics back in favor of conservatives by electing George Allen to the governorship. In this way, Wilder's historic victory is also characterized by a more alarming trend in American politics. The United States, experts contend, often oscillates between greater political access and more political restrictions.[10] Moments of political permissiveness are often followed by an era of deep political restriction.

River City Reclamation: Wilder's Early Years

Lawrence Douglas Wilder, the grandson of slaves, was born and raised in the former capital of the Confederacy, Richmond, Virginia. It is impossible to separate the world he grew up in from the politics of race and racial segregation. Wilder was born on January 17, 1931, just east of downtown in the deeply segregated Church Hill area of Richmond. Church Hill overlooked what was once a quasi-free community of enslaved people in Shockoe Valley. There, enslaved peoples once worked in Richmond's multimillion-dollar tobacco industry, iron foundries, and flour mills.[11] During the antebellum period, there were more free African Americans in Virginia (a large percentage lived in Richmond and throughout the Tidewater region) than in any other state in the American South.[12] Wilder was a legatee of this world—and the slave system cast a long shadow over twentieth-century Richmond. Roughly ten years after Wilder's birth, nearly 50 percent of Richmond's census tracts were almost exclusively African American, and nearly every Black Richmonder lived in a handful of almost exclusively segregated enclaves.[13]

Jim Crow segregation shaped Wilder. He attended both Armstrong High School and Virginia Union University. Armstrong, then located in the Jackson Ward area on Prentiss and Leigh Streets, was the first high school in the capital city exclusively set aside for African Americans. The American Baptist Home Mission Society established Virginia Union University during Reconstruction in 1865 in what was then Lumpkin's slave jail (also in Shockoe Valley).[14] Upon graduating from Virginia Union University in 1951 with a degree in chemistry, Wilder was drafted into the army and sent to fight in the Korean War, where he was awarded the Bronze Star for heroic service in combat.[15] Wilder returned to the United States, as did most Black veterans, a second-class (albeit decorated) citizen in a racially segregated world.

Howard University's law school shaped the professional that Wilder became. Like most of Virginia's African Americans during the 1950s, Wilder was unable to attain access to America's prominent White universities and so chose Howard University, where his roommate also happened to be a Richmond native. Henry Marsh III not only eventually became a legendary civil rights attorney, he was also the first African American mayor of Richmond (elected in 1977).

Charles Hamilton Houston, who died in 1950, cast a long shadow over the teaching of law at Howard. His vision of Black lawyering shaped Wilder and Marsh (it also influenced Oliver W. Hill, Spottswood Robinson, and, ultimately, Thurgood Marshall, all of whom were essential to the litigation strategy that upended de jure segregation in public schools).[16] As dean of Howard University's law school and past chief counsel of the NAACP, Houston instilled in Howard students a specific type of Black lawyering.

Houston spent the better portion of the mid-twentieth century turning Howard into a veritable cottage industry for churning out politicized Black lawyers, or what he called social engineers. These engineers were, according to Houston, to be spokesmen for Black communities.[17] Social engineering stressed the need for lawyers to appreciate both the intricacies of the law and the complexities of racial life in America. Inequity, discrimination, and the denial of full citizenship rights, according to Houston, should not be fought on moral grounds but rather should be challenged in the context of America's social contract, the Constitution of the United States.[18] For Houston, Black lawyers were the primary vehicles of social change. As experts on the law, they were mediators between African American communities and politics; they were representatives, leaders.

Both Wilder and Marsh earned law degrees from Howard University in 1959. And they were influenced by some of the greatest African American lawyers of the civil rights era. Wilder recalled, "I was a great admirer of

Spott, who, along with Hill, had been instrumental in the *Brown* decision and was Thurgood Marshall's right-hand man."[19] Wilder returned to Richmond where he established the law firm Wilder, Gregory & Associates. The politics of segregation too shaped Wilder's professional aspirations.

By the mid-1950s, Wilder and Virginia's African Americans had inherited a commonwealth run by oligarchs. In Richmond and in Virginia more broadly, Harry F. Byrd Sr. and his machine significantly influenced racial politics. Byrd, like the commonwealth's business elites, championed a form of racist civility that not only worked to restrain Whites from deploying mob violence to manage race relations but also made room for modest African American voter registration.[20] Byrd, before his tenure in the US Senate from 1933 to 1965, served as the commonwealth's governor between 1926 and 1930. Byrd, who believed mob violence was bad for Virginia's business culture (policymakers were particularly concerned that rigid racism might preclude Washington, DC, from expanding federal organizations and infrastructure into Virginia), had assumed almost total control over Virginia politics by World War II. Byrd's machine actually derived power by using poll taxes to eliminate voters (both Black and White), exploiting both Virginia's circuit court system (elected officials in the General Assembly appointed judges) and a state constitution that made it difficult to reapportion the General Assembly's districts. Until the mid-1950s, when urban populations began to outpace populations in the commonwealth's rural areas, rural Democrats (particularly from the heavily African American Southwest region of the state) were disproportionately represented in Richmond. The organization also kept rolls of loyal Democratic workers and voters, and Byrd himself often personally supervised a network of patronage and fees within the assembly and the court system.[21] In terms of race relations, unlike states below the Upper South that tolerated (and, often, encouraged) indiscriminate lynching practices, Senator Byrd supplanted mob violence with legal injustice.

Virginia's $1.50 poll tax kept most poor Whites and African Americans out of politics.[22] Early twentieth-century policymakers during the Constitutional Convention of 1901–1902 believed that African Americans lacked the intellectual capacity for politics. And poll taxes affirmed Virginians' belief that good government was synonymous with elite whiteness. Virginia's poll tax also eliminated voters who were more likely to vote against both elites and their political machines, resulting in a small yet manageable electorate that made it extremely difficult for weaker parties and independent candidates to run for office.[23] State law mandated that potential voters had to register for elections and primaries at least thirty days before an election. The annual $1.50 poll tax had to be paid at least six months prior to any particular election. Over time, these regulations ensured that Byrd's organization could pay lip service to limited Black political participation without conceding substantial political power.[24] Red tape often made it difficult for groups outside the Democratic machine to gain political traction. As long as the poll taxes helped Democrats control who voted, it was the Byrd machine that determined whose votes counted.[25] African Americans had other plans.

In Richmond and Virginia, African Americans had organized to meet the challenges of disenfranchisement long before the Voting Rights Act of 1965. To this day, one of the biggest misconceptions about southern politics prior to the Voting Rights Act is that African Americans were not voting at all. While the numbers were disproportionately low, the story of Richmond and Virginia speaks otherwise.

A number of Wilder's mentors found a chink in the Byrd machine's armor as early as the late 1940s. Oliver W. Hill, an integral member of the NAACP's Legal Defense Fund and a close companion of Thurgood Marshall, showed the way. In 1948 alone, Hill and Robinson (himself a graduate of Armstrong High School and Howard University's law program) brought approximately 124 cases against separate school jurisdictions throughout Virginia.[26] Backed by an organization called the Richmond Civil Council, Hill ran for and won a seat on Richmond's city council in 1948. In fact, the *Richmond Times-Dispatch* confirmed the city's interracial support for Hill's candidacy. The newspaper held that Hill had the "best chance of getting elected. . . . The general belief is that he will get enough

TABLE 5.1. Voting in Virginia before and after the Voting Rights Act of 1965

	Pre-VRA number of registered voters (%), 1964	Post-VRA number of registered voters (%), 1967
African American	144,259 (38.3)	234,000 (55.6)
White	1,070,168 (61.1)	1,190,000 (63.4)

Note: VRA, Voting Rights Act. These numbers were estimates from the Voter Education Project from various rolls throughout the Commonwealth of Virginia.

Source: John A. Hannah, *Political Participation: A Study of the Participation of Negroes in the Electoral and Political Process in 10 Southern States since the Passage of the Voting Rights Act of 1965* (Washington, DC: US Commission on Civil Rights, May 1968), 13.

supplemental votes from White citizens to win him a seat."[27] As it pertains to the politician that Doug Wilder became, Hill's interracial support cannot be understated. Hill became the first African American of the twentieth century to serve on a southern city council.[28] And he did it with interracial support, much as Wilder did in 1969, twenty years later. In a field of twenty-nine candidates, Hill finished ninth, receiving 9,097 votes, and a good number of those votes were from White Richmonders.[29] Some 4,095 of those votes were cast in precincts where at least 96 percent of the residents were White.[30] These trends continued into the 1950s.

Though Wilder was only tangentially affiliated with the Richmond Crusade for Voters, the organization shaped the politician that he became. No civic organization did more to democratize local politics in Virginia and Richmond than the Crusade for Voters.[31] Before Wilder ran for and won a seat in the General Assembly's senate, he watched the Crusade change the complexion of Richmond politics—and in time, Wilder took a page from the Crusade's playbook. In 1956, a group of five middle-class African Americans, William S. Thornton, William Ferguson Reid (who in 1967 became the first African American elected to Virginia's House of Delegates since 1891), John Brooks (the NAACP's national voter registration organizer), Ethel T. Overby, and Lola Hamilton, founded the Richmond Crusade for Voters to combat Virginia's "massive resistance" to public school integration. The organization changed Richmond politics in the following critical ways. First, the Crusade recognized that if it could organize to help enough Black people pay their poll taxes, it could swing the balance of power in local elections. Next, it not only remained nonpartisan, it also resolved to influence city council elections by *not* throwing Black votes behind one African American candidate (commonly referred to as single-shot voting). Instead, the organization resolved to manipulate Richmond's at-large voting system. By 1962 the Crusade had registered 27,823—there were roughly 91,000 total African Americans in Richmond in 1960.[32] Under Richmond's at-large system, voters selected nine council members from a slate of candidates. By the early 1960s, the organization's research committee had taken to sending out questionnaires to White candidates. They then threw the Black community's votes behind the least objectionable White candidates in an effort to render these candidates indebted to Black voters. Five years before passage of the Voting Rights Act, the Crusade argued, "If 9,000 colored voters all vote for the same 9 men, these 9,000 votes will put these 9 candidates ahead of the 13 others on the ticket. The same 'balance of power' which will assure election of the nine men who get support of 9,000 colored voters can at the same time unseat several councilmen who are definitely against the rights of colored citizens."[33]

The Crusade for Voters revolutionized Richmond politics (and, in time, paved the road Wilder walked to the state senate in 1970). By 1964 the Crusade had helped elect Richmond's second African American city councilman in the twentieth century, an insurance salesman, B. A. "Sonny" Cephas. One year after ratification of the Voting Rights Act, *Harper v. Virginia Board of Elections* (1966) transformed racial politics in Virginia. The Twenty-Fourth Amendment, which states ratified on January 23, 1964, banned poll taxes in federal elections. The use of these levies, however, was still constitutional in state and local elections. It was an African American from Fairfax County, Virginia, Annie Harper, who filed suit challenging the commonwealth's poll tax. In 1966 the Supreme Court confirmed the Voting Rights Act. It held that the poll taxes put an unconstitutional burden on voters by making income an electoral standard. These taxes, the court held 6–3, thus violated the Equal Protection Clause of the Fourteenth Amendment. The number of Blacks registered to vote jumped from 18,335 in 1964 to 29,388 in 1966; the number of Whites registered to vote, on the other hand, increased by only 4,868, from 52,179 to 57,047.[34] That same year the Crusade helped elect three African Americans to the Richmond City Council—Cephas, Henry Marsh III, and Winfred Mundle. Of Richmond's nine-member city council, then, three were African American a mere one year after ratification of the Voting Rights Act. One year later, Dr. William Ferguson Reid, a founding member of the Crusade for Voters, was elected to Virginia's House of Delegates. And Wilder, it turned out, had his own plans.[35]

Doug Wilder's entry into politics predated his election to the state senate by roughly five years. The future governor emerged in relative opposition to the Crusade. In 1964, Wilder, Ronald K. Charity, and Neverett A. Eggleston established an alternative to the Crusade, Church Hill's Voter's Voice. Both Charity and Eggleston had resolved to run for seats on Richmond's city council, and Wilder endorsed their candidacies by creating an organization on their behalf. Wilder held:

> I knew it was time for African Americans to start winning elections, but I was disenchanted with the organizations that were setting up and endorsing candidates. Our community didn't know its own mind. . . .
> A big part of the problem was that African Americans were organizing around solidarity to a ticket rather than focusing on the issues. I can

remember having frequent arguments, when I would say, "Don't you think we ought to expose people to what the issues are and what they mean?" And they'd reply, "No, we need to maximize solidarity. We need to make certain that people vote the right ticket and that they trust us." This was a point of view that was catastrophic to the cause of justice and equality. It was paternalistic and demeaning. The leaders, who should have known better, were saying, in effect, that African American folks didn't need to be educated, they didn't need to understand the issues, they just needed to vote the "right" way—the way they were told. It made me heartsick.

I knew I had to do something, so I formed my own group, along with three friends, called Voter's Voice.[36]

Charity, as it happened, was not just a nationally ranked tennis player, he was Arthur Ashe's first tennis coach. Eggleston was the owner and operator of Jackson Ward's Eggleston Hotel. The Eggleston Hotel on Second and Leigh Street was a recognized listing in the nationally circulated "Green Book"—a book that listed Black-friendly accommodations for African American travelers. It was one of only three hotels within Richmond's city limits that permitted Black guests. Those who patronized it included Jackie Robinson, James Brown, Martin Luther King Jr. (King actually stopped at the hotel for breakfast before his famous speech in Washington, DC, during the 1963 March on Washington), and Muhammad Ali.[37] All of these men were a part of Richmond's thriving yet segregated Black community. Nonetheless, Voter's Voice thought that Black Richmonders needed more diverse representation. Wilder argued, "The primary purpose of the Crusade is to encourage Negroes to register and vote. [Voter's Voice] is the first organization allowing full voter participation throughout a campaign." The need for political education, Wilder said, was "ever present," and he spent the better portion of the 1960s dedicated to legal and public life. Neither Eggleston nor Charity came close to being elected—it was a lesson that Wilder would not need to repeat again. He eventually cut his teeth in one of the most politicized African American communities below the Mason-Dixon line.

Voter's Voice: Wilder Enters the Political Arena

If local people created the conditions necessary for future elected officials such as Doug Wilder, the Voting Rights Act of 1965 revolutionized southern politics. It gave rise to an outburst of African American registration and voting, broke the nearly century-long stranglehold that segregationists had maintained over southern politics, and eventually led to a veritable complexion revolution in African American elected officials. Wilder was one of hundreds of elected officials who rode the rising tide of racial reform left over from the American civil rights movement.

The Voting Rights Act was the most full-bodied civil rights bill in American history. The act deviated from previous civil rights bills in that it contained both punitive and preventative provisions. It first suspended discriminatory tests and devices as conditions for voting in federal elections. Section 2 forbade voting qualifications, prerequisites, criteria, practices, and measures that might inhibit people from voting—namely, grandfather clauses and literacy tests. The preventative mechanisms went further. They authorized federal examiners to oversee and register voters in areas that were in violation of the law—this provision, detailed in section 4, contained a triggering formula. The triggering process had two specific mechanisms that strengthened the act's supervisory components. States and political subdivisions that used prerequisites for voting were now subject to direct federal scrutiny of the electoral process. These areas could also be subject to preclearance if less than half of voting-age adults had registered or voted on or after November 1, 1964. Section 5, known commonly as the preclearance clause, covered areas in violation of sections 2 and 4. The coverage formula in section 4 applied to all elections, federal, state, and local. Furthermore, the Voting Rights Act prohibited voting laws or election-based changes in states and subdivisions that fell under the triggering mechanism. The preclearance mechanism in section 5 required direct approval from the Department of Justice (the department had sixty days to determine whether the changes were discriminatory) or the district court of the District of Columbia. In other words, covered jurisdictions were prohibited from making any electoral changes without direct approval from Washington.

The years after the ratification of the Voting Rights Act were the most transformative in the history of southern politics.[38] Black southerners registered to vote in record numbers, and the number of voting-age registrants in Virginia rose by nearly 20 percent in two years.[39] The US Commission on Civil Rights estimated in a 1961 report on voting that 100,499 African Americans were registered to vote in Virginia—23 percent of the total voting-age population.[40] Between 1964 and 1972 the number of registered African American voters in Virginia rose by 130,741.[41] By the spring of 1967, the Department of Justice estimated that upward of 416,000 African American southerners had registered to vote. In fact, the number of registered African Americans rose to more than 50 percent in every state covered by the Voting Rights Act. These numbers had profound implications for Black officeholding. In 1966 the number of Black officeholders reached approximately 159. That number rose to 200 by 1967.[42] While the lion's share of Black elected officials held minor posts, African Americans began to change the demographic composition from the local level up.

The rise in African American political activity met firm resistance.[43]

The Voting Rights Act and the racial politics it engendered shook Virginia's segregationists to their core. One of the act's most vocal critics was none other than Harry F. Byrd himself. The ink had barely dried on President Lyndon B. Johnson's bill when segregationists invoked the politics of interposition and the doctrine of states' rights when Byrd was quoted in the Richmond Times-Dispatch, "This so-called Voting Rights Bill of 1965 will demonstrate the bias and prejudice under which the bill was conceived and with which it will be enforced. The bill is literally based on discrimination as between the states."[44] Byrd died roughly six months after the court's decision in Harper, on October 20, 1966. The abolition of poll taxes all but ensured the death of his machine. But it was slow, painful death. The steep increase in number of African Americans voters sounded the death knell for Byrd's constricted electorate.[45] Just before ratification of the Voting Rights Act, African American voters in Virginia numbered approximately 144,000. By 1967, that number had increased to roughly 243,000.[46] The rise in number of African American voters undermined nearly a century of one-party political rule in the Old Dominion. In time, Republicans slowly crept into Virginia politics, especially as African Americans moved into the Democratic Party and Whites moved out. This, of course, was a regional strategy that had implications for Richard Nixon's (and Kevin Phillips's) so-called Southern Strategy.[47] That shift was not immediate, however. Before that, segregationists had to come to terms, if begrudgingly, with Black officeholding.

It was within this context that Doug Wilder first aspired to elected office. A good number of segregationists, including Harry Byrd's son, Harry Byrd Jr., outlived the segregated system in Virginia. Yet the demographic diversification of Virginia politics also gave rise to a new brand of moderate White politicians. In time, no White politician would have a more significant impact on Wilder's initial bid for office in the state senate than a young Democrat in his thirties, Julian Sargeant "Sarge" Reynolds. Reynolds was the son of the founder of Henrico County's (an inner-ring suburb of Richmond) Reynolds Metal company. He was elected one of

TABLE 5.2. African American officeholders in Virginia after passage of the Voting Rights Act, 1965–67

Officeholder	Elected office	Location	Year
William Ferguson Reid	House of Delegates	Richmond	1967
B. A. Sonny Cephas	City Council	Richmond	1966
Henry L. Marsh III	City Council	Richmond	1966
Winfred Mundle	City Council	Richmond	1966
Embria Byrd	City Council	Port Royal	1966
Oliver Fortune	City Council	Port Royal	1966
H. E. Fauntleroy	City Council	Petersburg	1966
Joseph Owens	City Council	Petersburg	1966
Ernest A. Gaines	City Council	Tappahannock	1966
Rev. Lawrence A. Davis	City Council	Fredericksburg	1966
John Wilmer Porter	City Council	Dumfries	1966
Basham Simms	City Council	Purcellville	1966
Charles R. Turner	City Council	Middleburg	1966
James N. Bradby	Sheriff	Charles City County	1967
Iona W. Adkins	County clerk	Charles City County	1967
S. O. Sykes	Board of Supervisors	Southampton County	1967
Moses A. Riddick Jr.	Board of Supervisors	Nansemond County	1967
William M. Cooper	School Board	Hampton	1967
Dr. Thomas H. Henderson	School Board	Richmond	1965
Charles B. Hutcheson	School Board	Lynchburg	1965
David L. Muckler	School Board	Portsmouth	1965
Dr. Waldo Scott	School Board	Newport News	1965
Murrell Owens	Justice of the peace	Greensville	1967
Garland Faison	Justice of the peace	Greensville	1967

Source: Hannah, *Political Participation*, 221.

Richmond's eight representatives to the House of Delegates in 1965. In the years following his election, Sarge had proved himself to be a sincere friend of African American political leadership in Richmond. He came to African Americans' defense in 1966 when local council members attempted to dilute the strength of recently enfranchised voters by staggering elections.[48] Although Reynolds died suddenly in 1971 of a brain tumor, before that he was elected to the state senate and lieutenant governorship, and had befriended Wilder (Reynolds was also responsible for helping establish Virginia's community college system).[49] It was the African

American vote that helped elect Sarge to the House of Delegates. Wilder noted, "I also received help from Reynolds and many of his supporters."[50] According to Dr. Fergie Reid, interviewed in 2005, "After Reynolds sought us out, Whites felt even more comfortable."[51] In fact, moderate Whites started to vote for Black candidates with greater frequency. Even Richmond's city council had two staunch White allies in Howard Carwile and James "Jim" Carpenter.[52] Wilder, feeling the growing tide of interracial support, eventually threw his hat into the ring.

Wilder set the tone as a race-neutral candidate from the outset. The *Richmond Afro-American* announced Wilder's candidacy for the state senate on August 30, 1969. The special election was to be held on December 2, 1969. Wilder, whom many considered one of Richmond's up-and-coming lawyers, said Richmond needed broader Black representation in government.[53] He also recognized that winning an election without White support was an absolute impossibility. As such, Wilder ran, in his own words, not as a Black candidate exclusively but as "a bridge between poor and wealthy, young and the old, and black and white."[54] He was also green, while his opponents were not. Wilder was to face off against Republican Morrill M. Crowe, a former four-year Richmond mayor and third-term city council member, and Fred G. Pollard, a holdover from the segregated system who was a sixteen-year veteran of Virginia's House of Delegates, incumbent lieutenant governor, and Byrd machine Democrat. Wilder was in many ways running as an underdog against an old order. Yet he had unwavering African American support and the support of Black associations, namely, the Richmond Crusade for Voters and the *Richmond Afro-American*.

The matter of vote dilution, which solidified Black support for Reynolds, nearly tanked Wilder's campaign. Black voters met firm resistance after 1965. In 1968 the US Commission on Civil Rights released a report on the state of southern voting titled *Political Participation*. More than half the report was not dedicated to spelling out progress but rather delineated the methods southerners had recently devised to maintain control over Jim Crow legislatures. The most pressing matter was vote dilution (a means of weakening votes after they are cast). In the years after ratification of the Voting Rights Act, White powerbrokers had taken to changing election systems (at-large elections were Whites' system of choice), moving polling places, combining Black and White districts, and annexing predominantly White jurisdictions to dilute Black voting strength.[55] They had also continued older tactics. In the Deep South, Whites threatened candidates with economic reprisal and violence. Richmond took a more genteel, color-blind approach. Beginning in 1968, White officials attempted to annex a jurisdiction of nearly 44,000 White suburban residents of Chesterfield County, with the intent of combining it with the city of Richmond. The city claimed it needed these residents to shore up a weakening tax base. Black people claimed, and the Supreme Court eventually agreed, that the city wanted to annex Chesterfield County to keep Black people (who made up nearly half of Richmond's residents) from taking over city hall.[56] By 1969, Blacks constituted nearly 55 percent of Richmond's total population. The fact that Richmond already had three African American city council members piqued White anxiety about a Black takeover.

Wilder's negotiation of the annexation dilemma proved to be the first example of his brilliance on the campaign trail. He openly supported annexation. The *Richmond Times-Dispatch* stated, "As a negro aware of the fact that the bulk of his support would come from members of his own race, he [Wilder] could have pandered to them [Blacks]. Yet, he risked alienating some of them by advocating expansion of Richmond's boundaries."[57] On the one hand, in supporting annexation for tax reasons, Wilder sought to solidify some White support.[58] On the other hand, he supported annexation only if the city implemented a district-based system to replace the current at-large system used for city council elections. In fact, the Crusade for Voters endorsed annexation so long as Richmond switched from multimember to single-member districts (a strategy that the court eventually supported over the course of the 1970s). Wilder more specifically told the *Richmond News Leader*'s Carl Shires that the city of Richmond should allow for "appropriate district representation."[59] By arguing in favor of county annexation for financial reasons, Wilder petitioned Whites. By asking for appropriate district representation—indeed, an indirect call for single-member district elections—Wilder appealed to the Black political establishment. This pattern of political pandering would come to define the manner in which Wilder campaigned for governorship in 1989. The weekend prior to the election, Wilder visited nine African American churches and crisscrossed Richmond's predominantly Black enclaves in a forty-car motorcade.[60] The Crusade for Voters helped Wilder's efforts by sending out letters to Black residents urging them to vote for Wilder. It all worked out.

On December 2, 1969, Doug Wilder won an unexpected yet imposing victory. He mustered "tremendous margins in predominantly Negro precincts," according to the *Richmond Afro-American*.[61] Richmonders cast

15,839 votes for Wilder, including 2,500 White votes. Wilder's opponents split the White vote—Mayor Crowe garnered 10,318 votes and incumbent lieutenant governor Pollard received 6,115 votes.[62] Crowe carried thirty-seven precincts, Wilder carried thirty-two, Pollard carried none.[63] Wilder became Virginia's first Black state senator in the twentieth century.[64] Just days before the election, Wilder mentioned that he looked forward to a time when all candidates would have the opportunity to run on their own merits, not as a Black or a White candidate.[65] On Election Day, he said,

> I am very conscious that my margin of victory is a plurality and that the bulk of my support came from black citizens. To these supporters I pledge to be a long-needed listing post and vigorous spokesperson for their special concerns and needs. However, the returns indicate that I also received a gratifying number of white votes. I particularly appreciate this support and look forward to the time when all men can run as candidates on their qualifications and not as a Negro candidate or a white candidate.[66]

Wilder did not emerge from thin air. Black political will and the Voting Rights Act revolutionized politics in Virginia. Wilder's election to the state senate represented a new chapter in Virginia politics. Not only were African Americans voting in record numbers, their candidates were getting elected with some White support. Black folks, however, wanted more than symbolic political victories. They were not voting for voting's sake. After nearly a century of neglect, Black southerners saw politics as a way to empower their communities. Voting was a means to an end, a way to gain community control and snatch Black communities back from the clutches of White supremacy. For a good number of African Americans, Wilder's victory was more than symbolic. With the realization of voting rights and the prohibition of poll taxes, African Americans had the political resources to back their demands. But old habits die hard.

The Insider: The Road to the Lieutenant Governorship

Jim Crow institutions and the powerbrokers who maintained them outlived the segregated system. Voting rights ensured the election of Black candidates, but they did little effectively to diversify American politics. Wilder spent the next fifteen years relatively isolated—he was one of only a handful of statewide Black officials. Wilder may have campaigned on consensus, but once in office he established himself as a maverick. He eventually parlayed his position into tangible political power.

Virginia, like much of the South, was struggling to break free from the fetters of Jim Crow justice. The trends initially looked positive. The Voting Rights Act led to a cataclysmic shift in the racial diversification of politics in Virginia. It also forced the commonwealth to revise its fifty-year-old Jim Crow–era constitution. The Commission on Constitutional Revision, assembled by then governor Mills Godwin in 1968, eventually recommended that the commonwealth rewrite the constitution to meet federal civil rights standards. The commonwealth's lawmakers amended the discriminatory voting procedures in Article 2. They also finally mandated antidiscrimination on the basis of race, color, national origin, or sex. African Americans also instigated the demise of the one-party system that had dominated politics in the Old Dominion for most of the twentieth century.[67] Racial diversification split Virginia's Democratic Party, and right-of-center moderates—in particular, Linwood Holton, whom Virginians elected governor in 1969—initiated a trend of unprecedented Republican control of the governorship. Over the course of the 1970s, Virginia elected three consecutive Republican governors—Holton, Mills Godwin (a Byrd machine Democrat who defected from the party) in 1973, and John Dalton in 1977.

Party allegiances were still undergoing profound demographic shifts in the late 1960s and early 1970s. Many of Virginia's African Americans had yet to abandon what they still felt was the party of Lincoln. African Americans were predominantly responsible for Holton's governorship. Holton received roughly 54 percent of Virginia's urban vote and carried fourteen of Richmond's fifteen predominantly Black districts. "Holton," according to political scientist Larry Sabato, "received outright majorities of the black vote in many areas, primarily due to his endorsement by the Richmond Crusade for Voters and other local black organizations."[68] After Holton, Republican candidates, like their national counterparts, grew increasingly conservative. African Americans were just coming to terms with elected office.

Minority voting rights, despite the Machiavellian backlash that emerged in the late 1960s, worked. The tidal wave of political reform gave rise to real if glacial change in electoral results. African Americans in Richmond elected William Ferguson Reid, a respected physician and founder of the Crusade for Voters, to the House of Delegates in 1967 (he assumed office in 1968). William Robinson Sr. of Norfolk, Virginia, became the second

African American member of the House in 1970. "Doc" Robinson, a Nor-folk State political scientist (who, like Wilder, had also studied at Howard University's law school), was Norfolk's first Black elected official since Re-construction.[69] Reid served until 1973, while Robinson stepped away from office in 1982. The total number of African Americans in the General As-sembly never exceeded five members until 1984.

Wilder spent these years making his bones as a political insider. Wash-ington all but ensured Wilder would have little electoral competition in 1971. During that year the Justice Department, under the authority of the Voting Rights Act and the preclearance clause in section 5, demanded that Richmonders elect all state senators from single-member districts rather than at-large senate districts. In fact, Assistant Attorney General David Norman urged Richmond toward single-member districts because the Supreme Court decided to settle the matter of vote dilution. And the court did so by urging localities across the South to implement majority-minority district systems.[70] Most of the city's Black population, it turned out, was eventually packed into Wilder's district. Wilder ran unopposed until 1985, when he threw his hat into the ring for lieutenant governor.

Between 1970 and 1984, Wilder parlayed his position in the state sen-ate into actual political power. In the early 1970s, recently elected African American legislators held no power positions in the General Assembly. Until Robert "Bobby" Scott (now a Democratic US representative for Vir-ginia's Third Congressional District) joined Wilder in the upper chamber, the future governor was the sole Black senator for the commonwealth. His colleagues eventually appointed the future governor to positions of ac-tual influence. Much of this was attributable to Wilder's competence and charm as a politician. During his second term, the senate appointed Wilder to the Privileges and Elections Committee, and he eventually chaired that committee in 1984. He also chaired the Rehabilitation and Social Service Committee for two terms between 1976 and 1980 and led the Transportation Committee for two terms in the early 1980s. Just before leav-ing the senate in 1985 to serve as lieutenant governor, Wilder led the sen-ate's Democratic Steering Committee. Ultimately, he spent the years before 1985 laying the groundwork for executive office. Wilder, however, was more than just ambitious and a skilled political actor. As the first Afri-can American in the upper chamber, Wilder brought his experiences as an African American to bear on the legislative process.[71]

Wilder may have campaigned as a race-neutral candidate and trans-formed into a shrewd political actor, but he also used his political position to fight against the commonwealth's legacy of institutionalized White supremacy. One of Wilder's first challenges to the legacy of the Confederacy was to take on the Virginia state song, "Carry Me Back to Old Virginny." Mandated by a Jim Crow General Assembly in 1940, the state song was replete with racial undertones and overtly racist language. In his first speech on the assembly floor, Wilder openly objected to the song's verse, "That's where this old darkie's heart am long to go." The song had actually been sung at two social gathering for legislators. Even Governor Holton argued that "the appropriate thing would be to change language that is offensive . . . to something not offensive."[72] Wilder went further. On February 16, 1970, he put forward a bill to officially drop the song.[73] It took twenty-seven years to finally demote the song from official status. It took another ten years after 1975 to get the commonwealth to recognize Martin Luther King Jr. Day as an official holiday. No state in the former slave South has more monuments to the Confederacy than Virginia. Virginia also had an official state holiday recognizing fallen Confederate leaders Robert E. Lee and Thomas "Stonewall" Jackson, Lee-Jackson Day (celebrated on January 19). Wilder did not just put forward a bill to honor King, he initially insisted that the name King be added to Lee-Jackson Day. "The drumbeat," Wilder recalled, "against the bill was fierce and steady"[74]—so fierce and steady that Governor Mills Godwin vetoed the bill, which passed the legislature, twice. To which Wilder responded, "I think the Governor has emerged from a cocoon over the years which spelled him out to be a racist."[75]

Wilder's desire to mandate a statewide holiday was genuine, but it was also a clever political maneuver. He knew that a good number of Virginia legislators represented constituencies with large numbers of Confederate sympathizers. These sympathizers also disliked King, whom many White southerners still associated with communism (thanks in large part to the FBI). Proposing a King holiday was a means to draw racists out into the open. These were efforts to demonstrate just how much Virginia had not changed in the post–civil rights era. Wilder wrote in his memoirs, "I saw how much political courage it took for many of my colleagues to vote for the bill. It was embarrassing to some of the people who voted no. They'd apologize to me privately. They'd promise to support me behind the scenes."[76] Wilder's attack on the state song and his proposal to officially recognize King's birthday were just two examples of his growing political acumen.

Wilder also spent the years before 1984 cementing *actual* Black political power. He appointed a number of African American officials and forged alliances with Black political organizations. It was Wilder who proved instrumental in getting the first African American judges elected by the legislature. Virginia named Willard H. Douglas (a Howard University School of Law graduate) to Richmond's juvenile and domestic relations court in 1974. Douglas served as a staff attorney for the US Commission on Civil Rights and practiced law at Richmond's renowned firm Hill, Tucker & Marsh.[77] Wilder also had a role in Godwin's appointment of James Sheffield (yet another Howard University law graduate) to Richmond's circuit court in 1974. Along with Fergie Reid, Wilder was instrumental in establishing and maintaining the Virginia Democratic Black Caucus and the Legislative Black Caucus. These alliances were vital to his campaign efforts in 1984.

Wilder's campaign for lieutenant governor was replete with national and statewide implications. A number of national and state-level trends set the stage for Wilder's 1985 campaign. On the one hand, many of Virginia's White voters had been drifting toward Reaganism and into the Republican Party by the early 1980s. Virginia was the only state in the once solid South not to vote for Jimmy Carter in 1976. Four years later, 53 percent of the commonwealth voted for Ronald Reagan. On the other hand, 95.4 percent of African American voters voted for Reagan's opponent, President Jimmy Carter.[78] African American voter turnout, though only 75.4 percent of Blacks of voting age participated in the election of 1980, was still a force to be reckoned with in the early 1980s. Black voters were almost singlehandedly responsible for the three consecutive elected Democratic governors during the 1980s, starting with Charles "Chuck" Robb. Some 200,000 African Americans voted in Virginia's gubernatorial election in 1981. Experts noted that "since blacks voted overwhelmingly Democrat . . . and since the total black vote exceeded the plurality amassed by each victorious Democrat, black voters were clearly a decisive factor in all three races."[79] Chuck Robb beat his opponent, Marshall Coleman (who had taken a third of the Black vote in his earlier successful bid for attorney general) with 96.4 percent of the Black vote.[80] The right African American might be able to maximize these votes for statewide office.

By 1982, Wilder's reputation as a shrewd political actor was as firmly established as the Black vote. It is difficult to understand Wilder's campaign in 1989 without an understanding of how Richmond shaped the politician Wilder became and his tenure as a state senator. It might be next to impossible to grasp how Wilder won the governorship without coming to terms with his bid for the lieutenant governorship in 1985. Three years earlier, however, Wilder had already outflanked what was left of the conservative elements in the Democratic Party during the US Senate race. If the election of Chuck Robb to the governorship sounded the death knell for the Byrd machine, so too did the retirement of Byrd's son, Harry Byrd Jr., from the US Senate in 1982. A Byrd had held Virginia's US Senate seat for fifty years.[81] When delegate Owen Pickett of Virginia, an incumbent state party chairman, specifically mentioned the name Harry Byrd Jr. in his initial campaign speech, Wilder set out to tank Pickett's bid for the Democratic nomination. In a stroke of political genius, he threatened to leverage the commonwealth's African American vote by running as an independent. After negotiating privately with the Democratic machine, Wilder dropped out a day later. But he'd made his mark. More specifically, he had recognized that he could split the Democratic vote by running as an independent, which would all but guarantee the election of the Republican nominee. Wilder's maneuver not only instigated a drawn-out and deeply acrimonious relationship between himself and Chuck Robb; it also reinvigorated the age-old balance-of-power tactics that were used in the early 1960s to undermine the most objectionable White candidates. Wilder knew there were enough African American voters to swing the election for or against a Democratic candidate. He also demonstrated that he was willing to play hardball in matters of racial politics.

Wilder's skill as a politician and the African American vote aside, the odds of winning the lieutenant governorship were long. The year 1985 just was not that far removed from the Jim Crow era—Pickett had shown that. Put another way, the senior Black member of the General Assembly was not just Black but by Virginia's standards was liberal on social issues, and had been riddled with a host of personal problems. Wilder had been in and out of court for late tax payments, had a history of questionable attorney-client relationships, and had been cited for building code violations on a number of his Richmond properties.[82] Yet as early as January of 1984, Wilder was openly expressing interest in the office. In June 1984, the *Richmond Times-Dispatch* reported that Wilder seemed to be "maneuvering toward a bid for lieutenant governor."[83] The paper was right. In true fashion, Wilder declared his bid for the office on July 3, 1984, stating that he wanted to "see just how far the horizon has stretched" for Virginia's African Americans. He also very purposely made his announcement under a portrait of none other than Harry Byrd Sr.[84]

In his 1985 campaign for the lieutenant governorship, Wilder negotiated racial anxiety masterfully. Shrugging off some of the residual resentment left over from the Pickett ordeal, Wilder outmaneuvered his Republican opponent, John Chichester, in several ways. First, he ran as a color-blind candidate. In doing so he put his opponent on the defensive. Wilder said that referring to him as a liberal had racial rather than political implications. Second, Wilder embarked on the now legendary two-month, 4,000-mile wagon trek through Virginia's rural and small town areas. In his memoirs he recalled, "My nephew Michael was enlisted to drive the station wagon that would serve as my campaign 'bus,' and my son Larry, a law student, accompanied me. I still have the wall-size map detailing every stop of the tour through the heart of Virginia."[85] Wilder set out on the trail to familiarize himself with White voters who had historically proven reluctant to support Black candidates, starting the trek in one of Virginia's most racially rigid regions—the coal-mining regions of Southwest Virginia. He drew on his military service and Virginia values in engaging with Whites. Third, the future governor, along with his campaign manager, Paul Goldman, conserved campaign donations by relying on a thin staff, which allowed them to purchase the greatest amount of television advertising possible (one advertisement emphasized Wilder's tough approach to crime by featuring a rural White sheriff with a strong southern drawl). In time, Wilder outspent Chichester 2.5 to 1—he spent $400,000 on television time, compared to Chichester's $135,000. In total, Wilder spent nearly $700,000 to win the lieutenant governorship. Republicans, we know now, misjudged his candidacy. At the party convention in June one Republican stated, "If Chichester's alive on Election Day, he's in."[86]

Wilder's election in 1985 was nothing short of historic. Democrats swept the executive positions. Gerald Baliles beat Republican Wyatt Durrette by 149,786 votes and Mary Sue Terry beat W. R. Buster O'Brien even more convincingly, by 302,539 votes. Wilder's race was far and away the closest. He won by 48,634 votes. Wilder won 52.6 percent of votes in Virginia's urban corridor, 48.8 percent of the suburban vote, and 50.3 percent of the rural vote.[87] Although he lost the White vote by a 44 to 56 percent margin, the proportion of White votes he did get was historic. His road trip also paid huge dividends: Wilder won the Ninth Congressional District, the Southwest region of Virginia, 54.4 to 45.6 percent.[88] He won an astounding, if predictable, 96.6 percent of votes from African Americans in predominantly Black precincts. Terry did well with Black voters downticket in the race for attorney general, receiving 95.6 percent of votes in predominantly Black precincts. Baliles took 94.1 percent of votes from predominantly African American precincts to win the governorship.[89]

Larry Sabato has pointed out that a statewide sample of Election Day exit polls asked voters, "Are you aware of anything historically significant about this year's Virginia state election?"[90] Of those who answered,

46 percent of African Americans specifically referred to Wilder's race, while only 27 percent of Whites mentioned the Wilder race. In Virginia's most heavily populated areas with a sizable number of African Americans, Wilder soundly defeated Chichester. Wilder received 79.7 percent of the Black vote in Virginia Beach, 91 percent in Charlottesville, 87.8 percent in Hampton, roughly 98 percent in Newport News and Norfolk, 98.3 percent in Portsmouth, 97.5 percent in Richmond, and 95.9 in Petersburg. A total of 38,649 African Americans cast votes for Wilder in these districts. They wanted material results.

A Great Day for Virginia: The Campaign of 1989

In 1985, the movement from protest to politics seemed to be well under way, and Wilder's election to statewide office stamped the importance of federal voting rights mandates. The Voting Rights Act led to a seismic shift in Virginia and southern politics. African Americans, it seemed, had triumphed over the forces of disenfranchisement. Wilder's victory, however,

TABLE 5.3. Results of 1985 election for state executive positions

Candidate, 1985	Total no. of votes	Percentage
Governor		
Baliles (D)	742,438	55.2
Durrette (R)	601,652	44.8
Write-ins	153	—
Total	1,343,243	100.0
Lieutenant governor		
Wilder (D)	685,329	51.8
Chichester (R)	636,695	48.2
Write-ins	89	—
Total	1,322,113	100.0
Attorney general		
Terry (D)	814,808	61.4
O'Brien (R)	512,269	38.6
Write-ins	67	—
Total	1,327,144	100.0

Source: Sabato, *Virginia Votes 1983–1986*, 64, 87.

overshadowed an intensifying crisis in Virginia—many African American communities were no better off after ratification of the Voting Rights Act than before. If voting was a means to community control, statewide politics had done very little to redirect material resources and public service deliverables to some of the commonwealth's most vulnerable communities. Wilder's bid for the governorship was an even more delicate dance. By 1989, deepening economic and social problems characterized many of Virginia's African American communities, especially in Wilder's hometown of Richmond.

Jim Crow segregation gave rise to problems that outlived the segregated system. African Americans in Virginia were already struggling to recover from segregation by the 1970s. The achievement gap was staggering. African Americans made up roughly 18.5 percent of Virginia's population in 1970. Thirty percent of African American families were living below the poverty level—15 percent more than the national poverty rate for adults between the ages of eighteen and sixty-four. By 1980 African Americans made up roughly 19 percent of the commonwealth's population.[91] In 1970 the Black unemployment rate was 5.4 percent, more than double the White unemployment rate of 2.5 percent. By 1980 the unemployment rate had not merely risen, it was still more than double the rate of Whites—9.1 percent to 4.1 percent. In terms of educational attainment, in 1970, 72.2 percent of White Virginians had a high school education or more. The figure for African Americans was less than half that, at 46 percent.[92]

The economic and social disparities between Virginia's Whites and Blacks had barely improved by 1989, the same year Wilder campaigned for the governorship. By 1990, African Americans made up roughly 19 percent of Virginia's total population. The average household income for an African American family in Virginia was $27,053—White families were nearly double at $44,634. Some 7.4 percent of the commonwealth's Whites were living below the poverty level; that figure was triple for African Americans, 22.4 percent. African Americans' unemployment rate stood at 8.9 percent, while the White unemployment rate was 3.5 percent.[93] The situation in Wilder's hometown of Richmond was even more dire. The city of Richmond was more segregated by race and class in 1980 than it had been in 1940.[94] By 1985, Richmond's murder rate, 41.0 per 100,000 residents, was second only to that of Gary, Indiana—and Richmond was also the murder capital of the state of Virginia. Richmond, the *Times-Dispatch* held, was becoming "increasingly a city of the wealthiest Whites and the poorest Blacks." Thirty-eight of Richmond's sixty-nine total census tracts were predominantly, and in many cases almost entirely, racially homogeneous. Trends were under way at the Capitol, within earshot of many of Richmond's poorest African American communities, that belied the progressive narrative of the post–civil rights era.

During the late 1970s and 1980s, the General Assembly embarked on a campaign of anti-urbanism that had serious implications for racial politics during the late 1980s. Virginia's system of city and county independence, commonly referred to as Dillon's Rule, holds that cities and counties have no authority to work with one another without an explicit mandate from the General Assembly. By the 1970s, unprecedented White flight out of cities such as Richmond (which began, in part, as passive resistance to public school integration in the 1960) allowed great suburban and rural representation in state government. The suburbanization of jobs and politics followed the suburbanization of White people. As cities' tax bases depleted in the commonwealth, they, like most American cities, appealed to expand their borders to meet economic challenges. The commonwealth's policymakers responded to the deluge of annexation suits (appeals to expand city borders, sometimes to meet legitimate growth demands, at other times to preclude African Americans from assuming municipal power) during the 1960s by placing a moratorium on boundary expansions in cities with more than 125,000 residents.[95] Moratoriums on boundary expansions also had racial and political overtones. Most of Virginia's cities in the late 1970s and early 1980s with populations over 125,000 had large African American populations. In 1979 the General Assembly passed House Bill 603, which significantly altered all future annexation hearings in Virginia and gave counties the right to appeal for immunity from all future annexations. Chesterfield, Henrico, Prince William, Roanoke, and York Counties immediately filed for this immunity.[96] These counties and others nullified all future boundary expansion. In 1987 the General Assembly extended moratoriums on boundary expansions to include areas with populations greater than 50,000 or a density of 140 persons per square mile and 20,000 residents, or both.[97] Many of Virginia's cities remain landlocked to this day. These ostensibly color-blind initiatives had grave political implications for the late 1980s.

The shockingly low number of African American representatives during the 1980s was attributable to these initiatives and the political cartography that so often characterizes the drawing of district boundaries. The structure of elections matters. In 1980, only five of all of Virginia's counties were at least 50 percent African American. Of the commonwealth's 3,104 total elected officials, African Americans made up only 124, or roughly 4 percent (even though African Americans made up nearly 19 percent of Virginia's population). As late as the early 1980s there were only four African Americans in the House of Delegates—James S. Christian, Bobby Scott, Benjamin Lambert, and William P. Robinson Jr.—plus Wilder in the senate. Much of this was attributable not only to residential patterns but also to the districts that policymakers had drawn around them. Before 1983, Virginia's House of Delegates elected its one hundred members from twenty single-member districts, twenty at-large districts, and four single-member districts where the boundaries incorporated other districts (known as floater districts).[98] Only one multimember district in the House had the possibility of a Black voting majority. All of Virginia's four African Americans were elected, quite predictably, from safe minority districts. In other words, the possibility of gaining enough White votes to be elected to an at-large seat was still difficult for Virginia's Black candidates well into the 1980s. At the local level, in 1980, Virginia had forty-two counties that were at least 20 percent African American. In those counties, African Americans held thirty-three positions as county governing board officials and five as law enforcement officials, yet none on a school board. Nineteen of those forty-two counties had no Black county officials at all. Fifteen years after ratification of the Voting Rights Act, African Americans made up 4.1 percent of elected officials in the commonwealth: 124 of 3,041.[99] Efforts to preclude boundary expansions in Virginia also meant that suburban and rural constituencies were still disproportionately represented in the General Assembly (the politics of region remained a holdover from the Byrd era) during the early 1980s. By the 1980s, a good number of Virginia's legislators were from rural and suburban districts that were predominantly racially homogeneous. Even newly elected members were disproportionately rural.

This began to change slowly after 1982 when Washington, under the authority of the Voting Rights Act, and voting rights litigation specifically called into question the structure of state elections.[100] Following the 1987 legislative elections, Democrats still outnumbered Republicans in the House of Delegates by sixty-five to thirty-five and in the state senate by thirty to ten. Wilder and African American Virginians represented only a slim proportion of the commonwealth's lawmakers.[101]

The continuation of racist trends in Virginia's political culture forced Wilder to campaign differently than he governed. African Americans made up 18.9 percent of Virginia's total population in 1980.[102] As such, on the campaign trail, Wilder was less Jesse Jackson and more Tom Bradley; he campaigned as a moderate Black candidate whom racially liberal Whites found acceptable. He was, for all intents and purposes, the least objectionable Black candidate. In 1985, Wilder, who campaigned as a tough-on-crime, moderate Democrat, helped create a blueprint for African American candidates running for office in predominantly White areas. He was not alone. Wilder borrowed from a playbook devised by political pioneers, namely, mayors such as Carl Stokes, Wilson Goode, and Tom Bradley.[103] The story of African American politics in the twilight is awash with instances of technocratic, African American politicians who supplanted their civil rights era predecessors.[104] These Black politicians often emphasized economic pragmatism and political moderation. They also built public and private coalitions by downplaying appeals to racial favoritism and the Great Society. Urban planner and deputy mayor of New York City J. Philip Thompson contends that once Black politicians "accepted the practical limitations on advocacy and policy change required by their new, often fragile, coalitions with business and White liberal reformers," they often struggled to address the needs of increasingly vulnerable communities.[105] Wilder's contribution to race and American political development is that he used this strategy to campaign for statewide rather than municipal office.

Wilder's bid for the governorship against former state attorney general and Republican Marshall Coleman had gained significant momentum by January 1989. By the late 1980s, Wilder was already a political icon throughout Virginia's African American communities. After ten long years, in 1984 Wilder's push to officially honor Martin Luther King Jr. in

TABLE 5.4. Number of new members in Virginia general assembly, 1983–89

Year	Senate			House			Entire Assembly		
	Urban	Rural	Total	Urban	Rural	Total	Urban	Rural	Total
1983	3	2	5	6	0	6	9	2	11
1985	—	—	—	5	3	8	5	3	8
1987	5	1	6	6	6	12	11	7	18
1989	—	—	—	8	6	14	8	6	14

Note: Dash denotes no election.
Source: Data from Sabato, Virginia Votes 1987–1990, 75.

the commonwealth finally passed the General Assembly, and Governor Chuck Robb made Lee-Jackson-King Day official in April 1984. Honoring King along with Robert E. Lee and Stonewall Jackson epitomized the state of Virginia's political affairs in the 1980s. Wilder had to maintain Black support without alienating Whites. He very gingerly cozied up to Jesse Jackson, who was at the time running a strong campaign for the Democratic presidential nomination. In fact, Wilder was instrumental in helping Jackson win the Virginia primary with 45 percent of the vote in 1988. The Jackson association was not without controversy. Wilder's support for Jackson added to the already palpable sense of tension between Wilder and Chuck Robb, who was at the time running for the US Senate. Robb argued that Jackson should play an inspirational, not managerial, role in the presidential competition, enraging both the Black Democratic establishment and Virginia's African Americans generally.[106] Wilder's association with Jackson's campaign not only helped Wilder's cause with African American voters, it also gained the lieutenant governor a national audience. Yet Wilder would not win the governorship in Virginia running on Jackson's brand of hyperliberalism (designed to unite poor White and left-wing activists with African Americans). Wilder recognized that he would need to run a moderate, color-blind campaign. As Wilder recalled in his memoirs,

> Jesse Jackson's strong showing in the 1988 Democratic primaries helped me as voter registration efforts added new voters to the rolls. However, when Jackson won the Virginia primary with 45 percent of the vote, many mainstream Virginians were inclined to associate our party with far-left liberalism. I had to get my centrist message out against a tidal wave of anti-Jackson sentiment.[107]

By 1989, as the campaign gained momentum, it was clear that Wilder had no Black or liberal agenda.

The election of 1989 was one of the only two governor's races that year, and it drew both national and statewide attention. Not only was Wilder running as an African American in a state struggling to free itself from the shackles of segregation, his campaign also had to contend with the unforeseen issue of abortion and a mineworkers' strike in Southwest Virginia. Wilder ran unopposed in the primary. The Democratic Party feared that not nominating Wilder would alienate recently enfranchised African American communities—the very communities that were still struggling to come to terms with the end of segregation. The party also knew that Wilder was virtually guaranteed Black and liberal White votes. Indeed, the certainty of these votes gave Wilder the latitude he needed to move toward the center. As he had in 1969 and 1985, Wilder deemphasized the historic nature of his campaign. He ran as a candidate of consensus.[108] As it happened, abortion proved to be one of the most important issues of the campaign—even more than race. On July 3, 1989, the Supreme Court set the issue. The justices held (5–4, in *Webster v. Reproductive Health Services* [1989]) that states now had more authority to determine abortion policies.[109] The case engendered a tidal wave of pro-choice sentiment that Wilder resolved to capitalize on. Larry Sabato recalled that the abortion matter helped Wilder for two reasons. First, Wilder eventually endorsed a limitation on parental notification for minor-age girls seeking the procedure. This placated those in the middle of the issue. Second, he then tapped into the long-standing if implicit vein of libertarianism in Virginia politics by arguing that the state should keep out "of the most personal decision a woman will ever have to make." This stance, we know now, ingratiated Wilder with White women who might otherwise have been skeptical of his blackness. Ultimately, the issue helped Wilder portray his opponent as an extremist.[110]

The mineworkers' strike was a different matter altogether. It exposed deep weaknesses between Virginia's Democrats and working-class Whites in the Southwest. Wilder's second campaign road trip was different from the first; as lieutenant governor, he now had to answer for the Baliles administration's policies. This proved particularly difficult in Southwest Virginia (the same areas that added the momentum necessary for his successful campaign in 1984). In April 1984, roughly 1,400 of Virginia's United Mine Workers began a strike against Pittston Coal Group, a Pennsylvania company that ran the largest mine in the commonwealth. Wilder, who had carried Southwest Virginia handily in 1984, attempted to forge a middle ground (in the 1980s, unions in Virginia still voted heavily Democratic). Wilder not only tried to forge alliances between Pittston and the union, he attempted to deflect heat from his campaign by taunting Coleman. At various stops in Southwest Virginia, Wilder said of Coleman, "I dare him to come here." While Wilder attempted to drum up labor support by quietly maneuvering to undo Virginia's right-to-work laws, Coleman's campaign in Richmond frequently accused him of selling out to the union.[111] In reality, the coal miners began to associate Wilder with Baliles's deployment of state troopers. Wilder struggled to recover.

Unanticipated racial issues also dogged the campaign. Things particularly heated up in September during Greekfest, an event in Virginia Beach that involved thousands of primarily African American students from various colleges and universities on the East Coast. Greekfest had not been without controversy, and the city had attempted to ban the festival after several incidents between students and the police had transpired the previous year. In 1989, things got worse. Harry Kollatz Jr. of the *Richmond Magazine* recalled that "the students instead came in greater numbers, with groups chanting the refrain to the Public Enemy song 'Fight the Power.' As police attempted to clear the streets, rioting erupted, and young people collided with officers and National Guard troops. Arrests extended to bystanders who were not involved." After several days of looting and confrontations with the police, the incident died down. National and local pundits attempted to place blame solely in Wilder's lap. Republican strategist and columnist Pat Buchanan argued on *The McLaughlin Group* show that the incident would kill Wilder's chances.[112] Wilder again forged a middle ground between African Americans who were skeptical of the police and White critics who wanted the students punished for years of unruly behavior. He emerged relatively unscathed. His "soft-spoken, well-tailored, dignified, and nonthreatening" manner eclipsed the issues.[113]

Wilder's victory in 1989 was slim but historic. His hometown newspaper endorsed Coleman. The *Richmond Times-Dispatch* specifically referred to Wilder as duplicitous for attempting to undermine the state's right-to-work laws. By contrast, they said Coleman "has the experience, the integrity, the intelligence, and the temperament to make a superb governor."[114] Many Virginians disagreed. Wilder won the governorship by the slimmest margin in Virginia's twentieth-century political history. Out of 1,789,078 total votes, Doug Wilder beat Marshall Coleman by 6,741 votes. Coleman received more votes than any winning candidate during the past gubernatorial elections.[115] Democrats also swept the other executive office positions—Donald Beyer won lieutenant governor and Mary Sue Terry held on as attorney general. Wilder's victory owed in large part to Virginia's most heavily populated areas. He racked up large margins in Northern Virginia and Hampton Roads. While he lost much of the geography of the commonwealth, he again won Richmond, portions of Southwest Virginia, and a number of college towns, including Charlottesville–Albemarle County (the University of Virginia), Williamsburg (the College of William & Mary), and Montgomery County (Virginia Tech University).

The election of 1989 was chock-full of regional and racial implications. Wilder beat Coleman in five of Virginia's ten congressional districts.[116] Ninety-six percent of African Americans voted for Wilder. As the polls closed, it became clear that African Americans had made the difference in District 1, Newport News–Hampton; District 2, Norfolk–Virginia Beach; District 4, Tidewater; and Districts 8 and 10, Northern Virginia. Eighty-two percent of liberals voted for Wilder and, extraordinarily, so did 4 percent of conservatives.

Race aided Wilder's campaign in a number of ways. First, he ran unopposed in the primary because the commonwealth's Democrats did not want to alienate Black voters. His support for Jesse Jackson helped spotlight the election nationally. In fact, national Democrats contributed large amounts of money to his campaign. In terms of media attention, Wilder had always been a matinee idol. The 1989 contest was the only major election of the year. The national media not only focused their gaze on Virginia, the race also contributed to Wilder's favorability in the

TABLE 5.5. Results of 1989 election for state executive positions

Candidate, 1989	Total no. of votes	Percentage
Governor		
Wilder (D)	896,936	50.1
Coleman (R)	890,195	49.8
Write-ins	1947	0.1
Total	1,789,078	100.0
Lieutenant governor		
Beyer (D)	934,377	54.1
Dalton (R)	791,360	45.8
Write-ins	537	—
Total	1,726,274	100.0
Attorney general		
Terry (D)	1,096,095	63.2
Benedetti (R)	638,124	36.8
Write-ins	310	—
Total	1,734,529	100.0

Note: A dash indicates no election.
Source: Data from Sabato, *Virginia Votes 1987–1990*, chap. 5.

TABLE 5.6. Voting in selected predominantly black precincts, 1989

City	Number of precincts	Total votes cast	Percentage of registered voters voting	Coleman (R)	Wilder (D)
Charlottesville	1	736	67.8	13.5	86.2
Virginia Beach	1	1,131	59.7	24.5	75.5
Hampton	2	3.,258	74.4	9.4	90.6
Newport News	8	6.117	68.6	1.7	98.3
Norfolk	10	11,816	65.3	2.0	98.0
Portsmouth	2	3.216	81.0	1.4	98.6
Richmond	15	12,802	70.9	3.1	96.9
Emporia	1	298	74.0	7.8	92.2
Petersburg	4	2,919	74.5	4.0	96.0
Total	44	42,283	67.8	13.5	86.2
Average of all votes cast			72.6	3.8	96.2

Source: Data from Sabato, Virginia Votes 1987–1990, chap. 5.

media. His opponent was particularly disillusioned by the amount of favorable media attention Wilder received.[117] Coleman actually accused the news media of deploying a double standard in campaign coverage.[118] Virginia's cities disagreed. Fifty-three percent of urban Virginians favored Wilder over Coleman. He also won 58 percent of votes from moderates.[119] The issues mattered, too: Wilder garnered 55 percent of the vote among Virginians who believed that abortion was the campaign's most important issue.[120]

Doug Wilder and Virginians made history. Virginia's voters demonstrated that the election of 1985 was not a one-off, chance occurrence. In electing Doug Wilder to the governorship, Virginia, a former slaveholding state, did what no other state had accomplished. It elected an African American to the state's highest office and, in doing so, nudged the commonwealth a little further away from its tortured racial past. It would take more than political victories alone. By the early 1990s the pendulum had swung back toward not just conservatism, but racial conservatism. Wilder's election did little to beat back the forces of restriction that so often characterize racial advancements in the United States.

TABLE 5.7. Result of Coleman-Wilder gubernatorial contest by congressional district, 1989

Congressional district	Total number of votes	Percent of registered voters voting	Coleman (R), % of vote	Wilder (D), % of vote
1	193,547	71.4	48.9	51.1
2	147,470	64.3	44.4	55.4
3	221,280	71.4	51.6	48.2
4	185,939	72.7	47.8	52.2
5	174,761	71.2	57.9	42.1
6	170,596	71.4	54.0	45.9
7	185,098	67.2	57.2	42.7
8	187,004	56.7	44.2	55.5
9	141,475	64.6	51.8	48.2
10	204,072	58.8	40.5	59.3

Source: Sabato, Virginia Votes 1987–1990, chap. 5.

Conclusion: The Rise of the New Right

Doug Wilder's governorship was not nearly as notable as his election. Almost from the outset, an economic downturn across the United States forced Wilder to cut state spending dramatically. Struggling to close the state's $1.9 billion budget shortfall, Wilder suggested that up to 4,600 state employees retire early, proposed significant cuts to state programs, and recommended a $137 million foray into lottery profits.[121] Several months later Wilder, determined not to raise taxes, announced a $1.4 billion cut, which amounted to roughly 5 percent of the state's budget for two years.[122] In 1991, he signed a $13.1 billion budget, which was accompanied by a handful of vetoes directed at Republicans in the General Assembly. It set a tone of political one-upmanship that came to characterize Wilder's governorship.[123]

Again, Wilder proved more committed to racial issues than his campaign let on. Wilder granted unprecedented access in state government to African Americans and women. Administration figures show his appointments accounted for 40 percent of his agency heads, which doubled that of his immediate predecessor. The amount of state dollars that went to minority contractors also grew significantly, to $71.1 million in 1991 from $46.9 million in 1990. Not to be outdone, on his way out the door, one of

Wilder's final acts epitomized his sensitivity to the politics of race and, perhaps, racial symbolism. In December 1993, Wilder ordered Virginia native and future National Basketball Association star Allen Iverson released from jail. Iverson had been convicted and jailed for involvement in a February 1993 race-inspired brawl at a Hampton, Virginia, bowling alley. Racial implications saturated the incident. There had been long-standing tension between White and Black teens in and around the area. After the dust settled from the fight that sent three people to the hospital, African Americans bore the brunt of the legal charges. Iverson, who many say had little to do with the actual fighting, was made an example of. He was convicted of three felonies and sentenced to five years in prison by a White Hampton circuit judge, Nelson T. Overton. Virginians circled the race wagons over the Iverson incident. Wilder settled the matter in one of his last acts as governor. Wilder, ever the centrist, forged a middle ground—he granted Iverson conditional clemency.[124] There were more ominous political trends on the horizon.

The end of Wilder's governorship, perhaps more than his time as governor itself, contains important qualities that heighten our understanding of race and American political development. In terms of race, the arc of American political development is not linear; it is more like a pendulum. Moments of racial permissiveness and acceptance are almost always followed by eras of either racial restriction or racial conservatism.[125] Virginia politics after 1993 is no exception to this general observation. Wilder's governorship, for all its symbolism, sounded the death knell for Democratic control of state politics in Virginia. The politics of 1991 in Virginia might best be described as a Republican reclamation. For the first time in the twentieth century, Republicans posed a serious threat to Democratic control of the General Assembly. In 1991, thirty-six of the General Assembly's 140 seats changed hands. Republicans now had forty-one of the one hundred House seats, which they pulled off while a Democratic governor, Wilder, and a Democratic majority controlled the redistricting process. In fact, according to Larry Sabato, "Redistricting had effectively cost the GOP seven seats by placing 14 Republican incumbents together in just seven districts. Republicans made up the lost ground primarily by winning 10 of 16 open House seats where no incumbent was on the ballot." Republicans took fifteen of a total of twenty-five open seats.[126] In 1991, Democrats made up twenty-two members of the state senate and fifty-eight members of the House, a result of the Republicans gaining eight seats in the state senate to reach eighteen and two seats in the House to reach forty-one.[127]

Republicans inched closer to a near takeover of the General Assembly during the gubernatorial election of 1993. By 1993, Democrats—Robb, Baliles, and Wilder—had had executive control over the commonwealth for nearly twelve years. In the 1993 election Virginia fell short of making history twice when Republican George Allen obliterated Attorney General Mary Sue Terry in the general election. George Allen, a Republican member of the House of Delegates since 1983, represented parts of Albemarle and Nelson Counties. He ran as a Jeffersonian conservative and campaigned to abolish Virginia's "liberal parole system." He also capitalized on Democratic fatigue (with Wilder and President Bill Clinton) and the emerging rural plus suburban Republican revolt. Terry began her campaign with a "tenfold" advantage in funding and a remarkable twenty-nine-point lead in the polls.[128] Allen eventually soundly defeated Terry by roughly eighteen percentage points, 58 percent to Terry's 40.9 percent. Terry garnered 733,527 votes to Allen's 1,045, 319 votes. Regional politics again mattered. While cities favored Terry by 52.5 percent, she fell remarkably short of Wilder's 68.5 percent in 1989. In fact, Terry had received 72.7 percent of the urban vote in the previous election for attorney general. And Virginia's suburbs and rural areas particularly revolted. Allen received 59 percent of votes from the commonwealth's suburbs and 63 percent of the vote from Virginia's rural areas. Fifty-two percent of women favored Allen over Terry.[129] African American turnout (discussed below) was also remarkably low.

The extent to which antipathy toward Wilder contributed to Terry's defeat is still a matter of debate. A range of other factors contributed. Terry, who had rural Virginia roots and was a long-standing incumbent, seemed to be the clear favorite. She had been campaigning for the governorship since the summer of 1990; Virginians had elected her attorney general with one million votes, the highest voter turnout for the office in the commonwealth's history. Terry's mishaps on the campaign trial may have overshadowed voter fatigue with Wilder and Chuck Robb. In fact, Wilder's and Chuck Robb's growing dislike of one another had become a source of embarrassment for the commonwealth's Democrats (it had become so intense that *Harper's* magazine ran an article by Christine Bridge titled "Virginia Is for Enemies"—an obvious play on the state's motto, "Virginia is for Lovers").[130] Wilder, who planned to challenge Chuck Robb's Senate seat, had been in an enduring battle with the senator over various political power disputes. He eventually ran very briefly for Robb's seat in 1994 as an independent. To be sure, Terry's association with what Allen called the Robb-Wilder-Terry team certainly did not help her campaign. Yet Terry made matters worse by pushing for a five-day waiting period for handgun purchases in a pro–Second Amendment state.[131] There were also other matters at play, namely, racial politics.

African American voters, despite the suburban and rural revolt that characterized the election of 1993, generally failed to support Terry's campaign. Virginia's African American voters were still a force to be reckoned with in the early 1990s. Terry's campaign suffered in large part because African Americans did not show up to the polls. If the politics of hope and symbolism characterized the Black voter turnout during Wilder's campaign for governor, the politics of apathy and fatigue characterized Black support for Terry's campaign. In some ways, it proved to be the Obama-Clinton prequel. Many African Americans believed that Terry had taken their votes for granted. Those African Americans who did vote overwhelmingly favored Terry. She received 86.7 percent to George Allen's 11.4 percent of the Black vote. Yet only 50.5 percent of all registered African American voters showed up to vote in predominantly Black precincts. This number not only paled in comparison to the statewide turnout, which was 61.1 percent, but also in comparison to the previous election's turnout. During Wilder's campaign for the governorship, 72.6 percent of registered Black Virginians showed up to the polls.[132] Terry had openly disagreed with Wilder about tax increases during the recession of the early 1990s and failed to more closely hitch her campaign to his achievements. African Americans seemed to demonstrate their loyalty to Doug Wilder by failing to show up for Terry at the polls. It proved to be one of the first cases in a troubling trend until very recently: when African Americans were not on the ballot, Black Democrats failed to show up.

Even into the 1990s (and perhaps beyond), Doug Wilder's political career was a measure of larger trends in Virginia politics. He was a product of the segregated South. He came to symbolize the demise not only of de jure segregation but also of the promise of federal voting rights mandates. He was also the quintessential Richmonder—he recognized that interracial cooperation was essential to political success in the commonwealth. But so too were African American voters. In the 1970s, for all his appeals to racial moderation and race-neutral campaigning, Doug Wilder never turned his back on Black associationism. The demographic, economic, and political implications of a segregated system, however, outlasted Jim Crow itself.

Wilder, in mastering the art of appealing to White voters, paved the road that Barack Obama took to 1600 Pennsylvania Avenue. Perhaps more than any other elected Black official of the late twentieth century, Wilder negotiated the distance between a growing Black body politic and what remained of racial conservatives. His elections to statewide office were nothing short of remarkable, particularly in Virginia. He is also emblematic of the limitations of racial politics. At almost every step of his political career the forces of restriction were at work. In this way, he embodies the story of Black politics in the post–civil rights era. It is, in one sense, a narrative of triumph. In other ways, however, it epitomizes the forces of restriction that so often characterize (and continue to characterize) the continuity of America's tortured racial history.

Notes

1. Edward E. Baptist, *The Half Has Never Been Told: Slavery and the Making of American Capitalism* (New York: Basic Books, 2016).
2. On the Racial Integrity Act of 1924, see J. Douglas Smith, *Managing White Supremacy: Race, Politics, and Citizenship in Jim Crow Virginia* (Chapel Hill: University of North Carolina Press, 2002).
3. Donald P. Baker, "As Wilder Takes Oath, Virginia Makes History," *Washington Post*, January 14, 1990.
4. Robin Farmer, "Black Leaders across U.S. Salute Wilder, State," *Richmond Times-Dispatch*, November 8, 1989, A-11.
5. Judson L. Jeffries, "Press Coverage of Black Statewide Candidates: The Case of L. Douglas Wilder of Virginia," *Journal of Black Studies* 32, no. 6 (July 2002): 673–97.
6. Larry J. Sabato, "Virginia Governor's Race, 1989: Part 2: General Election," *University of Virginia Newsletter* 66, no. 6 (January 1990): 6.
7. On politicized African Americans in Richmond, see Julian Maxwell Hayter, *The Dream Is Lost: Voting Rights and the Politics of Race in Richmond, Virginia* (Lexington: University Press of Kentucky, 2017).
8. Sabato, "Virginia Governor's Race, 1989," 2.
9. This was particularly true for African American mayors. For more on these generational trends in Black politics, see J. Phillip Thompson, *Double Trouble: Black Mayors, Black Communities, and the Call for a Deep Democracy* (New York: Oxford University Press, 2006) and Clarence N. Stone, *Regime Politics: Governing Atlanta, 1946–1988* (Lawrence: University Press of Kansas, 1989).
10. Tova Andrea Wang, *The Politics of Voter Suppression: Defending and Expanding Americans' Right to Vote* (Ithaca, NY: Cornell University Press, 2012); Karen Orren and Stephen Skowornek, *The Search for American Political Development* (New York: Cambridge University Press, 2004).
11. To meet the challenges of industrialization and urban density, Richmond's industrial slave owners often allowed slaves to live apart. Prior to the

American Civil War, Richmond's slaves developed Black enclaves in areas like Shockoe Creek. These enclaves, instigated by economic need, and the process of hiring out eventually engendered a relative sense of African American autonomy. Not only did many free Blacks live in these areas, African Americans preserved kinship networks and established places of worship and businesses in them. On Richmond's slave community, see Midori Takagi, *Rearing Wolves to Our Own Destruction: Slavery in Richmond, Virginia, 1782–1865* (Charlottesville: University Press of Virginia, 1999), 1, and chap. 2.

12. Smith, *Managing White Supremacy,* 27.

13. Christopher Silver and John V. Moeser, *The Separate City: Black Communities in the Urban South, 1940–1968* (Lexington: University Press of Kentucky, 1995), 34.

14. Hayter, *The Dream Is Lost,* 23.

15. L. Douglas Wilder, *Son of Virginia: A Life in America's Political Arena* (New York: Lyons Press, 2015), 36.

16. For more on the NAACP's legal strategy on the verge of *Brown v. Board of Education,* see Mark V. Tushnet, *The NAACP's Legal Strategy against Segregated Education: 1925–1950* (Chapel Hill: University of North Carolina Press, 1987), chap. 7. For more on Oliver W. Hill and Spottswood Robinson, see Margaret Edds, *We Face the Dawn: Oliver Hill, Spottswood Robinson, and the Legal Team That Dismantled Jim Crow* (Charlottesville: University of Virginia Press, 2018).

17. Genna Rae McNeil, *Groundwork: Charles Hamilton Houston and the Struggle for Civil Rights* (Philadelphia: University of Pennsylvania Press, 1983), 85.

18. McNeil, *Groundwork,* 84.

19. Wilder, *Son of Virginia,* 45.

20. Virginians lynched eighty-six Blacks between 1880 and 1930 (twenty-three Blacks were lynched between 1900 and 1930), which was a relatively low number when compared with that in other southern states. The predominantly coal-mining region of Southwest Virginia had a lynching rate double that of the Tidewater region. Scholars attribute higher lynching rates in the southwestern portion of the state to labor disputes. On lynching, see W. Fitzhugh Brundage, *Lynching in the New South: Georgia and Virginia, 1880–1930* (Champaign: University of Illinois Press, 1993), chap. 1.

21. On the Byrd organization, see Ronald L. Heinemann, *Harry Byrd of Virginia* (Charlottesville: University Press of Virginia, 1996), 12, 44–45.

22. On the one hand, Virginia's poll tax was a panic reaction by White elites to the interracial politics of the late 1870s. William Mahone, a former Confederate general, and his interracial Readjuster Party sought to break the planter elite's ascendancy over state politics by promoting broad-based educational reforms. While the issue of interracial education led to the

Readjuster's demise in 1883, Virginia's policymakers passed literacy tests under the 1894 Walton Act. Rachleff, *Black Labor in Richmond, 1865–1890: Black Labor and the Struggle for Civil Rights after the Civil War* (Champaign: University of Illinois Press, 1989), chaps. 6 and 12.

23. Heinemann, *Harry Byrd of Virginia,* 12.

24. Robbins Gates, *The Making of Massive Resistance: Virginia's Politics of Public School Desegregation, 1954–1956* (Chapel Hill: University of North Carolina Press, 1964), 22.

25. Abigail M. Thernstrom, *Whose Votes Count: Affirmative Action and Minority Voting Rights* (Cambridge, MA: Harvard University Press, 1987).

26. Hill and Spottswood Robinson relentlessly pursued litigation aimed at destabilizing racial segregation by equalizing Black teachers' salaries. These salaries were exponentially lower than their White counterparts' even though most Black teachers had multiple degrees. Richard Kluger, *Simple Justice: The History of Brown v. Board of Education and Black America's Struggle for Equality* (New York: Vintage, 2004), 472.

27. *Richmond Times-Dispatch,* April 18, 1948, 1.

28. *Richmond Afro-American,* June 12, 1984, 1.

29. Ibid.

30. *Richmond Afro-American,* June 12, 1948, 1, and June 19, 1948, 1.

31. Hayter, *The Dream Is Lost,* 3.

32. Richard Wilson, "Crusade for Voters Estimates 8,500 Negroes Voted Tuesday," *Richmond Times-Dispatch,* June 16, 1960, 1; *Richmond Afro-American,* June 18, 1960.

33. *Richmond Afro-American,* June 11, 1960, 1, 6.

34. Lewis A. Randolph and Gayle T. Tate, *Rights for a Season: The Politics of Race, Class, and Gender in Richmond, Virginia* (Knoxville: University of Tennessee Press, 2003), 208.

35. Hayter, *The Dream Is Lost,* 70–73.

36. Wilder, *Son of Virginia,* 150–51.

37. For more on the history of the Eggleston Hotel, see https://www.wric.com /Black-history-month/hidden-history-jackson-ward-hotel-offered-safe -haven-to-Black-travelers-during-segregation/.

38. Charles S. Bullock III, Susan A. MacManus, Jeremy D. Mayer, and Mark J. Rozell, *The South and the Transformation of U.S. Politics* (New York: Oxford University Press, 2019), 83–107.

39. John A. Hannah, *Political Participation* (Washington, DC: US Commission on Civil Rights, May 1968), 12–15.

40. John A. Hannah, *Voting: 1961 Commission on Civil Rights Report* (Washington, DC: US Commission on Civil Rights, 1961), 307.

41. Arthur S. Flemming, *The Voting Rights Act: Ten Years After* (Washington, DC: US Commission on Civil Rights, January 1975), 41.

42. Hannah, *Political Participation*, 12–15.
43. Table with African American elected officials from Hannah, *Political Participation*, 221.
44. *Richmond Times-Dispatch*, August 15, 1965, 14-B.
45. On the demise of the Byrd machine, I have written elsewhere: "Token integration and compliance, which characterized public-school integration until the Court held that freedom of choice was unconstitutional in *Green v. County School Board of New Kent County* (1968), replaced Byrd's calls for massive resistance. Even before the demise of massive resistance, however, younger Democrats from Virginia's growing urban areas, many of them veterans of World War II, had challenged Byrd's tax-and-spend approach to infrastructure building and internal improvements. These Democrats could see around the corner: led by Mills Godwin, anti-machine Democrats supported the repeal of poll taxes, called for equitable redistricting of the General Assembly's districts, and favored more enlightened policies on racial segregation. The Court's ruling in *Reynolds v. Sims* (1964) also forced Virginia's General Assembly to redistrict in accordance with the state's growing urban and suburban populations. This redistricting, by reapportioning rural and urban districts in the commonwealth, was the actual death blow for Byrd's machine—particularly as the machine derived representative power from drawing district lines that favored a handful of rural officials. These forces allowed Godwin to win the governorship as an antimachine Democrat in 1966." Hayter, *The Dream Is Lost*, 73.
46. Hannah, *Political Participation*, 13.
47. See Kevin Phillips, *The Emerging Republican Majority* (New Rochelle, NY: Arlington House, 1969). Earl Black and Merle Black argue that the compression of Black voters into exclusively urban enclaves sped up the rise of the Republican South. Although African Americans often held district majorities in the South's urban enclaves, congressional districts in effect became "safe" Republican districts. Earl Black and Merle Black, *The Rise of Southern Republicans* (Cambridge, MA: Belknap Press of Harvard University Press, 2002), 331–37.
48. On the staggering dilemma, see Hayter, *The Dream Is Lost*, chap. 2.
49. On Reynolds, see Andrew P. Miller, "J. Sargeant Reynolds: What He Was Not, Not What He Might Have Been," *Virginia Law Review* 57, no. 8 (1971): 1312–14; Michael P. Gleason and Andrew McCutcheon, *Sarge Reynolds: In the Time of His Life* (Gwynn, VA: Gleason Publishing, 1996).
50. Wilder, *Son of Virginia*, 54.
51. Interview with Dr. Reid on July 21, 2005.
52. Ibid.
53. *Richmond Afro-American*, August 30, 1969, 1.

54. Wilder, *Son of Virginia*, 53.

55. Hayter, *The Dream Is Lost*, 130–32.

56. For more on the annexation dilemma, see Julian Maxwell Hayter, "From Intent to Effect: Richmond, Virginia, and the Protracted Struggle for Voting Rights, 1965–1977," *Journal of Policy History* 26, no. 4 (2014); John V. Moeser and Rutledge M. Dennis, *The Politics of Annexation: Oligarchic Power in a Southern City* (Richmond: Virginia Commonwealth Libraries, 2020); and *Holt v. City of Richmond*, 459 F.2d 1093 (4th Cir. 1972).

57. *Richmond Times-Dispatch*, December 3, 1969, A-18.

58. *Richmond News Leader*, November 28, 1969, 9.

59. Ibid.

60. *Richmond Afro-American*, December 1, 1969, 1.

61. *Richmond Afro-American*, December 2, 1969, 1.

62. *Richmond Times-Dispatch*, December 5, 1969, B-2.

63. Ibid, A-6.

64. *Richmond Afro-American*, December 3, 1969, 1.

65. *Richmond Times-Dispatch*, December 3, 1969, 1.

66. *Richmond Times-Dispatch*, December 4, 1969, 1.

67. Larry Sabato, *Virginia Votes 1983–1986* (Charlottesville: University of Virginia, Institute of Government, 1987), xxiii.

68. Larry Sabato, *Virginia Votes 1969–1974* (Charlottesville: University of Virginia, Institute of Government, 1976), 16.

69. For more on Robinson, see Michael L. Clemons and Charles E. Jones, "African American Legislative Politics in Virginia," in *African American State Legislative Politics* (special issue), *Journal of Black Studies* 30, no. 6 (July 2000): 744–67.

70. For more on majority-minority district systems and "equality of results" standards, see Hayter, *The Dream Is Lost*, chap. 3, and J. Morgan Kousser, *Colorblind Injustice: Minority Voting Rights and the Undoing of the Second Reconstruction* (Chapel Hill: University of North Carolina Press, 1999).

71. Clemons and Jones, "African American Legislative Politics in Virginia," 758.

72. "Carry Me Back . . . ," *Richmond Times-Dispatch*, February 13, 1970, D-4.

73. *Richmond Times-Dispatch*, February 17, 1970, B-1.

74. Wilder, *Son of Virginia*, 60.

75. *Richmond Times-Dispatch*, April 5, 1977, B-4.

76. Wilder, *Son of Virginia*, 61.

77. Wanda D. Stallings, *Richmond Free Press*, June 10, 2016.

78. Sabato, *Virginia Votes 1979–1982*, 29, 40.

79. Ibid.

80. Ibid., 75–76.

81. Ibid., 103.

82. Sabato, *Virginia Votes 1983–1986*, 104.

83. *Richmond Times-Dispatch*, January 5, 1984, C-1, and June 19, 1984, B-3.

84. *Richmond Times-Dispatch*, July 4, 1984, B-1.

85. Wilder, *Son of Virginia*, 80.

86. Sabato, *Virginia Votes 1983–1986*, 104–6.

87. Ibid., 80.

88. Ibid, 71, 72.

89. Ibid., 64, 87.

90. Figures from table; see Sabato, *Virginia Votes 1983–1986*, 64, 87.

91. US Bureau of the Census, "Census 1980," *Social Explorer* (database), https://www.socialexplorer.com/tables/C1980/R13225191 (accessed January 21, 2021).

92. US Bureau of the Census, "Census 1970," *Social Explorer* (database), https://www.socialexplorer.com/tables/C1970/R12741181, and US Bureau of the Census, "Census 1980," *Social Explorer* (database), https://www.socialexplorer.com/tables/RC1980/R12741193 (accessed January 21, 2021).

93. US Bureau of the Census, "Census 1990," *Social Explorer* (database), https://www.socialexplorer.com/tables/RC1980/R12741193 (accessed January 21, 2021).

94. Hayter, *The Dream Is Lost*, 15.

95. Following a series of studies from Virginia's Stuart Commission (1971–77) and the Michie Commission (1977–79), lawmakers clamped down significantly on boundary expansions. See Hayter, *The Dream Is Lost*, 149–50.

96. Ibid, 149.

97. Ibid., 201.

98. Arthur S. Flemming, *The Voting Rights Act: Unfulfilled Goals* (Washington, DC: US Commission on Civil Rights, September 1981), 56.

99. Flemming, *The Voting Rights Act*, 17, 15.

100. For more on federal voting rights enforcement in Virginia during the early 1980s, see Anita S. Earls, Kara Millonzi, Oni Seliski, and Torrey Dixon, "Voting Rights in Virginia: 1982–2006," *Review of Law and Social Justice* 17, no. 2 (2008): 761–799.

101. Sabato, *Virginia Votes 1987–1990*, 76.

102. US Bureau of the Census, "Race," 1980, *Social Explorer* (database), https://www.socialexplorer.com/tables/C1980/R12741164 (accessed January 21, 2021).

103. On Carl Stokes, see Leonard N. Moore, *Carl B. Stokes and the Rise of Black Political Power* (Urbana: University of Illinois Press, 2002). On Tom Bradley, see Frank D. Gilliam, "Exploring Minority Empowerment: Symbolic Politics, Governing Coalitions, and Traces of Political Style in Los Angeles," *American Journal of Political Science* 40, no. 1 (1966): 56–81. On Wilson Goode, see Matthew Countryman, *Up South: Civil Rights and Black Power in Philadelphia* (Philadelphia: University of Pennsylvania Press, 2006).

104. Hayter, *The Dream Is Lost*, 17.
105. J. Phillip Thompson, *Double Trouble: Black Mayors, Black Communities, and the Call for a Deep Democracy* (New York: Oxford University Press, 2006), 131–34.
106. Donald P. Baker, "Strike Protest Threatens to Crash Wilder's Party," *Washington Post*, June 9, 1989.
107. Wilder, *Son of Virginia*, 98.
108. Sabato, *Virginia Votes 1987–1990*, 91–92.
109. *Webster v. Reproductive Health Services*, 492 US 490 (1989).
110. Sabato, *Virginia Votes 1987–1990*, 92.
111. Kent Jenkins Jr., "Coal Miners' Discontent Gets Political," *Washington Post*, August 6, 1989.
112. Harry Kollatz Jr., "Election Night Nail-Biter," *Richmond Magazine*, November 1, 2019.
113. Brent Tarter, *The Grandees of Government: The Origins and Persistence of Undemocratic Politics in Virginia* (Charlottesville: University of Virginia Press, 2013), 363.
114. *Richmond Times-Dispatch*, November 7, 1989, A-16.
115. Sabato, "Virginia Governor's Race, 1989," 1.
116. Sabato, *Virginia Votes 1987–1990*, chap. 5.
117. Judson L. Jeffries, "Doug Wilder and the Continuing Significance of Race: An Analysis of the 1989 Gubernatorial Election," *Journal of Political Science* 23, no. 1 (1995): 91.
118. Sabato, *Virginia Votes 1987–1990*, 94; Mark J. Rozell, "Local v. National Press Assessments of Virginia's 1989 Gubernatorial Campaign," *Polity* 24, no. 1 (Fall 1991): 69–89.
119. Sabato, *Virginia Votes 1987–1990*, 77, 81.
120. Ibid, 93.
121. John F. Harris and Donald P. Baker, "Wilder Proposes Deeper Budget Cuts," *Washington Post*, December 18, 1990.
122. "Gov. Wilder's Cuts How Deep?," *Washington Post*, September 19, 1990.
123. John Ward Anderson, "Wilder Signs Budget Bill after Scuttling Foe's Ship," *Washington Post*, May 4, 1991.
124. Associated Press, "School Star Wins Clemency," *New York Times*, December 31, 1993.
125. On race and American political development, see Sidney M. Milkis, "The Modern Presidency, Social Movements, and the Administrative State: Lyndon Johnson and the Civil Rights Movement," in *Race and American Political Development*, ed. Joseph E. Lowndes, Julie Novkov, and Dorian Tod Warren (New York: Routledge, 2008).
126. Larry Sabato, *Virginia Votes 1991–1994* (Charlottesville: University of Virginia, Weldon Cooper Center for Public Service, 1996), 7.

127. Ibid, 13.
128. Mike Allen, *Wall Street Journal,* October 27, 1993, A-16.
129. Sabato, *Virginia Votes 1991–1994,* 66–68.
130. Allen, *Wall Street Journal,* A-16.
131. Ibid.
132. Sabato, *Virginia Votes 1991–1994,* 68–69.

6

The Rise of a Competitive Republican Party

GEORGE ALLEN AND THE ELECTION OF 1993

Warren Fiske and Robert Holsworth

George Allen's election to the governorship in 1993 was significant for three reasons. First, it ended twelve years of Democratic control of the statehouse and enabled Republicans to implement in Virginia conservative reforms that had been advanced at the federal level and in other statehouses. Second, Allen's term as governor brought about significant changes not only in policy areas such as criminal justice and education but also in the role that the Virginia governor assumed in promoting economic development. Finally, while Allen's major policy initiatives endured for decades, his embrace of social conservatism and his missteps on race not only damaged his own political aspirations but exposed the problems his fellow Republicans experienced in responding to the changing dynamics of twenty-first-century Virginia.

This chapter begins by examining Allen's 1993 gubernatorial race against Democrat Mary Sue Terry in which he came from far behind in the polls to win a landslide victory. It moves on to explore Allen's major policy initiatives and his redefinition of the governor as the commonwealth's chief economic development officer. It concludes by examining Allen's post-gubernatorial political career and the challenges to Republican success in contemporary Virginia.

The 1993 Governor's Race

CANDIDATE BACKGROUNDS

Mary Sue Terry was born in 1947 in Critz, Virginia, a rural crossroads in the once tobacco-growing Southside region of the state, ten miles from the North Carolina border. She is the eldest of three daughters whose parents were teachers and ran a five-hundred-acre family farm passed down through generations. Terry was one of two members of her high school class to attend college. She earned a BA in political science from West-hampton College of the University of Richmond and was elected student body president. She went on to study at the University of Virginia, where she received a master's degree and a law degree.

Terry returned to her native Patrick County and went to work for Commonwealth's Attorney Martin F. "Fill" Clark, the local Democratic political boss. Her break came in 1977, when Garry DeBruhl, the local member of the House of Delegates, did not seek reelection and Clark, who was considered next in line for the seat, chose not to run. Terry took Clark's place on a victorious three-member Democratic ticket that included A. L. Philpott, a venerable conservative Democratic legislator from neighboring Henry County who became one of her key mentors. When Terry took office the following January, she was among nine women in the hundred-member House.[1]

Philpott was elected House Speaker in 1980 and entrusted Terry to carry major Democratic initiatives, most notably successful bills that raised the state's drinking age from nineteen to twenty-one and toughened drunk driving laws. She was cautious in positioning herself and avoided being labeled a feminist, originally opposing the state's ratification of the Equal Rights Amendment, then embracing it after a survey showed her constituents supported the ERA. Terry participated in a tobacco-spitting contest with rural lawmakers while building ties with Democratic governor Charles S. Robb and his deep-pocketed supporters in vote-rich Northern Virginia, piecing together a coalition that she would ride to nomination in 1985 as attorney general. She became the first woman nominated for statewide office in Virginia, joining a historic Democratic ticket with Gerald L. Baliles, who was seeking to step up from attorney general to governor, and Richmond state senator L. Douglas Wilder, the first Black nominated for statewide office in Virginia, running for lieutenant governor. The ticket promised to continue Robb's popular conservative approach to budgeting and his liberal outlook on social issues.

Terry's opponent was Del. W. R. "Buster" O'Brien, a Virginia Beach Republican and legendary former quarterback at the University of Richmond. Her campaign, according to a November 1985 article in the *Washington Post*, "was designed to overcome concerns that a woman, particularly an unmarried one, could not win in Virginia. She stressed her experience as a county prosecutor, businesswoman and serious legislator."[2] Terry's

strategy was boosted by O'Brien's self-implosion through résumé inflation. Portraying himself as someone who had played quarterback for the
Washington Redskins, Virginia's favorite football team, when he had only
been a member of the practice squad, O'Brien needlessly imperiled his
campaign, which never got off the ground, and Terry coasted to victory.
She won 61 percent of the vote, beating O'Brien in each of ten congressional districts[3] and doubling his fundraising. Her 814,808 votes led the
victorious Democratic ticket.

The ticket's success came with peril, however, setting up Terry and
Wilder as rivals for the 1989 Democratic gubernatorial nomination. Terry
spared the party a bloodbath, one from which she was unlikely to emerge
victorious, by announcing in early 1989 that she would defer to Wilder
and seek reelection as attorney general. Her opponent that fall was state
senator Joseph B. Benedetti, an avuncular Republican with little identity
outside his Richmond district. Terry's advantage in name recognition
and fundraising was enhanced when a family illness prevented Benedetti
from waging a vigorous statewide campaign. Wilder's historic victory as
the nation's first African American elected governor was the major story
of 1989, but it was an exceptionally good year for Terry as well. She won
the most votes on the victorious Democratic ticket, gaining 1,096,095
votes—63 percent of the ballots in her race—and swept all congressional districts.[4]

Terry won another victory as well. Her concession to Wilder was deeply
appreciated within the state Democratic Party and all but guaranteed her
the nomination for governor four years later. The only obstacle was the
man who ran in the middle of the 1989 ticket: Lieutenant Governor Donald S. Beyer Jr., a Northern Virginia car dealer. While Beyer kept his options open during the first three years of his term, he increasingly signaled
that he would not challenge Terry for the gubernatorial nomination and
did little to counter Terry's big head start in fundraising. In October 1992,
Beyer conceded the nomination to Terry and announced he would seek
reelection as lieutenant governor, saying, "It was a good time to affirm the
ability of women and minorities to rise to leadership positions."[5] Terry,
forty-five, declared her long-expected candidacy on March 11, 1993, promising a cautious mix of no new taxes, streamlined state services, and more
local control of public schools. With "Working Girl" as her theme song,
she was nominated at a unified Democratic state convention on May 8–9.
The estimated three thousand delegates on hand also renominated Beyer
and selected William D. Dolan III of Arlington County to run for attorney general.

Far from Terry's rural roots, George Felix Allen was reared mostly in Chicago and Los Angeles, the oldest son and namesake of an NFL Hall of Fame head coach. The family lived in upscale neighborhoods and hobnobbed with a bevy of entertainment and political stars, including Richard Nixon and Ronald Reagan. The workaholic father stressed preparation and attention to detail, and brought Allen and his two brothers to practices to observe the work habits of his best football players. Allen was a star quarterback in high school and would later describe football as a "true meritocracy, and that level field is what America should strive to be."[6]

Allen came to the East Coast and enrolled at the University of Virginia in 1971 when his father became head coach of the Washington Redskins. Majoring in history, he embraced the state's past: revering Thomas Jefferson's concepts of limited government, decorating his dorm room with a Confederate flag, and putting a sticker of the Dixie banner on his pick-up truck. Allen was back-up quarterback of the football team and president of his senior class. He went on to the University of Virginia School of Law, then set up a small practice in Charlottesville, handling real estate closings and acting as his father's agent.

Allen's passion was not law but politics. Inspired by Ronald Reagan's ascent in the Republican Party, he joined the Kiwanis, volunteered on local Republican campaigns, and made friends with his outgoing personality and through his football connections. He lost a race for the House of Delegates in 1979, then narrowly won the seat three years later, running on issues that became his trademark: law and order, no new taxes, and welfare reform. Allen was essentially a backbencher in the General Assembly. Democrats were in firm control of the House of Delegates, and Republicans who received plum assignments were typically those whose partisan instincts were more muted. Allen obtained occasional visibility when his libertarian leanings, such as his opposition to mandatory motorcycle helmets, garnered media attention, but his legislative years were nondescript. Indeed, this was a major reason why so many Democrats in 1993 underestimated Allen and believed he did not threaten their continued dominance of statewide elections.

The GOP Nomination

Allen's chance to advance came in July 1991 when Representative D. French Slaughter Jr., a Seventh District Republican serving a fourth term in Congress, announced he was resigning after suffering a series of strokes. Allen announced his candidacy a week later and had a clear path to the GOP nomination after Slaughter's son dropped out of the race. In a

November special election, Allen defeated Slaughter's cousin—the Democrat Kay Slaughter, an environmental lawyer and Charlottesville City Council member—with 62 percent of the vote.

The victory was short-lived, however. Allen was sworn into office on November 5, and sixteen days later the Democratic-led General Assembly drew new election maps that put Allen in the same district with Representative Thomas J. Bliley Jr., a five-term incumbent Republican and former mayor of Richmond. Bob Ball, chair of the House Appropriations Committee, gleefully proclaimed that Congressman Bliley would need "a seeing eye dog" to get around his district. Allen denounced the new map as a "disgusting" gerrymander, but declined to run against Bliley and, after some consideration, also decided not to move to Northern Virginia and challenge another entrenched Republican, Representative Frank R. Wolf.[7] But what seemed to be Democratic checkmate on Allen's political career would prove illusory. Allen set his eyes on a 1993 gubernatorial bid. Bliley, owing Allen a favor, took charge of an exploratory committee in March 1992 named "The Friends of George Allen." A massive roadblock was removed the next month when US senator John W. Warner, who also was considering a run for the GOP nomination for governor, decided to remain in Washington.

Allen declared his candidacy on November 14, 1992, accusing Democrats of becoming arrogant and stale during their twelve-year reign in the governor's office. He promised no tax increases, tougher criminal sentencing laws, less public education bureaucracy, and a repeal of "unnecessary, burdensome" small business regulations. Allen became the second Republican to enter the race, joining Earle C. Williams of Fairfax County, a retired CEO of defense contractor BDM International. Clinton Miller, a longtime moderate Republican state delegate from Shenandoah County, joined the race in the first days of 1993.

Allen was the clear frontrunner in what many considered to be a B-list field for the GOP nomination. He was better known to Republican activists than either of his opponents and better organized, having gained endorsements from seven of eleven GOP district chairmen across the state. Much of the debate focused on whether he had even a slim chance to beat Terry in the fall. Terry held a twenty-seven percentage point lead over Allen in a mid-January statewide poll by Mason-Dixon Political/Media Research.[8] Her advantage expanded to twenty-nine points in an early May poll.[9] The good news for Allen was that his Republican opponents trailed by even greater margins. Terry was known by 97 percent of voters, and more than half viewed her positively. Williams and Miller portrayed the forty-year-old Allen as immature and lacking in real-life experience. Williams self-financed his campaign with $2 million. He argued that Terry, in her two successful runs for attorney general, had trounced legislator-lawyers just like Allen and Miller. He said his business experience was unique and touted his endorsement by an inner sanctum of Northern Virginia developers. Allen dismissed William's backing, saying the nomination would be decided by "more than ten people."[10]

On that count, Allen was right. The Republicans nominated their candidate in June through a statewide convention held at the Richmond Coliseum. This was a format far more favorable to Allen and his grass-roots supporters than a primary where Williams's financial resources may have made more of a difference. In addition, the 1993 GOP convention was marked by the highly unusual circumstance in which many of the record 13,109 delegates who jammed the arena came primarily to participate in the selection of the lieutenant governor candidate. Michael Farris, the legal counsel for a national home-schooling organization, had mobilized legions of evangelical supporters to attend the convention. His delegates were new to state politics and staunchly anti-abortion and pro-gun. Allen may not have been their ideal choice for governor because he did not embrace the absolutist pro-life position of opposing abortion under any circumstances that had doomed GOP gubernatorial candidate J. Marshall Coleman in his race against Wilder four years earlier. Allen said it was "my inclination to support unborn human life" and that he would be guided by scientific information. Still, he was far better positioned with the evangelical community than either of his opponents, who generally supported abortion rights. In addition, Allen was in sync with the delegates on firearms; he opposed Wilder's bill limiting Virginians to buying one handgun a month. His two opponents backed the legislation.

Allen won the nomination with 64 percent of the delegate votes.[11] Williams pulled in 29 percent and Miller 6 percent. In his acceptance speech, Allen urged the crowd to rise against "that arrogant Democratic machine that has manipulated Virginia government for its own purposes. They have controlled politics with an iron fist, and they've emptied our wallets with a power vacuum."[12] Farris easily won the nod for lieutenant governor, and James S. Gilmore III, a moderate-conservative commonwealth's attorney from Henrico County, was nominated for attorney general. Looking back at the convention eight months later, University of Virginia political scientist Larry J. Sabato wrote, "The Allen-Farris-Gilmore ticket was unquestionably the most conservative state ticket fielded by the Republicans in recent times, mainly due to Farris's presence."[13]

The General Election

It is hard to overestimate the negative impact that observers felt in the days after the convention that Farris's nomination might have on the Republican ticket. While the number and fervor of the delegates he brought to the convention were unprecedented, Allen now had a running mate who had called the public school system "a godless monstrosity."[14] How would Allen compete in the suburbs with voters who believed that support for the public school system was crucial to the future of their children? Besides the Farris dilemma and polls showing him trailing Terry by a 2–1 margin, the cost of his three-way battle for the nomination left Allen's campaign nearly broke. Terry, who sailed unopposed to the Democratic nomination, was sitting on a war chest approaching $2 million. Allen's campaign feared that Terry would launch a negative advertising blitz defining him as a captive of the religious right that Allen would lack funds to quell. Terry did not seize the opportunity, however, showing a cautious, play-not-to-lose strategy that would stall her campaign.

Campaign professionals pointed to Terry's decision not to hammer Allen when he was broke as the crucial tactical mistake of the campaign. In retrospect, however, the early polls and commentary often underestimated both the difficulties that Terry faced in reassembling the Democratic coalition that had led to three consecutive statewide victories and Allen's own strengths as a campaigner. Terry's first challenge came from across the Potomac. Virginia and New Jersey are the only states to hold odd-year gubernatorial elections the year after presidents are chosen. In the four gubernatorial cycles prior to 1993, the winner was from the opposite party of the president elected the previous year, a trend that became known in Virginia as the "presidential curse." President Bill Clinton had lost Virginia to George H. W. Bush in his successful 1992 campaign and, by mid-1993, his standing in the commonwealth had declined; a statewide poll showed only 28 percent of Virginia voters rated Clinton's performance in office as "excellent" or "good." Given these numbers, Terry hurried to distance herself from the president. Asked at her first debate with Allen whether she would repudiate Clinton's stance on raising taxes and gays in the military, Terry immediately responded "I repudiate."[15]

Terry's problems were compounded by the internal dynamics within the Virginia Democratic Party. Wilder's decision to capitalize on the accolades he had received from the national media for his gubernatorial performance and run for president in 1992 was poorly received inside the commonwealth and drove down his approval ratings. In addition, by 1993, Robb and Wilder, the two major figures in the Virginia Democratic Party, were at loggerheads. The tension between the two had been building for years. Staffers had engaged in a contentious proxy battle. Robb's people made it known that they believed Wilder was not sufficiently grateful for the support that Robb had given, while Wilder's supporters said Robb was trying to take undue credit for the governor's historic election.

The situation escalated in the early 1990s. Robb's reputation took a huge hit when media reports revealed he had had a dalliance with a beauty queen and partied with a fast crowd in Virginia Beach almost every other weekend when he was governor. In a bizarre effort to blame Wilder for the revelations, Robb staffers obtained and leaked to newspapers an illegally taped phone conversation between Wilder and a political supporter. While the tape showed that Wilder thought the revelations would be fatal to Robb's political career, it contained no indication that he had anything to do with the stories. The wiretapping infuriated Wilder and exposed Robb to a grand jury investigation about why his office had held and then released the tape of an illegally obtained phone call. In the public's mind, the "feud" damaged both Wilder and Robb, reducing their approval rating to 37 percent in 1993. One month after Terry was nominated, Wilder declared that he would seek Robb's Senate seat, either in a Democratic primary or as an independent.

Terry's own relationship with Wilder was also on tenterhooks and became a recurring problem in her quest to succeed him. Never especially close, they had publicly clashed in late 1992 when she began an investigation of legal fees paid by the state's pension fund, which was headed by Wilder appointees, including its first Black chairwoman. The governor fired Terry as the pension fund's lawyer, accusing her of waging a political "stunt" and saying it was an "ethical conflict" for her to simultaneously represent the retirement fund as attorney general and investigate it for potential wrongdoing.[16] Terry sued, and a judge ruled in December 1992 that Wilder could not block her from representing the fund. Terry portrayed the incident as an indication of her independence from Wilder. While she never pronounced the same "I repudiate" that she had concerning President Clinton, it was generally perceived that she was attempting to distance herself from Wilder.

Terry appeared to believe that her two previous landslide elections for attorney general had given her a constituency separate and distinct from that of other Democrats in Virginia. But while she may have entered the race with greater name recognition than Allen, she was not identified in the public's mind with a compelling issue or a distinct accomplishment. In the three gubernatorial elections from 1981 to 1989, the Democrats managed to garner more than 40 percent of the White vote and combined this with more than 90 percent of the Black vote to elect Robb, Baliles, and Wilder. Equally important, the Democratic coalition of the 1980s catalyzed historic turnout in the African American community, one that equaled and sometimes exceeded the turnout rate of White voters, a remarkable feat in light of how economic disparities had typically affected voter turnout. In two of these elections—1985 and 1989—Doug Wilder was on the ticket with a historic candidacy. It was not clear that Terry recognized how difficult it would be in 1993 for Democrats to replicate these successes without Wilder's full-throated backing, regardless of her performance in the attorney general elections.

Terry's natural cautiousness and pragmatic approach to politics meant she did not come to the campaign with a ready-made issue that had already galvanized a statewide constituency. In 1993, it was not evident how much emphasis the campaign should place on the historic nature of Terry's candidacy as potentially the first woman governor of Virginia. In her past races, Terry had not emphasized the gender barriers that her candidacy broke. Moreover, a not so silent whispering campaign had pointed to her status as a single woman to imply that she might be lesbian. In conversations that one of the authors had with Terry, it was evident that she had studied the obstacles faced by women candidates in some depth. She was aware that the public often gave women candidates high marks on trust but did not necessarily view women as chief executives and might be harsh in judging them when they made a misstep.

Terry chose to frame the campaign around a proposal to institute a five-day waiting period for handgun purchases, a state complement to the federal Brady bill, with a requirement even stricter than the three-day period in the national legislation. An early June poll showed 88 percent of registered voters in Virginia supported the waiting period and, for many Democrats, this signaled increased support for regulating guns to enhance public safety.[17] It was a surprising step for Terry. With her background in rural Virginia, she had never been at the forefront of the gun control legislation that had been supported by urban Democrats in the commonwealth. In 1993, however, Terry insisted that "if this saves one life, it's worth doing" and "I think this is an issue where the public is ahead of the lawmakers." It was a decision that proved politically fatal.

Allen, an ally of the National Rifle Association, immediately ridiculed the proposal as a "slogan" that would not reduce crime. He then skillfully turned the issue against Terry. Rejecting gun control, he focused on putting more people in prisons for a longer time. He made a galvanizing call in July to end Virginia's "liberal, lenient parole system" for violent criminals, and it became a motto for his campaign. He also called for a law that would allow juries to look at defendants' past records before deciding prison sentences. Allen gained traction at the end of August by winning the endorsement of the Virginia State Lodge of the Fraternal Order of Police, an organization that had backed Terry in her two runs for attorney general. "We haven't been concentrating our efforts on gun control," said Garth Wheeler, president of the influential group.[18]

Allen maintained that a waiting period for the purchase of guns would do little to counter the increase in crime that was, in his portrayal, the consequences of a parole policy that was letting convicted murderers, rapists, and other violent criminals back on the streets too quickly. The combination of parole rules and "good time" had led to large discrepancies between official sentencing terms and time actually served. Democratic-sponsored initiatives such as Wilder's Commission on Violent Crime had flagged significant problems with the parole system. But Allen took it to another level by making it the centerpiece of his gubernatorial campaign. It was an extraordinarily effective counter to Terry's waiting period proposal. And although the attorney general in Virginia is not responsible for most criminal justice issues, the public often perceives the role as top cop, and Allen had effectively placed the problem of parole on Terry's doorstep. As Allen put it, "for her to suddenly discover crime when for seven years she was the state's top law officer just shows how shallow and hollow her campaign is."[19]

Allen also framed the debate that summer by proposing that Virginia welfare recipients be required to work to receive benefits, and for tying runaway college tuition increases to inflation. Terry, rather than offering innovative policies of her own, spent much of the summer reacting to Allen's agenda. After her repudiation of Clinton and praise for Reagan, a few Black activists, including the state's NAACP director, began criticizing Terry's campaign for tilting to the right.[20]

With little money, the extroverted Allen spent long days on the campaign trail, where he was genial, self-deprecating, and interested in the voters he met. The introverted Terry, in contrast, was stiff on the hustings and avoided public campaign appearances. During a week in late August leading up to a debate, the *Washington Post* reported Allen had scheduled fourteen public events and Terry had none.[21] Wilder urged Terry to spend less time fundraising and more meeting voters. By Labor Day, her once impregnable twenty-nine percentage point lead had shrunk to six percentage points, and the slide never stopped.[22] Allen's growing chance of victory brought money to his campaign and, although he never matched Terry's war chest, he would have ample cash for the homestretch.

September brought continued woe to Terry. Mid-month polls showed the race had become a dead heat. The AFL-CIO, a longtime ally of Democrats, stayed neutral in the governor's race while endorsing Terry's two ticket mates; the organization was miffed at her actions as attorney general in a bloody 1989 coal strike. Terry also incurred Wilder's public wrath again, this time for opposing an unsuccessful compromise he had endorsed to avoid admitting women to Virginia Military Institute by starting a separate military-style program for women at a different, private Virginia college. The *Washington Post* reported that Wilder called Terry unethical for opposing the position that a former client, VMI, was taking in a case that was being adjudicated.[23]

October brought a decidedly nasty tone to the race when, hours before a statewide televised debate with George Allen, several media outlets reported a totally uncorroborated charge by a Roanoke psychiatrist facing disciplinary charges for having sexual relationships with his patients that he had treated Mary Sue Terry's lesbian lover for suicidal tendencies. Terry believed that the reports epitomized the double standard by which the media treated women candidates. Yet she felt compelled to deny the baseless accusation and note that she was heterosexual. In the ensuing weeks, she accused Allen of giving a go-ahead wink to surrogate speakers—including former Iran-Contra figure Oliver L. North—who were reminding crowds that Terry had never married.[24] From the stump and in television ads, she sought to tie Allen to the religious right and to Farris's calls for a school voucher system in Virginia. Allen remained unflappable; he had kept his distance from Farris and dodged taking a firm position on vouchers, saying the matter should be left to local governments. He portrayed Terry as the heir to an arrogant Democratic machine that, after twelve years, had run out of ideas. The final Mason-Dixon poll, conducted during the last week of the campaign, showed Allen ahead, 49 percent to 42 percent.

Wilder did join Terry on the trail for the waning days of the campaign, but the dynamics of the race had already been baked in. The surprise on Election Day was not that Allen won but the breadth of his victory. He trampled Terry, 58.3 percent to 40.9 percent, the largest margin of victory in a Virginia gubernatorial race in thirty-two years. Terry received the lowest vote percentage of any Democratic gubernatorial candidate in the records of the Virginia Department of Elections, which go back to 1852.[25] Allen became the first Virginia candidate for governor to exceed one million votes—he got 1,045,319, compared to Terry's 733,527. Allen won nine of Virginia's eleven congressional districts, carrying suburban and rural regions. He won two of three districts in Northern Virginia (the Tenth and Eleventh districts) and swept the suburbs of Richmond and Hampton Roads. Allen's romp ran through the rural Shenandoah Valley and Terry's native Southside region. Allen won every locality in the coal-mining Ninth Congressional District in the Southwest region and became the first Republican gubernatorial candidate in the century to carry strongly unionized Wise County near the state's westernmost corner. He carried eighty-nine of Virginia's ninety-five counties and twenty-eight of its thirty-eight cities.[26] Exit polls showed that Allen won with both men and women voters and that turnout among African Americans had dipped considerably from the previous decade.[27]

Terry, in contrast, won only two congressional districts: the majority-Black Third District, stretching from portions of Norfolk to South Richmond, and the heavily Democratic Eighth District in Northern Virginia. Allen also had long coattails as Republicans performed strongly in other elections. Gilmore won the attorney general's race with 56.1 percent of the votes, compared to Dolan's 43.9 percent. Gilmore's results correlated with Allen's; he ran within four percentage points of the governor-elect in each congressional district. Republicans also gained six seats in races for the House of Delegates, narrowing the Democratic majority in the chamber to fifty-two of one hundred seats—at that point the low-water mark of the century.[28] Republicans won each of five seats left open by retiring Democrats that fall and ousted one incumbent. Three of the new seats were in Southwest Virginia, further signaling a shift in the once solidly Democratic coalfields. The lone GOP defeat came in the lieutenant governor's race, where Democrat Beyer won a second term with 54.5 percent of the vote compared to 45.5 percent for Farris.

Although Democrats still had control of the General Assembly by a narrow margin, the overwhelming size of Allen's victory gave Virginia Republicans the opportunity to act on their beliefs and policy ideas in a manner that had been denied for over a decade. In Allen, the party had a leader who was willing to interpret the mandate he had been given by the voters expansively and spend every ounce of political capital he had to implement it. The next four years were characterized by Allen's relentless push to advance the most ambitious set of conservative reforms that modern Virginia ever witnessed.

A Consequential Governorship

Allen's electoral victory in 1993 was followed by a governorship that implemented a wide range of conservative reforms in criminal justice, education, and social services and established the governor of Virginia as the chief economic development officer of the commonwealth. With Republicans back in the Executive Mansion for the first time in twelve years, there was pent-up demand from conservatives to bring to the state level the kind of reforms that President Ronald Reagan had advocated on the national stage. Allen's inaugural address boldly announced this new era. He portrayed himself as the head of an insurgency, a "revolutionary army that was victorious in taking back Virginia's government [from] the stolid, status quo, monarchical elitists." Virginians, Allen asserted, understood that "government had been whittling away at their freedoms . . . diminishing opportunity and stifling initiative under the heavy, grimy boot of excessive taxation and spending and regulation." He claimed that Virginia had replaced wise and frugal government with "massive" government spending increases. Allen maintained that the "primary duty of government to 'restrain men from injuring one another,' has been neglected as our Commonwealth has experienced an epidemic of violent crime, much of it the result of offenses committed by career criminals out on early parole."[29]

Democrats reacted angrily to what they considered to be Allen's excessively partisan address.[30] But while Allen's initial State of the Commonwealth speech the next week was less adversarial and more policy-oriented, there was no doubt that he intended to preside over a major transformation of Virginia state government. In 1994, Virginia was one of the few states that prohibited governors from running for reelection in consecutive terms—a governor would have to sit out four years before seeking office again. For this reason, newly elected governors understood they had to act quickly and decisively in defining and pursuing their agenda. Allen also recognized that with a Democratic majority in the General Assembly, it was critical that his mandate from November's election be fresh in the members' minds while they were deliberating on his priorities.

CRIMINAL JUSTICE REFORM

In the late 1980s and early 1990s, the upward trend in violent crime became an increasingly salient political issue in Virginia and across the country. The growing use of crack cocaine and the violence associated with its sale and distribution were perceived as a national epidemic. Virginia's location on the I-95 corridor and its permissive gun-purchasing laws made it a haven for those involved in the drug trade wishing to purchase large quantities of weapons. Drug and gun traffickers from out of state used local straw purchasers to amass large quantities of weapons in Virginia and transport them up the coast. The commonwealth's reputation was damaged by a series of reports in which law enforcement officials in the Northeast said that guns purchased in Virginia were used in firefights and murders in their states. In response, Wilder proposed and successfully passed a One-Handgun-a-Month law that limited the quantity of handguns that could be purchased by individual buyers. Wilder brought together a broad coalition of Democrats, Republicans, business leaders, and law enforcement officers to address bulk sales by straw purchasers. The bill was one of the most important pieces of legislation passed during his administration and was the key feature of his final legislative session in 1993. Subsequent research published by the *Journal of the American Medical Association* and the Virginia State Crime Commission provided strong evidence that the legislation achieved its aim.[31]

Allen's landslide victory dramatically altered the legislative orientation in Virginia on criminal justice. Allen immediately established the Commission on Parole Abolition and Sentencing Reform, composed of a bipartisan group of "judges, crime victims, business leaders, prosecutors, law enforcement officers and legal professionals," for the purpose, as Allen described it, "to stop the bleeding" as a prelude to calling a special session of the General Assembly to address its recommendations. The commission was cochaired by former US attorney general William Barr and Richard Cullen, a former US attorney who had partnered with Wilder on the one-handgun-a-month bill. Prior to the special session, Allen barnstormed the state, making the case once again for the arguments that had been central to his campaign success.[32]

In a 2015 retrospective, criminal justice researcher Dr. Sarah Scarbrough provided a comprehensive summary and analysis of the commission's recommendations and the Allen administration's proposed legislation. Its major recommendations focused on three areas:

Elimination of discretionary parole: Ending the practice whereby violent criminals were serving, on average, one-third to one-sixth of the official sentence.

Increased prison time for violent offenders: The legislation required that all violent offenders serve at least 85 percent of their sentence. Prison time would increase 100 percent for first-time violent offenders; 125 percent for first-time rapists, armed robbers, and murderers; 300 percent for those with previous convictions for assault, burglary, and malicious wounding; and 500 percent for those with previous convictions for murder, armed robbery, and rape. As Barr noted, the "most effective method of prevention is to take the rapist off the street for 12 years instead of four."

Establishment of a major prison construction program: The Allen administration did not provide a specific cost estimate but acknowledged that it would require the construction of new prisons, even if sentences for nonviolent offenders were not increased and, in some instances, diverted to work camps.

Advocates within the criminal justice community objected to the package, arguing that it amounted to a "declaration of war on young black males."[33] But in the environment of 1994, the argument did not gain traction. Democrats, chastened by the election results, did not defend the existing parole system or raise significant objections to the substance of Allen's legislative recommendations. For the most part, they focused on the cost of the plan and the lack of specifics as to how it would be funded. Some even claimed he was essentially proposing measures that they had advocated for years. Allen's program was passed overwhelmingly by the General Assembly, 89–7 in the House and 34–4 in the Senate. Parole was eliminated, "good time" was reduced, twenty new prisons were approved, and, because of legislative changes, alternative programs for nonviolent offenders were established that increased electronic monitoring and intensive supervised parole.[34]

Overreach on Taxes but Success on Welfare Reform

Buoyed by his success with criminal justice reform in his initial legislative session, Allen came forward in the lead-up to the 1995 General Assembly session with an aggressive series of proposals calling for tax reductions, spending cuts, welfare reform, and enhanced prison construction. He proposed a $2.1 billion five-year package of tax cuts. It included increasing the personal exemption on the state income tax over a five-year period from $800 to $2,400, placing it at the same level as the federal income tax. He also proposed eliminating the Business and Professional Occupational License (BPOL) tax. BPOL was a local tax collected by the separate jurisdictions in Virginia, and Allen's plan proposed using state dollars to hold localities harmless for a five-year period. To pay for the tax cuts, Allen proposed a series of spending reductions that would affect funding for the arts, colleges and universities, state parks, mental health facilities, and Medicaid coverage for teenagers. Describing his plans in the annual State of the Commonwealth address, Allen framed the matter as an existential choice. "We stand at a fork in the road," he said. "Will our state continue down the path of bigger government, increased spending and taxes, deepening dependency, and declining values? Or we will make government smaller and more focused on core governmental duties—allowing you to keep more of your hard-earned money?"[35]

While the Allen camp did not expect the overwhelming bipartisan agreement that accompanied parole abolition, it believed that a substantial number of moderate-conservative Democrats would be reluctant to vote against tax cuts in an election year. It was apparently taken aback by the capacity of the Democratic legislative leadership to oppose the proposals and by how widespread and vehement the criticism became. The opposition to Allen's proposals came from multiple quarters in Virginia's political ecosystem, and the bipartisan agreements that had been forged around criminal justice reform rapidly evaporated. A broadside from Democratic Lieutenant Governor Beyer asserted that Allen would make state support for colleges among the lowest in the nation; "eliminate mental health services for tens of thousands; kill health clinics that diagnose children with disabilities; and cut millions of dollars targeted to prevent high school dropouts. . . . [It's] cruel and reckless."[36] Two former governors from different sides of the ideological spectrum, Mills Godwin and Gerald Baliles, reiterated the concern about Allen's higher education choices. Baliles warned that a "once proud university system was in danger of being driven into the nation's bottom because of the reductions in state spending." These positions were echoed by university presidents, who argued that the continuing reduction in state support was fundamentally transforming the Virginia system of higher education. Outside higher ed, advocates for mental health, the disability community, and K–12 education joined the chorus denouncing Allen's priorities. And local governments, which already had little trust in state promises, were not pleased with the prospect of a disappearing revenue source, even if the Allen proposal held local revenues harmless for five years.

Allen and his allies dismissed the criticisms as the predictable response of liberals out of touch with the people. His cuts, he argued, were targeted to top-heavy administrators and other forms of bureaucratic bloat and that ordinary "folks will not suffer." Convinced that most of the public was supportive, Allen pointed to the upcoming legislative elections, making it clear he would put Democrats on the defensive for supporting a tax increase if they did not vote for his reductions. The Democratic leadership in the assembly was undeterred by the implicit political threat. Energized by the determination of the advocates and boosted by polling that showed the unpopularity of the cuts, they summarily killed the legislative package in committee. This tactic effectively ensured that party members who might have supported tax cut legislation if it got to the floor were not put in the uncomfortable position of casting a vote. According to the *Washington Post,* Democrats issued "one of the strongest repudiations of any Governor in decades. . . . They spiked his plans to overhaul welfare, build prisons, create state-financed charter schools, and require that parents be notified before their teen-age daughters get an abortion." Allen denounced what he labeled the "Thursday night massacre," blasting the Democrats for not giving his plans the opportunity to reach the floor, declaring that "we do not feel compelled to hide our convictions by casting our votes in smoke-filled committee rooms late in the day or under the cover of darkness."[37]

There were many reasons offered for Allen's defeat. While he had spoken rhetorically in his gubernatorial race against Terry about Democratic spending and taxes, he had not specifically campaigned on the issue. Nor had he taken the issue directly to the public across the commonwealth as he had done the previous year with parole abolition. Fellow Republican legislators blamed a "my way or the highway" approach that ignored the potential for compromise and Allen's failure to consult with them prior to the time that the proposed spending cuts became public. A leading GOP legislator, state senator John Chichester of Stafford County, told the *Washington Post,* "No one can do that, parties notwithstanding, without bouncing that off the people who've got to carry the ball. . . . They got what they deserved."[38]

At its core, however, the proposal fundamentally misread the public's position on the state income tax and the programs supported by taxpayer dollars. Allen's heated rhetoric about the grimy boot of taxation was not well matched to Virginians' perception of their 5.75 percent state income tax rate. Data did not indicate that Virginia's state income tax rate was high when compared to that of most other states. Perhaps more important, when taken out of a weekly or biweekly paycheck, the public did not experience it as an especially onerous obligation. (In fact, critics of Virginia's state income tax had typically lamented its lack of progressivity since the 5.75 percent rate did not escalate as one's income increased.) Nor was the public concerned by the imposition of a business and professional license tax by most localities. With Virginia having just been named the best-managed state in the country for two consecutive years during the Wilder administration, Virginians consistently rated the quality of state government far higher than they did the quality of the federal government. In addition, polls consistently indicated majority support (and even a potential willingness to pay more) for the most important functions that state government provided, such as K–12 education. Allen's bargain, which appeared to provide an average taxpayer with a $40 break in its first year, did not appear to be a great deal when potential service reductions were balanced against it. Allen's legislative defeat in 1995 did not prove that Virginians loved taxes but that targeting the personal exemption on the state income tax had little visceral appeal to the public. Virginia's tax revolt would have to wait until Allen's Republican successor, Jim Gilmore, targeted elimination of a much more hated levy, the local car tax.

At the same time, Allen did achieve a major eleventh-hour victory on welfare reform in the 1995 session. It originally appeared that Democrats would successfully stymie his welfare reform proposals, which contained rigorous work requirements and reduced the amount of time that benefits could be received by supporting what Republicans viewed as a weaker alternative proposed by Democratic Lieutenant Governor Don Beyer. Rejecting the Beyer plan as not real reform, Allen essentially gave the Democrats an either-or choice: support his plan or elevate welfare reform to the central issue of the November elections. The Democrats blinked and provided Allen with a significant victory. In the ensuing decades, there has been an intense scholarly debate about whether welfare reform's acknowledged success in taking people off the rolls, in Virginia and nationally, has actually resulted in the reduction of poverty and an increase in family formation. But in 1995 it was clear that Virginia Democrats had no stomach for running an election campaign that would allow Allen to make welfare reform that year's version of parole abolition.

THE 1995 ELECTIONS AND EDUCATION REFORM

Stung by the legislative defeat of his tax-cutting agenda in 1995, Allen looked to November's upcoming legislative elections to flip control of the General Assembly to the Republicans, remove the obstacles to his policy agenda, and usher in a Republic majority in the assembly for the first time since Reconstruction. Even before Allen took office, the Republican Party had made significant advances as voter support for political parties began to divide more clearly on ideological grounds. Conservative "Virginia Democrats" found it increasingly difficult to hold seats against Republican challengers. By 1995 the composition of the House was fifty-two Democrats, forty-seven Republicans, and one Republican-leaning independent; the forty-seat Senate was twenty-two Democrats and eighteen Republicans. Sensing a crucial political opportunity, Allen became more engaged than governors traditionally had been in assembly elections. He was instrumental in shaping the GOP strategy; he traveled the state, lending his popularity to GOP candidates; and he appeared in ads for Republican candidates. Allen especially targeted Democratic House members and senators who represented Republican-leaning districts across the state, including Senate Majority Leader Hunter Andrews of Hampton, perhaps the most powerful figure in the assembly and an avowed opponent of Allen's tax cut and spending cut agenda. Allen's political action committee called for removing "liberal, big spending Democrats" in order to "bring more honest change to Virginia."

Allen's personal popularity ultimately did not translate into the hoped-for Republican takeover of the assembly in 1995. There was no overall change in the House as Democrats retained the same 52-47-1 margin they held after the 1993 elections. In the Senate, the Republicans did make gains, but not enough to flip the body. The GOP picked up five Democratic seats, including knocking off Andrews. But the Democrats defeated three Republican incumbents in Roanoke, Charlottesville, and Northern Virginia to keep the chamber at a 20–20 tie. With Beyer, the Democratic lieutenant governor, having the tie-breaking vote, the Democrats retained effective control, though the Republicans were able to force a historic power-sharing agreement.[39]

Several of Allen's fellow Republicans blamed him for the party's performance. Northern Virginia Republicans, supporters of spending on education and transportation, felt that Allen's tax-cutting message was detrimental in the region. State GOP chair Pat McSweeney, a long-time

Allen critic, said, "We have never in this century . . . had a situation in a midterm election in Virginia where an appeal from an incumbent chief executive brought anybody in."[40] Democrats saw the results as a repudiation of Allen and Republican policies in Washington. Beyer claimed a major victory for the Democrats, asserting that the results "were a rejection of the Gingrich revolution. . . . People want change, but they want to be sensible. You can't cut your way to prosperity." His position was echoed by Don Fowler, chair of the Democratic National Committee, who said Allen "made it clear to everyone that the '95 election was a referendum on him or his policies and he lost. He's under severe pressure now to see if he can recover anything from his last two years in office."[41]

If Allen had not raised the stakes of the election by making the elimination of Democratic control the measuring stick, the power-sharing agreement in the Senate and the removal of his most significant adversary in the Senate might have been interpreted more positively. In any case, Fowler and Beyer underestimated Allen's resilience and his capacity to lead the Republican Party of Virginia to future electoral success. He accomplished far more than Fowler's "anything." After the legislative and electoral defeats, of 1995, Allen recalibrated. He achieved significant compromises with Democrats in the remaining two years on several crucial initiatives. On juvenile justice, he was able to get legislative support for trying teenagers as young as fourteen for murder and other violent crimes by agreeing to increased support for prevention and rehabilitation programs. He won support for a tuition freeze at Virginia public colleges and universities by agreeing to provide more state support. And, in 1997, he was able to achieve a long-term goal of social conservatives with passage of a bill requiring parental consent for abortions for teenagers sixteen and younger. He left office with a 68 percent approval rating, and the 1997 election was another Republican landslide in which his successor, Gilmore, ran on a quintessential Allen platform—no car tax—eliminating the hated tax by which Virginians who owned a relatively new car might pay upward of $1,000 per year in a single payment to their local government.

But Allen's most important and enduring achievement was his passage of a major educational reform initiative in 1996. By the early 1990s, the performance of Virginia's public schools was coming under increasing scrutiny. Student scores on state and national tests were declining. A literacy passport test that Virginia had implemented for testing sixth graders' fundamental skills had at least a single section failed by one in three test takers. And there were continuing complaints from employers that graduates from Virginia's high schools were not job ready and required extensive training before becoming capable of performing job-related tasks.[42] Many conservatives believed the situation was unfixable unless the system was infused with fundamental reform. They pointed to the almost insurmountable difficulty of establishing charter schools in Virginia's public school system and advocated allowing parents to use vouchers to move their children out a failing public school system into available parochial and private schools. In 1995, Allen's effort to expand charter schools in Virginia was rejected by the assembly. In 1996, he successfully passed a major educational reform package that deemphasized charters and vouchers by focusing on standards, accountability, and school-based transparency.

Allen had established a forty-nine-member Commission on Champion Schools in 1995 under the leadership of Dr. William Bosher, the state superintendent of public instruction. At its formation, it was not clear precisely what direction the group was likely to take. Allen, who had supported public school choice in his campaign statements, urged the panel to be "bold and creative. I want you to look at options like charter schools and school choice and to find ways to encourage cooperation and competition." Its membership included several people, including a member of the State Board of Education, who supported using vouchers to support private schools. Robley Jones, president of the Virginia Education Association, worried that "we are already in a fiscal crisis in Virginia public schools, ands school choice would rob the public schools of a billion dollars in state funding."[43] Bosher, a former superintendent of Henrico County Public Schools, was an innovative leader who had introduced popular "choices" within the public school system at the secondary level by establishing thematic specialty centers at each Henrico high school that were open to students throughout the county. Bosher understood that the public would support reform, but that it had to be framed in terms of improving schools and not blowing them up. He emphasized that the commission's biggest challenge was that "we not malign the strong local programs that exist while at the same time identifying our weaknesses."

The commission's final recommendations avoided the highly charged areas of vouchers and charter schools and did not necessarily please the most ardent conservatives among Allen's supporters. The report focused most prominently on elevating educational standards and imposing accountability at the school and district level in the public school system. In terms of content, the panel focused on strengthening and specifying the Standards of Learning, a vehicle that had been introduced in the 1980s and had been used by the Wilder administration as the focal point of its own educational reform efforts. The commission's recommendations went through a public comment process and were eventually refined and approved by the Virginia Board of Education to include new, more detailed and more stringent requirements in English, math, history, and science. Bosher described the new Standards of Learning as "the most rigorous set of standards in math, science, English and social studies that Virginia has ever known."[44] In 1996, Allen officially proposed "to put accountability behind the new educational standards through the development of a comprehensive Virginia-based testing program geared to standards." In his annual State of the Commonwealth address, he noted that test scores had not increased, despite additional funding, and asked the General Assembly to dedicate new funds to support the testing and accountability program.[45]

In a 2001 retrospective, Allen's policy director, Mark Christie, outlined the four key elements of the Standards of Learning. These were the development of academic standards for K–12; high-stakes testing in grades three, five, eight, and high school; the linkage of student achievement to graduation and school accreditation; and the transparent reporting of school performance to all parents of public school students in Virginia. The ambitiousness and magnitude of these reforms far surpassed what is involved in a typical legislative initiative. Allen was striving to change the entire operation of the K–12 system, a conservative reform that only a few states had tried. The follow-up that was required to implement the reforms included rewriting entire curricula, developing an extensive series of tests, establishing criteria for linking consequences for students and schools related to performance, and developing a communication strategy for informing the public about the performance of Virginia students and schools on a granular level. All this had to be done with the cooperation of educators across the state, including those who were not convinced that the outcomes would be worth the effort. Just setting the system in place was a multiyear endeavor that would extend beyond Allen's term.[46]

Perhaps most significant about Allen's Standards of Learning reforms was the attention and effort that Christie, Board of Education chair Kirk T. Schroder, and other supporters of the reforms devoted to implementing the standards and the accompanying accountability and transparency measures over multiple years. It was certainly vital that Allen's Republican successor, Gilmore, was committed to their implementation. But the Standards of Learning reforms were, in many ways, the type of complicated, multifaceted initiative that could have been watered down at many points in the implementation process, especially in light of the initial opposition from segments of the education establishment. Standards of Learning skeptics always questioned whether the reforms sacrificed critical thinking to rote learning and teaching to the test. But using their appointed positions on the state Board of Education, the Standards of Learning proponents obtained sufficient buy-in from education leaders. They listened to feedback and modified tests and requirements, and they developed school-based reports that were widely publicized in almost every local community. The Standards of Learning became the operating framework of Virginia K–12 education policy for a generation.

If Allen did not lead a charge in Virginia for charter schools and vouchers, he did align with conservative organizations such as the Virginia Family Foundation in his refusal to accept federal Goals 2000 money to assist his reform efforts. Allen refused to apply for an available $6.7 million in federal funds from the program, arguing that the money would come with so many strings attached that it would undermine Virginia's reform efforts. Michelle Easton, an Allen appointee on the Virginia Board of Education, said, "The nature of the federal beast is to start quietly and then begin to dictate . . . , bully . . . , and audit."[47] Allen's refusal catalyzed a two-year battle with Virginia Democrats and education advocates. Virginia was one of two states to refuse the dollars, and, by the time Allen relented and applied for the dollars to fund technology improvements, Virginia was the only state that had not accepted federal funding. It was a fruitless ideological stance that provided Democrats with an election issue; it was incomprehensible to most local districts and eventually lost the support of the GOP caucus in the assembly. The kerfuffle over Goals 2000 funds did not, in the final tally, detract from the significance of Allen's signature education initiative. But it did indicate the kind of stubbornness that, in later years, may have damaged Allen's political aspirations.

CHIEF ECONOMIC DEVELOPMENT OFFICER

George Allen's populism did not always fit comfortably with the prevalent outlook in Virginia's business community, especially for leaders in Northern Virginia. Allen's call for lower taxes, reduced spending, and smaller government was often perceived to be more appropriately applied at the federal level than to state government. There were two specific issues on which these leaders were consistently at odds with the priorities of the Allen administration. First, Northern Virginians continually argued that the commonwealth's inability to fund needed transportation improvements not only was choking automobile traffic, it was having a detrimental effect on economic development. Some form of tax increase—either the state gas tax or tolls on commuters—was contained in almost every call to address the detested gridlock. Second, groups such as the Virginia Business Higher Education Council believed that maintaining and improving Virginia's higher education system was essential to the state's long-term economic future. They opposed the Wilder administration's decision in the recession of the early 1990s to allow colleges and universities to raise tuition by double digits to minimize social service cuts for the most vulnerable and avoid raising taxes. In the first two years of the Allen administration, they opposed cuts to higher education budgets and what they considered to be the appointment of political hacks and not higher education advocates to the State Council of Higher Education for Virginia.

At the same time, Allen embraced the role of Virginia's chief economic development officer with unsurpassed vigor. The Wilder administration had achieved national recognition for Virginia as the "best-managed state" in the country. Campaigning on the slogan that Virginia was open for business, Allen saw attracting out-of-state investment to the commonwealth through business relocation or expansion as an essential part of his gubernatorial role. He continually pitched the advantages of the commonwealth on overseas trade missions. He proposed legislation that would enable the state to compete more successfully with other states on incentive packages for business considering relocating. And he said that he spent more time on economic development than on any other aspect of his governorship.

Allen's initial high-profile recruitment—attracting Disney America to build a history theme park in northern Virginia—came to naught. Disney had acquired nearly three thousand acres of vacant land in Haymarket, a town in Prince William County. Shortly after his election in 1993, the company proposed building a history theme park with residential development and office space that was forecast to create three thousand jobs and $12 million in county tax revenues. Disney chairman and CEO Michael Eisner said the park would "touch upon the more painful, disturbing and agonizing parts of American history." The Allen administration convinced the General Assembly to seal the deal by offering Disney $163 million in incentives. But local landowners and preservationists continued to oppose the project, arguing that it would be located too close to an actual Civil War site at Bull Run. And the opposition was given an extraordinary assist when a group of prominent Civil War historians and the documentarian Ken Burns publicly denounced it. As Dr. Ed Ayers, a well-known historian and former president of the University of Richmond, explained in a 2019 retrospective on the controversy, "What people found alarming about Disney, other than the fact that it was displacing a real historical place, was they were taking away something real and replacing it with something made up."[48] In the wake of this opposition, Disney abandoned the project, thinking the bad publicity was not worth the price.

During the remainder of his administration, however, Allen was instrumental in attracting a host of well-known companies to Virginia, especially high-tech firms to the thriving Northern Virginia suburbs outside Washington, DC. He put together an impressive list of successes as Motorola, Siemens, Toshiba, Gateway, and Oracle all made commitments to Virginia during the final years of Allen's administration. Not every commitment fulfilled its original goals. Motorola, for example, ultimately decided not to build a plant in Virginia. But there is no doubt that Virginia's reputation as a business locale was significantly enhanced during this period. Allen viewed these efforts as his most important legacy. Speaking to the *Washington Post* in 1997, Allen said that twenty to thirty years in the future, these recruitments would be "monuments" to his administration. "It changed the way that Virginians looked at themselves and their capabilities, and the way that the rest of the world looked at Virginia."[49]

To be sure, several forces that had little to do with Allen were making Virginia attractive to high-tech companies. Ironically, the Virginia business community was the beneficiary, to a large extent, of the growth of big government in Washington that Allen so loudly and consistently denounced. With the growth of defense budgets in the 1980s and the increasing reliance of the federal government on technology to deliver and monitor almost all its services, it is not surprising that the nation's leading high-tech firms would want to have a sizable presence next door to the seat of government, where its spending was dependent on what Allen labeled the "heavy, grimy boot of taxation." In addition, Northern Virginia business leaders continued to voice their concern that the unwillingness of the Allen administration to address financing issues (read: tolls and taxes) for road improvements was causing quality-of-life issues that were bound to stunt the attractiveness of the region. Still, there can be little doubt that Allen's success on this front permanently elevated the role of the Virginia governor as the commonwealth's chief economic development officer. In the ensuing years, the number of jobs created in Virginia became a measure by which almost all administrations were judged.

The Postgovernorship Elections

After leaving the governorship, Allen was involved in three US Senate elections. In 2000, he defeated Democratic incumbent Chuck Robb, maintaining that the sitting senator had abandoned commonsense "Virginia values" in favor of the liberal outlook of the national Democratic Party. By the time he ran for reelection in 2006, Allen was being mentioned as a potential Republican presidential candidate. But his ascent came to an unexpected halt when he was upset by Democratic challenger Jim Webb, a loss attributed in part to a self-inflicted wound—the infamous "Macaca moment" in which Allen insulted an Indian American Democratic operative who was shadowing his campaign. When Webb declined to run for reelection, Allen attempted to regain his seat in 2012, but lost decisively to former Democratic governor Tim Kaine in a race that demonstrated the declining appeal of Allen's brand of conservatism in a changing Virginia.

2000 RACE

Allen was riding nearly 70 percent approval ratings in December 1997[50]— the final month of his gubernatorial term—when he announced at a statewide Republican Party meeting that he was all but certain to challenge two-term incumbent Robb for his US Senate seat in 2000. A year later, at the same annual GOP meeting, he officially declared his candidacy and characterized Robb in the same way he had depicted Terry: as a remnant of a burnt-out state Democratic regime. But his starting block for the race would be much different this time. Allen had begun his campaign against Terry as a prohibitive underdog. This time, against Robb, he was the front-runner, with a ten percentage point lead.[51]

Robb, the son-in-law of ex-president Lyndon Johnson, made a dashing entry into Virginia politics in the 1970s. He was a square-jawed former Marine captain who had commanded a rifle company in Vietnam, and who, at a time when the Democratic Party was drifting to the left and losing support, urged the party to realign in the center. Flush with Johnson family money and connections, Robb was elected lieutenant governor in 1977 and governor in 1981, ending a twelve-year GOP era at the state's helm. His agenda of being fiscally conservative, liberal on social issues, and strongly pro–public schools created a playbook that would lead Democrats to victory in the next two gubernatorial elections (a streak eventually broken by Allen). He aligned with a group of southern Democrats, including Bill Clinton, that pushed the national party to a more centrist platform. Robb won an open US Senate seat in 1988, easily beating a weak Republican opponent to become the state's first Democratic senator in sixteen years. There was chatter about Robb as a future presidential candidate. Few guessed at this moment that he had peaked.

Robb was tarnished in 1991 and 1992 by reports of marriage infidelity and weekend partying during his days as governor, by the escalating tensions with Wilder over the wiretapping incident, and by the subsequent federal investigation, which could have resulted in criminal charges. In 1994, Robb was reelected in a close race over Republican Oliver North, the central figure in the Iran-Contra scandal of the 1980s and perhaps the only GOP candidate that a weakened Robb could have defeated. Instrumental to Robb's victory was the support of John Warner, Virginia's popular senior senator, for Marshall Coleman, an independent Republican candidate who entered the race for the sole purpose of damaging North. Robb received 45.6 percent of the vote in the three-way race. He had held on to his seat, but Republicans were convinced that a stronger candidate would have led to a different result. The 2000 Allen-Robb campaign was marked by vigorous debate and negative, misleading ads that were often funded by a then astounding $5.9 million spent by the Democratic National Committee and $4.3 million by the Republican National Committee.[52]

Robb prided himself on being a senator who would make "difficult" votes on both social and economic issues. In 1996, he was one of a handful of fourteen senators and the only one from the South who voted against the Defense of Marriage Act, an antigay bill enshrining the position that marriage was an act that took place between a man and a woman. Robb's Democratic colleague, Barbara Boxer of California, had urged Robb not to vote against DOMA, telling him that "it is going to kill you in Virginia." But Robb not only voted against the bill but gave an impassioned speech on the floor, calling it a basic civil rights issue and warning that, in forty years, supporters of the bill would be embarrassed by their position. Ultimately, both Boxer and Robb turned out to be correct.

Robb also positioned himself as budget hawk who had cast hard votes to help Clinton create surpluses for the first time in a generation. But some of these difficult votes were for tax increases that Allen routinely criticized. By contrast, Allen proposed a plan to give families $1,000 per year to buy school supplies and supported a $2 trillion tax cut over ten years that was a centerpiece of Republican presidential nominee George W. Bush's campaign—policies Robb called "irresponsible."

Allen, who had never served in the military, tried to offset Robb's combat experience by calling for a constitutional amendment banning desecration of the American flag; Robb strongly opposed the idea. Robb portrayed Allen as an opponent of abortion rights. Allen criticized Robb's 87 percent voting record with Clinton, who remained unpopular in Virginia.[53] In the closing weeks of the campaign, Allen's lead had shrunk to three points, and Robb, who had been campaigning heavily in Black precincts, attacked Allen for being insensitive to racial issues. Robb issued a list of complaints. including Allen's display seven years earlier of a Confederate flag in his home, his opposition to a separate state holiday for Martin Luther King, a proclamation he signed as governor creating a Confederate History Month, and his abolition of parole as governor. Allen called Robb's criticism "desperate."

Allen won the election 52–48 percent, running well in suburban and rural Virginia and benefiting from a strong showing by Bush in the state's presidential race. The victory was testament to another disciplined campaign by Allen and his ease with voters compared to Robb's wooden style. Allen also sailed in strong Republican tailwinds that he had helped create in Virginia during the decade. In the late 1990s, Republicans gained control of both General Assembly chambers for the first time since Reconstruction. Allen's victory gave Republicans brief possession of Virginia's five state elected offices—governor, lieutenant governor, attorney general, and two US Senate seats—for the first and only time.

2006

In the Senate, Allen drew far more accolades for his political skills than for his attention to policy. He was chairman of the National Republican Senatorial Committee from 2003 to 2005, a powerful party branch that raises money for GOP Senate candidates. Republicans added one seat to their Senate majority during Allen's tenure.[54] The chairmanship allowed Allen to travel the country, meeting prominent Republican donors and local party activists. He made a good impression and sparked talk about his possible future in the White House. In April 2005, Allen finished first in a poll by the *National Journal* that asked eighty-five Republican insiders to predict their party's 2008 presidential nominee.[55] Allen parted ways with Jay Timmons, his longtime chief of staff and Virginia campaign adviser who was credited with keeping Allen on message. Timmons was replaced by Dick Wadhams, a well-regarded campaign consultant from Colorado, and Allen hired others on his Senate staff who also had political experience in other states. After his term as NRSC chairman expired and his 2006 Senate campaign approached, Allen continued to visit Iowa and New Hampshire—key early states in presidential nominations. He told Virginia reporters that he was solely focused on winning reelection to the Senate but refused to promise that he would serve out his term if he won.[56]

Allen might not have been so bold if he had thought he faced strong competition for reelection. But the Democrat who posed the biggest threat, former governor Mark Warner, chose to sit out the election before mounting a successful Senate campaign in 2008. That left two Democratic challengers vying to take on Allen, both making their first run for elective office: one-time Republican Jim Webb, a novelist and former secretary of the navy under Ronald Reagan, and Harris Miller, a wealthy Washington lobbyist. Webb won a June primary that drew only 156,000 voters and entered the general election campaign facing obstacles: Allen had a sixteen-point lead in the polls[57] and a $7.5 million war chest, compared to the $200,000 Webb had in the bank.[58]

Webb portrayed Allen as a yes-man to President George W. Bush, noting that he had a 96 percent voting record in support of the president's positions.[59] Much of the debate focused on Bush's increasingly unpopular invasion of Iraq in 2003 under the false premise that the hostile nation had weapons of mass destruction. Webb, a much-decorated Marine combat officer in Vietnam, opposed the Iraq War; Allen supported it. Webb wanted to repeal corporate tax cuts Bush had signed into law; Allen defended them. But these issues took a back seat to a series of astounding gaffes by Allen that again raised questions about his racial sensitivity and triggered his political downfall.

The bombshell moment came on August 11, 2006. Allen, addressing a mostly White crowd in rural Dickenson County, departed from his script and pointed to a videographer of Indian descent who was working for Webb. "This fellow here, over here with the yellow shirt, Macaca, or whatever his name is. He's with my opponent. He's following us around everywhere," Allen said. "Let's give a welcome to Macaca here. Welcome to America and the real world of Virginia."[60] The comments were widely perceived as racial slur: The photographer he welcomed to the United States was a native of Fairfax County attending the University of Virginia, and *Macaca* is a monkey genus.[61] Although Allen eventually apologized, his campaign bungled the initial response, suggesting that it was simply a media-driven issue that did not warrant an explanation. But the speech went viral and remained in national and state headlines for the rest of the campaign. The issue caught added wind a month later when three people who attended the University of Virginia with Allen said he used a derogatory term to describe Blacks when he was a student. Allen called the allegations "ludicrously false."[62]

Another strained moment occurred during a televised debate when Allen, who had been raised as a Presbyterian, berated a panelist who asked him to comment on a report that his mother was likely born Jewish. Allen said the question was irrelevant and, as far as he knew, the report was wrong. A day later, he acknowledged he knew his mother was Jewish; she had kept her origin secret out of lifelong fear after her father was arrested by the Nazis.[63] "I still had a ham sandwich for lunch," he told a reporter from the *Richmond Times-Dispatch*.[64]

By the end of September, the race had become a dead heat, and a plurality (49–37 percent) of likely Virginia voters said Allen should not run for president.[65] Webb would never have a campaign bank account as large as Allen's, but he outraised his opponent during the final months of the contest. On Election Day, Webb edged Allen by 8,941 votes out of almost 2.4 million cast. Although Allen was entitled to a taxpayer-funded recount, he decided two days later not to seek one, saying it would not change the election's outcome.

2012

Allen remained active in politics after his loss to Webb, maintaining a fundraising apparatus, traveling the state to support Republican candidates, and criticizing passage of the Affordable Care Act. He founded the American Energy Freedom Center, a nonprofit organization advocating for free-market energy and environmental policies. Allen was coy about his own political plans, but few doubted he was eyeing a 2012 rematch against Webb for his old Senate seat. Allen announced his candidacy in January 2011, saying he had been chastened by the Macaca incident. Two weeks later, Webb announced he would not seek a second term. His decision was not shocking: Webb was innovative and engaged on policy matters but had little patience for political glad-handing. He was anxious to return to private life as a globe-trotting writer. Democrats quickly turned to former governor Tim Kaine, a quick-witted Harvard Law School graduate who had led the state from 2006 to 2010. Kaine demurred at first but, with urging from President Barack Obama, announced his candidacy in April 2011 and had a clear path to his party's nomination. Allen easily won a four-way Republican primary, garnering 66 percent of the vote.[66]

What followed was a civil campaign that, in the aftermath of the Great Recession, centered on fiscal issues. Allen rarely strayed from his talking points. With the rise of the tea party wing of the Republican Party, he cast himself as a budget hawk, focusing on debt reduction by less spending, a balanced budget amendment, and a presidential line-item veto. Kaine said Allen's rhetoric clashed with his Senate record from 2001 to 2007, which began with an $86 billion national budget surplus and ended with a $342 billion deficit.[67] He repeatedly criticized Allen for backing expensive Bush administration initiatives that relied on borrowing, including tax cuts, a Medicaid prescription program, and the Iraq War. Kaine backed the 2011 sequestration compromise that would require equal, automatic cuts to defense and social programs if Congress could not agree to a ten-year debt reduction plan. Allen opposed sequestration, saying Virginia stood to lose 207,000 jobs from the automatic cuts.[68]

Allen and Kaine vigorously debated their economic records as governors, although they served facing different challenges. Allen was governor during boom years and signed budgets that increased general fund spending by 46 percent. Kaine, who had governed during the Great Recession, often noted that he cut general spending by 2 percent during his term.[69] Allen pointed out that the spending went down because the Republican-led House of Delegates repeatedly rejected Kaine proposals to raise taxes.

But perhaps more than anything else, the 2012 race was shaped by the broader landscape of Virginia politics, one that had dramatically shifted from Allen's election as governor in 1993 and first Senate race in 2000. President Barack Obama was up for reelection, and Allen tried to make Kaine's closeness to the chief executive an issue. Other than Rod Blagojevich from Obama's home state of Illinois, Kaine had been the first governor to endorse Obama's 2008 presidential campaign and had served, during the last year of his term, as Obama's hand-picked chair of the Democratic National Committee.[70] Allen criticized Kaine for backing Obama's Affordable Care Act and predicted he would be a yes-man for the president in the Senate. But it was a message that no longer resonated with the growing diversity in Virginia's suburbs. These voters, especially in the growing and increasingly diverse suburbs of Northern Virginia, were far more comfortable with Kaine's inclusiveness and social progressivism than they were with Allen's social conservatism. Culturally, lingering questions about Allen's racial sensitivities related to his declaration of Confederate History Month as governor and the 2006 campaign made his candidacy far less appealing in the suburbs than it had been when he ran for governor in 1993.

Allen and Kaine started their campaign even in polls, and Kaine gradually pulled to a small but consistent lead. More than $80 million poured into the campaign, about two-thirds of it coming from super PACs.[71] On Election Day, Kaine won a convincing 53 percent of the vote, with more than the margin of his 225,000-vote victory coming from Northern Virginia.[72] Allen, days after the election, said he would not run for office again.[73]

Allen's Legacy

Since the abolition of parole and Allen's truth-in-sentencing reforms, violent crime in Virginia clearly declined. Allen himself cited the positive statistics when responding to a commission that Governor Terry McAuliffe formed in 2015 to examine the continuing desirability of parole abolition. Allen noted that the "Commonwealth has remained well below the national property crime average for over a decade and we rank eighth lowest in the country. When Governor McAuliffe was elected [in 2013], Virginia had the third lowest violent crime rate in the country. Those are the positive results of our public safety reforms and there should be no backtracking. . . . [The commission] should avoid sanctimonious, blissful wishing away of the principle of holding criminals personally responsible for their acts."[74] Academic researchers have debated the causes of the nationwide reduction in crime that has occurred for years. Some researchers have suggested that property and violent crime rates were dropping in Virginia and nationally even before parole was abolished. And they have maintained that demographic and economic influences may have been more important than parole and sentencing policies. From Allen's perspective, however, it was simply common sense that if repeat offenders were responsible for a significant percentage of violent crime, keeping rapists in jail for twelve years rather than four, and murderers for thirty years rather than twelve, would have a salutary impact on public safety.

Regardless of how much impact could be directly attributed to Allen for the reduction in violent crime, there was a political irony in the result. It became increasingly difficult for Republicans in Virginia to capitalize on their tough-on-crime stance in future elections. As crime became a less salient issue to voters in suburban Virginia, it ranked far lower on their priority lists than jobs, transportation, and education. In 2005 the Republican candidate for governor, Jerry Kilgore, made Kaine's personal opposition to the death penalty an integral part of his campaign, accompanied by a gut-wrenching campaign ad in which the widow of a slain police officer noted that Kaine, if he had his way, would not support the death penalty for her husband's murderer. But Kaine easily parried Kilgore's attacks, noting that he would carry out his constitutional duties and suggesting that criticism of his "pro-life stance" was an attack on his religious beliefs. In his 2017 campaign for governor, Republican Ed Gillespie pointed to gang violence in Northern Virginia and attributed it to the spread of the MS-13 gang, which originated in Los Angeles. Gillespie directed this claim at suburban women who left the Democratic Party, but it did not help. Virginia voters linked all Republicans to their distaste of Donald Trump, and Gillespie lost in a landslide.

In the years after 2017, Democrats began to focus on racial inequities in the criminal justice system and truly began to modify the framework that Allen had established almost thirty years prior. Democrats abolished the death penalty, promoted the legalization of marijuana, and combined this with efforts to expunge the criminal records of those convicted of or in jail for marijuana-related crimes; they also supported the elimination of mandatory minimum penalties to give judges more discretion and to provide a greater incentive for rehabilitation. Republicans considering runs for statewide office once again saw an opening similar to what George Allen perceived in 1994 when Mary Sue Terry embraced gun control as a central issue. Denouncing "liberal overreach," prominent candidates for the Republican gubernatorial and attorney general nominations in 2021 claimed that Democratic support for reducing mandatory minimum sentences would put violent criminals back on the streets and serve as evidence that Democrats were more supportive of criminals than Virginia families. A generation after his abolition of parole, Allen's signature initiative was still at the heart of Virginia's political debate.

Allen's education reforms in establishing stringent content standards, linking them to graduation requirements and school performance, and providing the public with transparent annual reports on school and district performance also established the framework in which K–12 policy was set in Virginia for a generation. The standards and tests themselves were continuously tweaked to ensure they were aligned with the program's principal goals and to allow "rigorous assessment" such as Advanced Placement tests and the International Baccalaureate to substitute for specified exams. The clearest sign that the standards had become embedded was that Allen's successors—Republican Gilmore and Democrats Warner and Kaine—maintained the program's fundamental structure while they established practices to improve the performance of students and schools. Under Gilmore, for example, a statewide system of support was created to focus on helping students in early reading and algebra. The Warner administration created an Office of School Improvement and Project Graduation to enhance the capacity of low-performing schools and to enable students to meet the more rigorous graduation requirements. The Kaine administration focused resources intensively on the school districts in the state that needed the most assistance while recognizing programs that exceeded state and federal standards. Governors and legislators of both parties consistently referred to the above-average performance of Virginia students on national tests as a signature example of what Virginia was doing right.

Nearly a quarter century after Allen left office, the focus of Virginia's educational policy began to shift toward aligning the K–12 system with the changing economic conditions of the twenty-first century, emphasizing critical thinking, problem solving, and teamwork. As business leaders still maintained that graduates were often unprepared for the workforce, more emphasis was placed on strengthening the links between public education and workforce development. Career pathways programs were started, introducing students to potential career choices as early as middle school. High school students attended dual enrollment programs with community colleges, enabling them to graduate not only with a high school diploma but also with a credential or even an associate's degree that gave them immediate marketability. And specialty programs in coding and other technical skills became far more widespread. These changes were accompanied by reductions in some of the testing requirements that had been advanced over the years. Yet Allen's emphasis on school accountability and transparency to the public remained an integral part of Virginia's K–12 system.

Allen's elevation of the governor as Virginia's chief economic development officer has only grown in importance in the last quarter century. Every governor since him, regardless of party, has worked to maintain the commonwealth's reputation as a good place to do business and an even better place to relocate one. Allen and Terry McAuliffe, for example, could hardly have had more different governing philosophies and policy priorities, yet they were extraordinarily similar in how much they relished pitching Virginia to out-of-state firms, both indefatigable salesmen when a business relocation opportunity presented itself. Virginia governors have consistently taken credit for the jobs they "created" when the Governor's Opportunity Fund, an incentive program for relocation and expansion, is used to bring jobs to, or expand jobs in, the state. Indeed, on several occasions the General Assembly has found it necessary to rein in gubernatorial exuberance by imposing strict performance criteria on the use of incentive funds and raising concerns when, for example, the McAuliffe administration provided incentives to a Chinese firm that had no intention (and no capability) of bringing business to Virginia.

Allen's vision of transforming Virginia into a high-tech oasis was also carried forward by his successors. Mark Warner, for example, ran for governor in 2001 on a promise to use his experience as a pioneering cell phone entrepreneur to position Virginia at the forefront of the twenty-first-century economic competition among the states and to bring innovative solutions to address rural economic decline. In 2019, Allen's vision was realized when Virginia won a competition with almost every other major state to land a second Amazon headquarters in Northern Virginia. While some cynical observers believed that Amazon had created an artificial competition to extract a better deal for a decision it would have made under any circumstance, Virginians saw it as validation of its sophisticated approach to economic development, offering much less in monetary incentives that most other serious competitors but linking the Amazon headquarters to investments the state would make in its universities and community colleges to ensure that the company would have the highly skilled workforce it required. Ralph Northam, the Democratic governor who finalized the deal, touted Virginia's return to the CNBC rankings as the "best state for business" as one of the major accomplishments of his administration.

Allen's defeats in 2006 and 2012 coincided with a dramatic Republic electoral slide from 2005 to 2020. In this period, Virginia Republicans won only a single election for president, senator, and governor—Bob McDonnell's gubernatorial victory over Creigh Deeds, a rural-based, pro-gun Democrat. During this time, Virginia cycled through the entire political color palette in presidential elections, moving from reliably red to purple to blue. Although Republicans were making historic gains in rural Virginia during this period, GOP appeal in the suburbs declined precipitously. Suburbs such as Henrico County that had been red turned blue; others, such as Virginia Beach and Chesterfield County, shifted from red to purple; and the populous Northern Virginia suburbs became a Democratic fortress. In the gubernatorial election of 2017 won by Northam, Kaine's senatorial victory in 2018, and Warner's reelection as US senator in 2020, the Democrats carried all ten most populous jurisdictions in the commonwealth. Undoubtedly, there was a negative Trump effect that became an albatross around the necks of Virginia Republicans, but recreating a coalition that attracts pro-gun social conservatives and moderate suburban voters had become a genuine challenge for the state's GOP.

The Republican message that had proved so potent in the 1990s—low taxes, tough on crime, welfare reform—had lost its power to mobilize suburban voters. Improving transportation, investing in schools, and addressing social inequities have become more potent messages for a population that has grown far more diverse and more sympathetic to the message of national Democrats. Perhaps equally as important, Allen and conservative Virginia Republicans embraced social issues that suburbanites have turned against. The pro-gun Second Amendment perspective of Republicans has been increasingly rejected by suburban voters in favor of what they consider to be commonsense gun safety reforms. Efforts to restrict access to abortion that go beyond the advocacy of parental consent have come up against the belief that the GOP is advocating excessive government intrusion in the personal choices of women. Opposition to gay marriage and to antidiscrimination legislation designed to offer protections to the LGBTQ community has been perceived as mean-spirited by young people, with whom the GOP is gaining a toxic reputation. And statewide campaigns focused on the preservation of Confederate monuments have become directly antithetical to efforts to rebrand Virginia as a tech-friendly state.

In the final tally, Allen surely transformed the Virginia political landscape, bringing his party to power after twelve years of Democratic rule and implementing reforms in criminal justice and education that became embedded in the policy landscape of the commonwealth for a generation. At the same time, Allen's own political career foundered as he found it increasingly difficult to negotiate the changing dynamics of Virginia politics—he became identified with a national party that was losing favor in the commonwealth. His positions on a range of social issues became increasingly out of step with the suburban voters who had helped propel him to the governorship in 1993 and to the US Senate in 2000. And his "Macaca moment" in 2006 became emblematic of a Republican Party that was insensitive to issues of race and ethnicity and that was harming Republican chances with the very demographic groups that were growing most quickly in Virginia. In the 1990s Allen was able to bring rural Republicans and suburban voters together over a common agenda. At the beginning of the third decade of the twenty-first century, Virginia Republicans needed to find issues and candidates that could replicate his success in a vastly altered political environment.

In 2021, the impact of the COVID-19 pandemic provided that opportunity for Republican gubernatorial candidate Glenn Youngkin. He capitalized on parental discontent with the closing of public schools and its replacement with twelve to fifteen months of remote learning, along with the rapid increase in inflation that had followed in COVID-19's wake. Borrowing from Allen's playbook, he adopted a signature sartorial note, a red fleece vest; promised to keep schools open; employed the slogan "Parents Matter" to contrast with what he decried as his opponent's indifference to their concerns; and, pledged to reduce the tax burden on hard-working Virginians. Allen himself was a happy warrior once again, crisscrossing the commonwealth on behalf of a candidate and ticket that stood for the continuing relevance of the ideas that had animated his career.

Notes

1. Mario Sequeira Quesada, "Va. General Assembly Reaches Highest Women Representation in History," Capital News Service, November 6, 2019.
2. Tom Sherwood and Molly Moore, "Mary Sue Terry: The Next Big Step," *Washington Post*, November 9, 1985.
3. Virginia Department of Elections, 1985, https://historical.elections.virginia .gov/data/serve_file_pages_for_item/47736/Election/.
4. Virginia Department of Elections, 1989, https://historical.elections.virginia .gov/data/serve_file_pages_for_item/47459/Election/.
5. Tyler Whitley, "Beyer Discloses Race News—Tells Rally He'll Run, but Not for Governor," *Richmond Times-Dispatch*, October 17, 1992.
6. Warren Fiske, "Competing against the Odds Drives Hard-Working Allen," *Virginian-Pilot*, October 17, 1993.
7. On the disgusting gerrymander, see "Redistricting Hopes for N.Va. Revived; Democrats Settle Key Dispute," *Washington Post*, November 20, 1991.
8. Rob Eure, "Terry Has Strong Lead," *Virginian-Pilot*, January 22, 1993.
9. Warren Fiske, "Poll: Terry Outscores Closest Competitor 2–1," *Virginian-Pilot*, May 7, 1993.
10. *Washington Post*, February 17, 1993.
11. John F. Harris and Donald P. Baker, "GOP Taps Allen for Va. Governor," *Washington Post*, June 5, 1993.
12. Ibid.
13. Larry Sabato, "Virginia's 1993 Elections: The 12-Year Itch Returns," *University of Virginia Newsletter* 70, no. 2 (January 1994).
14. Harris and Baker, "GOP Taps Allen for Va. Governor."
15. Donald P. Baker, "In Debate, Terry Leans Right; Allen Tries to Capitalize on Democrat's Critique of Clinton," *Washington Post*, August 1, 1993.

16. John F. Harris, "Terry Sues Wilder over VRS Post," *Washington Post*, December 18, 1993.

17. "Va. Gun Poll Shows Support for 5-Day Waiting Period," *Washington Post*, June 17, 1993.

18. Tyler Whitley, "State FOP Supports Allen," *Richmond Times-Dispatch*, August 31, 1993.

19. John F. Harris and Donald P. Baker, "Terry Wants 5-Day Wait to Buy Guns; Issue Could Influence Race for Va. Governor," *Washington Post*, June 9, 1993.

20. Baker, "In Debate, Terry Leans Right."

21. John F. Harris, "Wilder Says Terry Should Hit the Trail; Take Message to Voters, Governor Urges," *Washington Post*, August 27, 1993.

22. Dale Eisman, "Allen Pulls Nearly Even with Terry in New Poll," *Virginian-Pilot*, September 1, 1993.

23. John F. Harris, "Wilder Says Terry Was Unethical: Governor Criticizes Statements on VMI," *Washington Post*, September 29, 1993.

24. Margaret Edds, "Terry's Marital Status Comes Up in Candidates' Debate," *Virginian-Pilot*, October 16, 1993.

25. Virginia Department of Elections, historical elections database, https://historical.elections.virginia.gov/.

26. Virginia Department of Elections, historical elections database, 1993 Governor General Election, https://historical.elections.virginia.gov/.

27. Sabato, "Virginia's 1993 Elections."

28. Virginia Department of Elections, historical elections database.

29. George Allen, "Inaugural Address," January 15, 1994, https://rga.lis.virginia.gov/Published/1994/SD1B.

30. Peter Baker and Donald P. Baker, "Allen Assails Democrats at Inauguration: Virginia Governor's Address Unusually Partisan," *Washington Post*, January 16, 1994.

31. Virginia Center for Public Safety, "Fact Sheet on Virginia's One-Handgun-A-Month Law."

32. Peter Baker, "Allen Offers Plan to Abolish Parole, *Washington Post*," August 17, 1994.

33. Sarah Scarbrough, "Abolition of Parole in Virginia," *Bacon's Rebellion*, March 19, 2015.

34. David Lerman and Bob Evans, "Allen Wins Parole Reform," *Daily Press*, October 1, 1994.

35. Peter Baker and Spencer S. Hsu, "Allen's Key Address Falls on Empty Chambers," *Washington Post*, January 12, 1995.

36. Ibid.

37. Peter Baker and Spencer S. Hsu, "Virginia Legislators Shred Allen's Agenda," *Washington Post*, February 3, 1995. See also Frank Atkinson, *Virginia in the Vanguard* (Lanham, MD: Rowman & Littlefield, 2006), 135–37.

38. Chichester quoted in Baker and Hsu, "Virginia Legislators Shred Allen Agenda."
39. Larry J. Sabato, "The 1995 Elections: Running in Place," *University of Virginia Newsletter* 72, no. 1 (January 1996).
40. Peter Baker and Spencer S. Hsu, "Republicans Criticize Tone Allen Gave Virginia Elections," *Washington Post,* November 15, 1995.
41. Richard L. Berke, "Republican Drive Fails to Advance around Country," *New York Times,* November 8, 1995.
42. Mark Christie, "Virginia's Education Reform Works," *University of Virginia Newsletter* 77, no. 5 (August 2001).
43. Jessica Portner, "Virginia Governor's Agenda Gets Mixed Reception," *Education Week,* June 1, 1994.
44. Virginia Department of Education, "Historical Overview of the Standards of Learning Program," https://www.doe.virginia.gov/home/show publisheddocument/1466/637947310184070000/.
45. Spencer S. Hsu and Ellen Nakashima, "Allen Embraces Democrats in Address," *Washington Post,* January 11, 1996.
46. Christie, "Virginia's Education Reform Works."
47. Spencer Hsu, "Allen Shuns U.S. Aid," *Washington Post,* May 26, 1995.
48. Ayers quoted in C. Suarez Rojas, "Disney's 'Lost America': History Derailed Virginia Theme Park 25 Years Ago," *Richmond Times-Dispatch,* August 17, 2019.
49. Allen quoted in Spencer S. Hsu, "The Transformation of Governor Allen—and Virginia," *Washington Post,* January 9, 1998.
50. Warren Fiske, "Already on the Campaign Trail?," *Virginian-Pilot,* June 26, 2005.
51. "Surveys Show Virginians Favor Allen in Senate Race," staff report, *Virginian-Pilot,* July 20, 2000.
52. Warren Fiske, "Allen Beats Robb in Senate Race," *Virginian-Pilot,* November 8, 2000.
53. Holly Heyser, "Robb, Allen Tangle in first Senate Debate," *Virginian-Pilot,* August 6, 2000.
54. See the website at https://www.senate.gov/history/partydiv.htm.
55. "Insiders Poll," *National Journal,* April 30, 2005.
56. Fiske, "Already on the Campaign Trail?"
57. "Allen Holds Big Lead over Webb in Poll of State Voters," *Virginian-Pilot,* July 30, 2006.
58. "Voters Pit Webb against Allen," *Virginian-Pilot,* June 14, 2006.
59. "In State and Nation, Allen's on the Move," *Virginian-Pilot,* March 19, 2006.
60. *George Allen Introduces Macaca,* YouTube video, August 11, 2006.
61. "'Macaca' New Call to Arms for Democrats," *Washington Post,* March 18, 2012.

62. "Ex-Classmates Charge That Allen Has Used Racial Epithet," *Virginian-Pilot,* September 26, 2006.
63. "U.S. Sen. George Allen Reveals: 'I Have Jewish Roots,'" *Virginian-Pilot,* September 20, 2006.
64. "Allen Tells of His Jewish Heritage," *Richmond Times-Dispatch,* September 20, 2006.
65. "For Allen, Support for Bid in 2008 Is Dwindling," *Virginian-Pilot,* September 12, 2006.
66. Virginia Department of Elections, historical elections database.
67. Office of Budget Management historical tables.
68. "Allen Releases New TV Ad Today about Defense Cuts," *Richmond Times-Dispatch,* October 8, 2012.
69. "Dueling Governors," *Richmond Times-Dispatch,* October 7, 2012.
70. "Kaine Endorses Obama at Richmond Fundraiser," *Virginian-Pilot,* February 18, 2007.
71. "Kaine Cut into GOP Strongholds en Route to Defeating Allen," *Richmond Times-Dispatch,* November 7, 2012.
72. Virginia Department of Elections, historical elections database.
73. "Allen Reflects on Failed Senate Bid; Won't Run Again," *Richmond Times-Dispatch,* November 13, 2012.
74. Allen quoted in Laura Vozzella, "George Allen Warns against Bringing 'Dangerously Lenient' Parole Back to Virginia," *Washington Post,* June 25, 2015.

The New Dominion in the Twenty-First Century

John G. Milliken and Wendy Chen

> The outcome of every conflict is determined by the extent to which the audience becomes involved in it.
>
> —E. E. Schattschneider, *The Semisovereign People*

Virginia has voted increasingly Democratic in the first two decades of the twenty-first century. Of the six governors elected since 2000, four have been Democrats. In five elections to the US Senate, four Democrats have won (longtime incumbent senator John Warner won in 2002 with no Democratic opposition). Following the 2020 election, the state's federal delegation in the House of Representatives was 7–4 Democratic. The state legislative House of Delegates, which had been controlled by the Republican Party since 2000, flipped to the Democrats in 2019, then back again to the Republicans in 2021. Is this all a sudden new phenomenon, or has it been building for a time? In this chapter we show that the drivers of the shift have been at work for more than half a century, clawing away at the foundations of the earlier order and putting in place the pieces of a new political framework. It is not rocket science, it is numbers: who the voters are and where they live. It's as simple as that. And the changes started as early as the 1940s and built, with some back and forth, to what we see today. More and more people, new arrivals in Virginia and those previously barred from voting, began to participate, and the tight little oligarchy that Yale professor V. O. Key had characterized as running Virginia began to lose control.[1] To understand this fully, we need to examine Virginia's population and politics beginning in the years immediately following World War II and trace the dramatic changes that have occurred in the ensuing decades.

As the twentieth century progressed, election outcomes came increasingly to be driven by demographics, both in the size (which is a function of population, voter eligibility, and motivation) and in the racial composition of the electorate. Virginia's population in 1940 was 2,677,773. By 1960 it had grown to 3,966,949, an increase of more than 48 percent. In the next sixty years it doubled to more than 8.6 million. But the change was in more than total numbers. The location of those new residents and the dramatic increase in voting participation by African Americans, the state's largest minority population, transformed state politics in the last half of the twentieth century and propelled it into the modern era. These changes did not necessarily benefit one party or the other but instead helped whichever candidate or party addressed such issues as education and voting rights, issues that mattered in the fast-growing suburbs and in the cities and counties with large African American populations.

As Ron Heinemann makes clear in chapter 1, the Martin and Byrd organizations, which dominated Virginia politics for more than sixty years, until the mid-1960s, relied on a controlled electorate based in the rural counties of Southside and the Shenandoah Valley. In their one-party state where access to voting was limited by law and practice, elections could be won with between 6 and 10 percent of the voting-age population. It was, as V. O. Key described it, "a museum piece . . . control[led] by an oligarchy."[2] To the extent there was competition, it was in the Democratic primary, not the general election.[3]

But population growth meant new people coming from different places, people who were not steeped in Virginia tradition and who in elementary school had not read about the Lost Cause and the valor of gray-clad Civil War generals. For the most part, these new people did not settle on the farms or in the small towns that were the base of organization strength but instead found homes in the communities where jobs were plentiful, especially in the counties just outside Washington, DC, and around the shipyards and the many military facilities in the cities of Hampton Roads. And increasingly, the children and grandchildren of those on the farms also drifted into those same communities in search of employment.

At the same time that the population was growing and its locus was shifting, there was an increase in electoral participation by the state's African American population. It was these two dramatic changes in the demographics of Virginia voting that shaped and continue to shape the contours of state politics.

Population Changes and the Emergence of a New Geographic Majority

It is not coincidence that in the forty years (1926–66) that the Byrd organization dominated Virginia politics, nine of the ten governors elected with Byrd support were from nonurban parts of the commonwealth, and most had their political origins in the rural communities of Southside and the Shenandoah Valley.[4] Only John Garland Pollard, whom Byrd reluctantly supported in 1929, was from a city, Richmond, and he had actually been raised in rural King and Queen County. These rural and farming communities were the political heart of the Byrd organization and the drivers of the early twentieth-century Virginia economy. Local politics centered on the courthouses of those rural counties. Its leaders were often the local political officials, whose offices provided sources of patronage and kept the organization in close touch with local issues: the sheriff, the local prosecutor (commonwealth's attorney), the clerk of the court, and the commissioner of revenue and treasurer, who managed the local tax rolls. And once elected, the officeholder was often there until he (rarely, if ever, a she) died or voluntarily retired. In that event, the resulting vacancy was filled by appointment by the local circuit judge, so that the electorate rarely saw anyone on the ballot other than an incumbent. And the circuit judge, frequently a former legislator, held office for an eight-year term and was selected by his former colleagues in the General Assembly. The circle was very small and very closed.[5]

But demographic changes would soon outrun rural roots and organization ties, forcing the old order to give way. The rural base that had set the tone and determined the policies of the Byrd organization slowly gave way to superior numbers. The personal campaign through the courthouses of rural Southside counties that had once been a political necessity for any candidate hoping to win was replaced by the suburban shopping center and transit bus stop visits that were the mainstay of personal campaigning in the final decades of the twentieth century. To see these changes most dramatically, it is useful to focus on the fifty-year period of 1950–2000, when the changes were most dramatic and impactful.

In 1950, Virginia's population was 3,318,610. By 2000 it had more than doubled, to 7,079,057. But in the midst of this statewide increase there were significant disparities among the many counties and cities. Twenty counties actually lost population over those fifty years, and another seven counties grew by less than 10 percent. In contrast, the population of the nine jurisdictions constituting what is commonly thought of as Northern Virginia—Arlington, Alexandria, Falls Church, Fairfax County and City, Prince William County (including Manassas and Manassas Park), and Loudoun County—grew from 346,142 in 1950 to 2,230,623 in 2000. Growth occurred elsewhere as well, but nowhere was it as dramatic as in Northern Virginia.

The New Deal, World War II, and the steady growth of the federal bureaucracy had brought thousands of new people to the nation's capital to fill the exploding number of federal and contractor jobs. And many of these same people moved into the newly built garden apartments and single-family homes in the nearby Virginia communities of Alexandria, Falls Church, Fairfax, and Arlington. In 1950 the population of these four jurisdictions was 303,328, or 9.1 percent of the state's total population; by 2000 it was 1,464,216, or 20.0 percent of the state's population. The next concentric ring of counties, Prince William and Loudoun, would explode in growth beginning in the 1990s and into the twenty-first century, increasing even further the disparity in regional growth patterns between Northern Virginia and most of the rest of the state. In contrast to Northern Virginia, eight jurisdictions in the heart of the Byrd organization–dominated Southside Virginia lost population over that same fifty-year period, falling from being 7 percent of the state's population in 1950 to being less than 3 percent by 2000.

For example, in 1950 the population of Brunswick County, on the North Carolina border, was 20,136; by 2000 it had fallen to 17,434. In Charlotte County the 1950 population was 14,057; it fell to 12,576 in 2000. Population declines (or, at best, very modest increases) occurred in the rural counties all along the North Carolina border, in the Piedmont area, in the jurisdictions flanking Chesapeake Bay, and in the mountain counties west of the Shenandoah Valley.

Who were the new people in Northern Virginia, and where did they come from? For the most part they had grown up elsewhere.[6] They had little knowledge of Virginia history (other than the names of some of the founding fathers) and little regard for, and even a suspicion of, the state political culture and its leaders. As a general proposition, the new northern Virginians were more open to an activist government, as most of them worked for the federal government as employees or contractors or had family or neighbors who did. They were comfortable with government and did not support candidates who attacked it. That was reflected in the votes they cast. In the hotly contested 1949 Democratic primary for governor, Arlington County split its vote almost evenly between the candidate favored by the established political organization headed by US senator Harry F. Byrd and his insurgent, more progressive opponent, Francis Pickens Miller, giving each about 4,500 votes.[7] By 1966, Arlington's population growth was evident, and the Byrd organization's candidates for the two US Senate seats up for election that year each received about 6,300 votes, while the insurgents each received close to 11,500. In Fairfax County that same year, the nonorganization candidates received nearly 20,000 votes each, while the established candidates could muster only 8,800 each. Those numbers continued to grow even as the designation of who made up the establishment changed, and the fight shifted from one solely within the Democratic Party to a contest between the parties in the general election. Whatever candidate and party seemed favored by the business and professional establishment based in Richmond would usually be opposed by a majority of the voters in the growing Northern Virginia suburbs.

What was the impact of these changes on the politics of the commonwealth? To examine that, we chose seven general elections for governor and the 1966 Democratic primary race for the US Senate seat held by Harry F. Byrd Jr.[8] These specific elections were chosen because in each one it is clear which candidate was a supporter of the status quo (i.e., the candidate favored by the Richmond-based establishment) and which was the "reformer."[9] When the results are examined county by county, the dilemma of the defender of the status quo becomes apparent. In each race until 2005, a significant part of the defender's political support came from jurisdictions with shrinking populations. In 2005, Tim Kaine, the Democratic incumbent lieutenant governor running to succeed an outgoing Democratic governor, became the first status quo candidate to rely wholly on the fast-growing jurisdictions of the urban corridor for his victory.[10]

The Byrd organization had relied heavily on a base of rural voters in the counties across Southside, from the edge of the cities of Hampton Roads west to the mountains of Appalachia. But those were the parts of Virginia that would lose population beginning in the 1950s, leaving the Byrd organization and those that succeeded it with a diminishing political base. For example, in the 1953 race for governor, the Byrd-supported candidate faced a strong Republican challenge and won with less than 55 percent of the vote, unusually low for a Byrd-supported candidate. He carried twenty-two of the twenty-eight counties that were to lose population or gain less than 10 percent over the ensuing fifty years.[11] Similarly, when Harry Byrd Jr. defended his US Senate seat in 1966, his thin margin in the Democratic primary was largely based in those same jurisdictions. He won nineteen of the twenty-eight jurisdictions.[12]

In 1977, when Republican John Dalton ran for governor against populist Henry Howell, Dalton carried eighteen of those same shrinking jurisdictions. Twenty years later Republican Jim Gilmore won the governorship carrying twenty-three of the twenty-eight jurisdictions. By that time the demographic handwriting had been on the wall for forty years and was becoming more and more legible. Candidates could not win unless they also carried parts of the fast-growing urban corridor stretching from Northern Virginia through the cities of Hampton Roads, something both Dalton and Gilmore did, carrying Fairfax, Loudoun, and Prince William Counties along with the city of Virginia Beach. A combination of the traditional rural areas with parts of the urban corridor worked without regard to political party, as the 1981 election of Charles S. Robb as governor showed. Robb carried twenty of the twenty-eight counties with shrinking population but combined that with majorities in vote-rich Fairfax and Arlington Counties.

That same combination gave Mark Warner a victory twenty years later, but he relied more on the new, fast-growing communities and less on the traditional rural base. He carried twenty-two of the twenty-eight shrinking jurisdictions but only by a total of 15,534 votes, while amassing a margin of nearly 60,000 in Arlington, Alexandria, and Fairfax County and City. From that point forward, the fast-growing communities dominated. Party mattered less if the candidate could appeal to the fast-growing areas, setting the pattern for the twenty-first century. By 2005 the twenty-eight jurisdictions losing population would play a minor role in Tim Kaine's election as governor. Though he carried twelve of the twenty-eight counties, he lost the collective vote of those twenty-eight by more than 17,000. In that same election he carried Arlington County by 29,000 and Fairfax County by over 50,000. The two Republican candidates for governor who have been successful in the twenty-first century, Bob McDonnell in 2009 and Glenn Youngkin in 2021, relied on strong support from their home community and the community in which each had grown up: Youngkin, with a home community in Fairfax County and raised in Virginia Beach, and the reverse for Bob McDonnell, raised in part in Fairfax County and with a home community in Virginia Beach. Each combined that base with support from the traditional rural counties to win statewide.

These statistics do not diminish the importance of policy and personality in Virginia politics. But they make clear where those policies and personalities need to find support, and they give guidance to the type of policies that will prevail. For most of the twentieth century, the politics of Virginia reflected the needs of the rural communities that delivered the vote to the prevailing organization, whether that organization was the Byrd Democrats or the post-Holton, Obenshain-led Republicans of the 1970s. The trend was clear as early as the mid-1960s that the balance was shifting to the faster-growing, heavily populated areas constituting the urban corridor. What had been the reform, anti–status quo jurisdictions for most of the century had become the new establishment region by the turn of the century, and it successfully elected all six governors from 2001 to 2021.

But there were a few rural communities that lost population that had sided with the reformers as early as the late 1960s. Counties such as Surry, Sussex, and Greensville had the common characteristic of a large African American population that became active as a result of the efforts by civil rights organizations to increase Black participation in the political process. Their story is the second major driver of Virginia politics in the last half of the twentieth century.

The Rise of the African American Vote

As the twentieth century opened, the principal political issue in Virginia was whether to call a convention to rewrite the state constitution. Those pushing for the convention pointed out that Virginia elections has become increasingly "corrupt" and that reform was needed.[13] When the convention met in June 1901, racial issues dominated, and the convention focused on ways to limit access to the ballot, particularly for the Negro. Carter Glass, then a delegate to the convention and later a US senator, called for disenfranchisement of the Negro to "simplify the race problem and end political rascality." A poll tax was instituted, as were several practices that gave local registrars considerable discretion to accept or reject a particular request to register.[14] As a result, the number of Virginians voting in the 1904 presidential election was only half the number who had voted four years earlier. And the Democratic primary, which, as a practical matter, served as the real forum for choosing candidates, was run not by the state but by the Democratic Party, which had a "White only" rule. Officially, the "White only" rule was struck down by the courts as a violation of the Fourteenth and Fifteenth Amendments to the US Constitution in 1930,[15] but the practical restrictions enforced by local registrars remained: poll taxes, the use of "blank" forms for registration,[16] and selective questioning of an applicant by the local registrar. The poll tax was $1.50 per year but had to be paid for three successive years of voting eligibility before a person could qualify to register. And it had to be paid at least three months before a primary election and six months before a general election. Since the tax was voluntary (as voting was not compulsory), most local political groups had no interest in encouraging its payment by notifying citizens of a due date unless that citizen was a recognized supporter of that political group.

And even if one paid the required poll tax, registration was not automatic. A person seeking to register was subject to questioning by the local registrar. In 1931 the State Supreme Court of Appeals struck down unrestricted questioning of an applicant for registration.[17] It ruled that questions posed by the registrar must be limited to ones that pertained to his "qualification as elector" and could not properly extend to more general questions designed to determine the applicant's knowledge of state law or policy. The court further ruled that an applicant could not be disqualified based on answers exhibiting a general lack of education so long as the applicant wrote out in his own hand the qualifying information of name, age, place of residence, and employment and provided evidence of payment of poll taxes, all in the presence of the registrar and without the aid of a third person. This led to the widespread use of a "blank page" registration form that required the applicant to write out all of the required information with no indication from the registrar as to what information was required.

Despite these victories in court, the level of Black participation did not change appreciably in the first half of the twentieth century. Legal and practical barriers continued, and many African Americans joined the tens of thousands from across the South who migrated to cities in the North and West to escape the oppressive Jim Crow environment and in search of jobs. In 1900, African Americans constituted more than 35 percent of the total Virginia population. By 1970 that share had fallen to 18.5 percent.[18]

Voting statistics during those years were compiled by Luther P. Jackson, a history professor at Virginia State College and the founder and longtime head of the Petersburg-based Virginia Voters League.[19] Professor Jackson relied on reports from local courthouses across the state and calculated that 25,441 Negroes met the poll tax requirement in 1941, an increase of only 4,500 from the number in 1904. Over that same period the African

American population over the age of twenty-one had increased from 146,122 to 354,144.[20]

The end of World War II brought thousands of young men, Black and White, back home to complete their education, return to jobs, and start families.[21] In Europe and the Pacific these young men had fought to defend their country and its values. Returning to America, many were struck by the contrast between the principles they had defended abroad and the reality of life at home. Nationwide, membership in the NAACP, which had grown rapidly during the war years, continued to gain, largely as a product of its court successes.

But in Virginia, voting participation continued to lag. In the mid-1950s, organizations such as the Richmond Crusade for Voters (the Crusade) and the Virginia Independent Voters League were formed to focus on registering new voters and increasing African American turnout. Their formation was a direct effort to address the low level of voting in Negro neighborhoods. Of the 8,500 registered African American voters in Richmond, fewer than 4,000 voted in 1956.[22] The statewide numbers grew, but slowly, from 92,757 total registrations in 1958 to 100,424 in 1960.[23]

African Americans, like other Virginians, were moving from rural to more urban areas. Richmond's African American population grew from 53,719 in 1950 to 92,331 in 1960, Norfolk's from 45,376 to 80,621.[24] Early efforts to register African Americans were having some success in those two cities, although in Richmond the total Negro registration in 1960 was only 15,651, and in Norfolk it was 11,486.[25]

Those numbers changed dramatically in the 1960s as national attention on the importance of voting grew and concerted efforts to organize registration took place in the South, including Virginia. From the first sit-ins in 1960 through the passage of the federal Voting Rights Act in 1965, the national attention on civil rights frequently translated into local efforts to register new voters. In Virginia, both national and local organizations were at work. Locally, organizations such as the Crusade in Richmond and Norfolk's Concerned Citizens for Political Education devoted their energies to increasing the number of African American who registered and voted.

The Crusade, founded in 1956, grew out of the Committee to Save Our Public Schools, an interracial group formed to oppose the 1956 referendum designed to avoid compliance with the 1954 Supreme Court decision in *Brown v. Board of Education of Topeka*. The statewide referendum had been approved by a wide margin, and leaders of the Schools Committee were disappointed in the low level of African American voting. In the same period the NAACP, which had been the leading civil rights group in Virginia, was openly attacked in the state legislature, resulting in the enactment of laws limiting its practical ability to act. Its membership suffered. In Richmond, several local NAACP leaders who had been active on the Schools Committee formed the Crusade for Voters to focus on increasing the levels of Black political participation.[26] That meant both registration and voting on Election Day.

Norfolk's Concerned Citizens for Political Education grew out of unsuccessful efforts to elect Black candidates to local office in the 1950s and early 1960s and was originally called the Committee of Forty. The Committee of Forty and its successor organizations became best known for the "Goldenrod Ballot," a voter guide distributed in the days before an election identifying the candidates with the group's endorsement. The group's initial goal was to increase the number of Black citizens who registered and voted, particularly in city council and state legislative races. Other local groups in counties and cities across the state, such as the Nansemond County–based Independent Voters League,[27] made similar efforts, but the sheer numbers in Richmond and Norfolk made the Crusade and Concerned Citizens the most prominent of the Virginia-based groups.

These local efforts were spurred by what was being shown daily on America's television screens, from the 1961 Freedom Riders to the 1963 March on Washington and the 1965 travesty on the Pettus Bridge in Selma, Alabama. A pivotal meeting occurred in Attorney General Robert Kennedy's office in June 1961. He had invited Diane Nash and other leaders of the Student Nonviolent Coordinating Committee (SNCC) and the Congress of Racial Equality (CORE) to his office to convince them to change tactics and focus on voter education and participation instead of Freedom Rides and sit-ins. His motives were mixed, of course, and he had little success in tempering the efforts of the young leaders with whom he met, but the idea of the Voter Education Project emerged largely as a result of that meeting.

The Voter Education Project (VEP), a nonprofit organization funded by several private foundations, became the source of grant funding to hundreds of groups working to register voters in cities and counties across the South. The VEP was housed in the Southern Regional Council (SRC) in Atlanta, as a neutral location, thus sidestepping the natural rivalry among the major civil rights organizations. The affiliation with the SRC also gave the new organization early credibility. The SRC's history stretched back to 1919, and it had long published studies on issues of race relations, including an early 1950s study on Black disenfranchisement in the South. But to that point it had remained a research and educational organization seen widely as a reliable source of information on southern race relations.[28]

The SRC agreed to be the home of the new VEP, which was set up in the SRC's Atlanta headquarters with its own executive director. Stephen Currier of the Taconic Foundation (based in Fauquier County, Virginia) led the fundraising efforts and, after a series of meetings, all the major civil rights organizations—the NAACP, CORE, the National Urban League, the SNCC, and the Southern Christian Leadership Conference (SCLC)—agreed to participate in the effort, recognizing it to be an important source of funding for voter registration. In March 1962 the initial grants were made.[29]

From 1962 through 1970 the VEP awarded seventy-one grants to support local Virginia voter registration efforts. The largest of the grants was a multiyear grant of $11,500 in support of the SCLC's registration efforts in the Fourth Congressional District, a predominantly rural area in the heart of Southside, south and east of Richmond along the North Carolina border, the traditional base of the Byrd organization. Additional, smaller amounts in support of that same effort were given each year, often to county-specific projects. Other sustained efforts were through the NAACP in Petersburg. Typical grants were in the $1,000–$2,500 range.

These efforts were, of course, not happening in a vacuum. In January 1964 the ratification of the Twenty-Fourth Amendment to the US Constitution had banned the use of a poll tax as a prerequisite to voting in federal elections. The registration efforts that followed led to a significant increase in African American registration across the state. A couple of examples compiled by the Virginia State Board of Elections show the dramatic impact of those efforts.

Most important, in 1965 Congress passed and the president signed the Voting Rights Act, which barred the use of various techniques to discourage registration and established procedures for federal monitoring. Widely used practices such as limited hours and locations for registration and various forms of literacy tests were outlawed, and changes in a state's laws or rules affecting registration and voting were subject to preclearance by the Department of Justice in any jurisdiction where fewer than half of the age-eligible adults had not registered or voted prior to adoption of the act.[30]

The tearing down of barriers to participation and the increasing efforts to register voters were making a difference, year by year, voter by voter.

TABLE 7.1. Number of African American registrants before and after the banning of the poll tax in federal elections

City or County	April 1964	October 1964
Arlington	1,263	2,525
Buckingham	480	825
Charles City County	793	943
Greensville	1,078	1,890
Hampton	4,076	5,789
James City County	375	960
Newport News	6,511	8,307
Norfolk	10,071	15,801
Petersburg	2,881	3,919
Southampton	1,245	2,045

Source: Data from Virginia State Board of Elections.

One example illustrates the point. Herbert V. Coulton was the director of the Petersburg division of the SCLC and had responsibility for the SCLC's voter registration efforts across Southside. In a March 1964 report to head-quarters in Atlanta, he detailed efforts in the city of Petersburg for the month of February. Two paid and thirty volunteer workers had registered fifty-seven persons that month. He cited the limited hours for registration (noon to 3 p.m.) and the poll tax as the major obstacles. "We have had no success in getting the hours changed so that a greater number of people can register."[31]

The US Commission on Civil Rights issued a report in May 1968 stating that 144,259 non-White persons were registered to vote in Virginia in March 1965, just prior to the effective date of the Voting Rights Act. By September 1967 that number was 243,000.[32]

And the increased registration resulted in increased Election Day turnout, particularly in those jurisdictions where local groups led the effort. In Richmond, for example, African American voting can be tracked with a reasonable certainty because of segregated living patterns, particularly in the last half of the twentieth century. Scholars have identified fifteen precincts in Richmond where the vote is close to 100 percent African American.[33] The total turnout in those fifteen precincts in the 1965 general election for governor was 7,031. By 1969 the turnout had risen to 11,256.

Similarly, the ten predominantly African American precincts in Norfolk cast 3,514 votes in 1965 and 8,766 in 1969. In rural Charles City

County, where most of the citizens were African American, the turnout in 1965 was 767; in 1969 it was 1,267. In the Firehouse precinct in Charlottesville the turnout was 305 in 1965; in 1969 it was 484. Similar percentage increases occurred in most Virginia cities. While new registrations in the more urban areas were due partly to population growth, more of the increase stemmed from successful registration of existing residents, long effectively barred from participating. In the rural areas, the growth was entirely from existing residents.

Beginning in the 1960s, African American voters supported national Democratic candidates. Such had not always been the case. There had been strong support in the Negro press and among Negro leaders for the Eisenhower civil rights policy and the early efforts of candidate Richard Nixon to support a continuation of that policy. But the failure of the Nixon campaign to follow up and the embrace of Nixon's candidacy by the leaders of the Byrd organization pushed African American voters toward the candidacy of Democrat John F. Kennedy. Support for the candidates of the national Democratic Party accelerated throughout the 1960s as the party identified nationally more and more with the goals of the civil rights movement.

Virginia statewide and local elections were a different story. African American voters supported anti–Byrd organization candidates in Democratic primaries but then frequently supported Republican candidates in the general election. In the 1966 Democratic primary for two US Senate seats, African American voters overwhelmingly supported the candidates opposing incumbent senators Harry F. Byrd Jr. and A. Willis Robertson. In the fifteen predominantly African American Richmond precincts, challengers Armistead Boothe and William B. Spong received more than 95 percent of the 8,637 votes cast. Similar margins were tallied in the Negro precincts of Norfolk, Portsmouth, Hampton, and parts of Newport News. But in the general election that fall, that vote was won by Bill Spong, the Democrat, and by the Republican challenger to Harry Byrd, Lawrence M. Traylor.[34] Despite leaning toward Democratic candidates generally, African American voters were not willing to support a member of the Byrd family, which for so long had been the symbol of the old segregationist order.

In the 1969 general election, Republican gubernatorial nominee A. Linwood Holton actively sought African American support and succeeded in splitting the Negro vote, winning nearly 60 percent of the 11,256 votes cast in the fifteen precincts in Richmond but less than 20 percent in

African American precincts in Norfolk, Portsmouth, and Hampton.[35] In endorsing Holton's candidacy, the Crusade for Voters declared that "a vote for Battle (Holton's Democratic opponent) would be a vote for the Byrd machine."[36] Holton went on to become the first Republican elected to statewide office since Reconstruction by weaving together support from groups like the Crusade with significant backing from parts of the business and professional community that had long supported Harry Byrd Sr. and the Byrd organization.

But that level of African American support for a statewide Republican was never repeated as the more progressive Holton wing of the Republican Party gave way to an emerging coalition of conservative Republicans and what remained of the traditional Byrd organization. That coalition swept statewide elections in 1972 and 1973, returning former Byrd organization Democrat Mills Godwin to the governor's office, this time as a Republican. In the fifteen predominantly African American precincts in Richmond, former Democrat Henry Howell, running as an independent, garnered 10,288 votes, 96.3 percent of the total cast. Similar margins were produced in African American precincts in urban areas across the state, although across the state the turnout percentages had leveled off after the sharp increases during the 1960s.[37]

Conclusion

The last half of the twentieth century was all about the forming of a new governing geography in Virginia, based in the fast-growing communities of Northern Virginia and the cities in the urban corridor from Richmond to Hampton Roads. It relied on the expansion of the electorate, the very thing that the old Byrd organization had worked hardest to prevent.

The growth patterns have continued, albeit more slowly, through the first twenty years of the new century and have spread to other parts of the state, including the suburban areas around Fredericksburg, Charlottesville, and Williamsburg. While the African American population continues to play a large role in the politics of the state, the greatest growth in population has been in other racial and ethnic minorities. The US Census Bureau's American Community Survey for 2019 estimates that in that year, 12 percent of Virginia's population had been born outside the United States, a number that had been growing steadily since the 1960s.[38] In the 2020 census, African Americans remained the largest minority group, with 20.9 percent of the population. But the fastest growing was Virginia's

Hispanic population, constituting 10.6 percent of the total, followed by the Asian population with 9.1 percent and the self-described multirace population and "other" population, also with 9.1 percent.[39]

As the 2021 election results made clear, statewide candidates will need to compete in this new geography and appeal to this increasingly diverse electorate. Each party will need to examine closely and reflect on what happened in 2021 and whatever may happen in the next two years in order to prepare for the next quadrennial election of the Virginia governor. Political parties have always adapted over time to meet new realities and will likely continue to do so.

Notes

1. V. O. Key, Jr. *Southern Politics* (New York: Vintage Books, 1949), 19.
2. Ibid.
3. In five of the seven gubernatorial elections between 1925 and 1949, the turnout for the Democratic primary exceeded that for the general election. Ralph Eisenberg, *Virginia Votes 1924–1968* (Charlottesville: University of Virginia, Institute of Government, 1971).
4. Harry F. Byrd (Clarke County), John Garland Pollard (King and Queen County plus City of Richmond), George C. Peery (Tazewell County), Colgate Darden (Southampton County), Bill Tuck (Halifax County), John S. Battle (Albemarle County), Tom Stanley (Henry County), J. Lindsay Almond (Roanoke County), Albertis S. Harrison (Brunswick County), Mills E. Godwin (Nansemond County).
5. J. Harvie Wilkinson III, *Harry Flood Byrd and the Changing Face of Virginia Politics* (Charlottesville: University Press of Virginia, 1968), 30–38.
6. In 1940 more than 82 percent of the population of Virginia had been born in Virginia and another 9 percent in a southern state. By 2019 only 49 percent of the population had been born in Virginia.
7. The dividing line in this and subsequent years was not always conservative versus progressive. The real divide was between the candidate supported by the established business and professional community centered in Richmond and the "outsider" running against more traditional Virginia.
8. The general elections for governor occurred in 1953, 1973, 1977, 1981, 1993, 2001, and 2005.
9. For the most part, presidential elections and most elections to the US Senate are not a reliable measure of Virginia state politics.
10. "Status quo" does not carry a connotation of liberal or conservative but only who was the candidate largely supported by those then in power. Kaine, the incumbent lieutenant governor, was running to succeed his ally

and predecessor, Governor Mark Warner. Though more liberal than his Republican opponent, Kaine was the candidate to continue the status quo.

11. Four of the six counties he lost were in the far Southwest, an area hostile to the Byrd organization and with a strong Republican Party dating from divisions originating in the Civil War.

12. Six of the jurisdictions Byrd lost were in the anti–Byrd organization areas of Southwest Virginia.

13. Virginius Dabney, *Virginia: The New Dominion* (New York: Doubleday, 1971), 430.

14. The disproportionate disenfranchisement of Negroes is well documented in Andrew Buni, *The Negro in Virginia Politics, 1902–1965* (Charlottesville: University Press of Virginia, 1967), 25–33.

15. *West v. Bliley,* 33 F.2d 177, 42 F.2d 101 (1930).

16. The 1902 state constitution and implementing statutes set rules that registrars widely interpreted to allow the use of a "blank" form, which meant that the applicant was handed a blank sheet of paper and had to write out all of the information required by statute without prompting by the registrar or help from any other person. This blank form was widely used to deny registration to African Americans and others not favored by local organization leaders.

17. *Davis v. Allen,* 157 Va. 84 (1931).

18. US Bureau of the Census, *Historical Census Statistics by Race,* Working Paper no. 56 (Washington, DC, 2002).

19. At its height in the late 1940s, the Virginia Voters League had chapters in virtually every county and city in the state, largely owing to its partnership with the Virginia State Teachers Association, the organization to which most Black teachers belonged. See Kimberly S. Johnson, *From Politics to Protest: African American Voting in Virginia in the Pre–Civil Rights Movement Era, 1940–1954* (New York: Cambridge University Press, 2017).

20. Ibid., 27–28.

21. More than 1,150,000 African Americans joined the military between 1941 and 1946. Harvard Sitkoff, "African American Militancy in the World War II South," in *Remaking Dixie: The Impact of World War II on the American South* (Jackson: University Press of Mississippi, 1997), 70–92.

22. Kimberly A. Matthews, *The Richmond Crusade for Voters* (Charleston, SC: Arcadia, 2017).

23. Buni, *The Negro in Virginia Politics, 1902–1965,* 197.

24. US Census Bureau, "Negro Population by County, 1960 and 1950" (Washington, DC, 1960), 58–60.

25. Buni, *The Negro in Virginia Politics, 1902–1965,* 206.

26. See Julian Maxwell Hayter, *The Dream Is Lost* (Lexington: University Press of Kentucky, 2017), 37–45, and Robert A. Rankin, "The Richmond Crusade

for Voters: The Quest for Black Power," *University of Virginia Institute of Government Newsletter* 51, no. 1 (1974).

27. The Virginia Independent Voters League was the successor organization to the Virginia Voters League, formed in 1965 with the merger of that organization, the Virginia Freedom Democrats, and the Independent Voters League of Suffolk and Nansemond County.

28. Evan Faulkenbury, *Poll Power* (Chapel Hill: University of North Carolina Press, 2019), 57–92.

29. After the initial funding, later funding was received from a wide range of private foundations, including the Ford Foundation, the Rockefeller Brothers Fund, the Field Foundation, the Mary Reynolds Babcock Foundation, the New World Foundation, and others. Faulkenbury, *Poll Power,* 103.

30. Charles S. Bullock III, Susan A. MacManus, Jeremy D. Mayer, and Mark J. Rozell, *The South and the Transformation of U.S. Politics* (New York: Oxford University Press, 2019), 91–94.

31. Records of the Southern Christian Leadership Conference (1954–1970) Voter Registration Reports, Records of Andrew Young (New Haven: Yale University Library), microform.

32. US Commission on Civil Rights, *A Report of the United States Commission on Civil Rights* (Washington, DC, 1968); "Political Participation: A Study of the Participation by Negroes in the Electoral Process in 10 Southern States since Passage of the Voting Rights Act of 1965," https://www2.law .umaryland.edu/marshall/usccr/subjlist.html?subjectid=23.

33. Ralph Eisenberg, *NEWS Letter of the Institute of Government* (Charlottesville: University of Virginia, Institute of Government, various years). Mr. Eisenberg published studies on several elections and in the 1960s included precinct-level data from selected African American precincts in eight Virginia cities, always using the same precincts, thus allowing comparisons across elections. His work was continued into the 1970s by Professor Larry Sabato and also published by the Institute of Government.

34. Eisenberg, *NEWS Letter of the Institute of Government* 43, nos. 5 and 9 (January and May 1967).

35. Eisenberg, *NEWS Letter of the Institute of Government* 46, no. 9 (May 1970).

36. Frank B. Atkinson, *The Dynamic Dominion* (Fairfax, VA: George Mason University Press, 1992), 192.

37. Larry J. Sabato, *NEWS Letter of the Institute of Government* 50, no. 12 (August 1974).

38. US Census Bureau, "American Community Survey 2019," table ID B05002 (Washington, DC, 2020).

39. US Census Bureau, "2020 Census Count by Race (Virginia)"; see also Qian Cai, "A Decade of Change in Virginia's Population," *NEWS Letter of the Institute of Government* 87, no. 4 (June 2011).

CONTRIBUTORS

FRANK B. ATKINSON is a partner in the law firm of McGuireWoods LLP and senior adviser with the firm's public affairs affiliate, McGuireWoods Consulting LLC. He is author of the books *The Dynamic Dominion* (George Mason University Press, 1992) and *Virginia in the Vanguard: Political Leadership in the 400-Year-Old Cradle of American Democracy, 1981–2006* (Rowman & Littlefield, 2006).

SALLY BURKLEY is a first-year law student at the College of William & Mary. In 2022, she graduated with honors from the University of Mary Washington.

WENDY CHEN is assistant professor of political science at Texas Tech University. Her research interests lie in local politics, political history, public management, and regional development. She is a Founders' Fellow at the American Society for Public Administration.

STEPHEN J. FARNSWORTH is professor of political science at the University of Mary Washington. He is the author or co-author of seven books on US politics, including *Late Night with Trump: Political Humor and the American Presidency* (Routledge, 2020) and *Presidential Communication and Character: White House News Management from Clinton and Cable to Twitter and Trump* (Routledge, 2018).

WARREN FISKE is a journalist who has covered Virginia politics and government since 1985 for the *Virginian-Pilot* and the *Richmond Times-Dispatch*. He is currently PolitiFact Virginia editor at VPM Public Radio in Richmond.

STEPHEN P. HANNA is professor of geography at the University of Mary Washington and the cartography editor for the American Association of Geographers. His recent work includes the co-written book, *Remembering Enslavement: Reassembling the Southern Plantation Museum* (University of Georgia Press, 2022).

JULIAN HAYTER is associate professor of leadership studies at the University of Richmond. He is the author of *The Dream Is Lost: Voting Rights and the Politics of Race in Richmond, Virginia* (University Press of Kentucky, 2017).

RONALD L. HEINEMANN was Squires Professor Emeritus of History at Hampden-Sydney College, where he taught nineteenth- and twentieth-century American history courses from 1968 to 2020. Among his notable publications are *Harry Bird of Virginia* (University of Virginia Press, 1996) and *Old Dominion, New Commonwealth: A History of Virginia, 1607–2007* (University of Virginia Press, 2007).

ROBERT HOLSWORTH is managing partner of Decide Smart. Prior to joining the firm, he was the founding director of the Center for Public Policy and the L. Douglas Wilder School of Government and Public Affairs at Virginia Commonwealth University. He also served as dean of the College of Humanities and Sciences.

JOHN G. MILLIKEN served as chairman of the Board of Commissioners of the Virginia Port Authority under five Virginia governors, concluding his service in 2022. He is also a member of the Virginia Committee on International Trade. Prior to his service on the Port Board, he served in a number of transportation-related elected and appointed positions in state and local government, including as the Commonwealth's Secretary of Transportation, member and chairman of the Board of the Washington Metropolitan Area Transit Authority, three terms as an elected member of the Arlington County Board, and, for eight years, a member of the Transportation Planning Board of the Washington Metropolitan Council of Governments. A graduate of Haverford College and the University of Virginia School of Law, he practiced infrastructure law until his retirement from Venable LLP in 2015. Currently he serves as Senior Fellow in Residence at the Schar School of Policy and Government at George Mason University.

MARK J. ROZELL is founding dean of the Schar School of Policy and Government at George Mason University, where he holds the Ruth D. and John T. Hazel Faculty Chair in Public Policy. Among his recent co-written books are *African American Statewide Candidates in the New South* (2022), *Federalism: A Very Short Introduction* (2019), and *The South and the Transformation of U.S. Politics* (2018), all with Oxford University Press.

INDEX

Printed in the USA
CPSIA information can be obtained
at www.ICGtesting.com
CBHW020226210524
8864CB00002B/64

9 780813 949710